VAN FLEET'S
MASTER GUIDE
FOR MANAGERS

Other books by the author

How to Use the Dynamics of Motivation

Guide to Managing People

How to Put Yourself Across with People

Miracle People Power

Power with People

Twenty-Two Biggest Mistakes Managers Make and How to Correct Them

Van Fleet's

Master Guide

For Managers

JAMES K. VAN FLEET

PARKER PUBLISHING COMPANY, INC. WEST NYACK, N.Y.

Library of Congress Cataloging in Publication Data

Van Fleet, James K
  Van Fleet's master guide for managers.

  1. Management. I. Title. II. Title: Master
guide for managers.
HD31.V35 1978   658.4   78-2959
ISBN 0-13-940452-X

Printed in the United States of America

This book is dedicated to those who have filled
my life with abundant joy and happiness:

My wife, Belva LaVonne Van Fleet

My children, Robert James Van Fleet
                Teresa Lynne Van Fleet Spain
                Lawrence Lee Van Fleet

My daughter's husband, G. Arch Spain

My grandchildren, Adam Lucas Spain
                   Joel Van Spain

What This Book Will Do For You

What is the definition of successful management? It is the process whereby the resources of *people, money, materials, time,* and *facilities* are all properly utilized to accomplish the mission of any organization, be it large or small, profit or non-profit, civilian or military.

When I entered the management field more than 35 years ago, I found that my college courses in business administration had adequately prepared me in the general aspects of four of these five areas of management: the proper utilization of finances, material resources, time, and facilities to accomplish the mission. And I was able to learn in short order the particular methods and procedures of these four specific facets of management in the corporation I went to work for. In fact, I was able to solve with comparative ease the problems I encountered in these areas.

But the management of people was something else entirely. It was the most difficult area of all to master, and my preparation for the management and leadership of people had been badly neglected in my college courses. I had received no education whatever in the applied psychology of handling people. To tell the truth, the only formal training in the leadership and management of people I could remember had been when I was in the Boy Scouts!

Yet fully 98 percent of the problems I was called on to solve each day were caused by people—not by machines or computers. And the problems in the other four areas of management—money, materials, time, and facilities—were also caused mainly by people. Almost every mistake I saw could be traced back to some kind of human error.

I quickly found I was not alone. The vagaries of human behavior left most managers and executives feeling utterly helpless. To get rid of their problems in managing people, they would quickly pass the buck to anyone they could find: the front-line supervisor—that last white collar link between management and labor . . . the personnel manager . . . the person in charge of industrial or labor relations.

When I asked my superior, the vice-president in charge of manufacturing for the corporation, what his hardest job was, he replied without a moment's hestiation.

"Managing people is my biggest problem, Jim," he said. "Or I should say, solving the problems caused by people. I have no trouble taking care of finances, materials, facilities, and time. I have good managers to help me solve any manufacturing problem in these areas rapidly and efficiently.

"But managing people . . . well, now, that's quite a different story. When you add two or more people together—no one can accurately predict what the exact outcome is going to be. Only a few persons in the entire organization really know how to manage and control people.

"If you want to get ahead in business or industry, Jim, my advice is simply this: know your specialty, of course . . . learn all the various aspects of management . . . but above all, *learn how to manage people and control their actions*. You can't help but succeed when you do this and you'll never really succeed until you do."

Although that conversation took place more than 35 years ago, it has guided my actions in management ever since. I soon found there were no adequate books or journals I could turn to for the answers I needed so much. I realized, then, the management of people would have to be learned from actual experience, by trial and error.

So I set about the formidable task of experimenting, searching, sifting, discarding, compiling, and filing information. I would try first one solution to a problem, then another. If a particular method did not work, I threw it away. Techniques that worked I kept, honing them to the sharpest possible degree of effectiveness.

Little by little over the years there evolved a thick heavy notebook that I kept on my desk and referred to constantly for help and guidance in solving my people-management problems. It contained only the methods and procedures I found to be the most important in the management of people. The techniques I retained in my notebook were the key ones, those I knew to be the most effective in solving people problems. They represented a distillation, a sifting, the results of years of research and experimentation, the cream of the crop.

My notebook had 12 major subdivisions which have since become the 12 chapters in the book you're now reading. In my notebook I called those subdivisions the *12 Master Keys to Management Success.* In this book each master key has a more explanatory chapter title, but the basic contents and original theme are still the same.

When I started my notebook on the techniques of managing people many years ago, I had no intention of ever publishing it as a book. I had compiled it only for my own personal use. But recently a number of magazine and newspaper articles telling how certain companies were using new and innovative techniques to solve their management problems came to my attention. I read those articles with great interest hoping to discover some new procedures I might use.

But to my surprise I found that most of these "new and innovative" techniques were already recorded in my notebook and had been there for quite some time. Without a doubt, then, what were brand-new techniques to many other people were old, true, and time-tested procedures to me. Up to then, I simply had not fully realized the true value of the material I had gathered over the years.

Another factor that greatly influenced my decision to publish my notebook was this. I asked a close friend of mine, the president and chief executive officer of a large and extremely successful computer manufacturing company, to look over my management notebook and give me his honest opinion about whether I should publish it or not.

When Ray returned my notebook a few weeks later, he said,

"Get it published, Jim. It will be invaluable for managers and executives at all levels of management."

Naturally, I was highly pleased with Ray's words, but I wondered just how my notebook would be useful to a person in a top management position as he was.

"Jim, let me put it this way," Ray said in answer to my question. "I've been in this management business so long I do most things by instinct. I make management decisions almost subconsciously. Many times I can identify situations that will lead to problems and stop them even before they happen. But I'm not able to give my knowledge to others. One of my hardest jobs is passing what I know along to my subordinates in key management positions. And even if I knew how to do that, I still wouldn't have time to do it. Your book will help me and thousands of others in that same situation solve that problem. It will help all of us bridge that difficult communication gap."

HOW THIS BOOK IS ORGANIZED

When I started my management notebook many years ago, I knew if ever I was to learn the secret of how to manage and control a person's actions and reactions, I would need to learn everything I could about human behavior. I would have to know what a person's innermost needs and desires were . . . why he reacted the way he did to certain stimuli . . . what he thought, how he felt, what turned him on, what made him tick. I have included the important information I learned in this area in Chapter 1, *Understanding, Predicting, and Controlling People's Behavior: The First Master Key to Management Success*. I'll tell you about the learned desires all people have and how you can use them to your own advantage. I have also included in this first chapter specific techniques you can use to motivate people to do what you want them to do.

Chapter 2, *The Master Power Play that Never Fails*, and Chapter 3, *Power Psychology at Its Best*, both show you how to implement the information you learned about people in Chapter 1. They give you techniques you can use to control and guide a person's behavior. For instance, Chapter 2 shows you how to fulfill one of a person's deepest desires . . . the desire to be important. The need for importance, the drive to be recognized and receive attention, is one of a person's biggest prime movers. It is one of the most useful tools you can ever use to motivate people. Chapter 3 will show you how to win people to your way of thinking as if by magic. It will reveal the secret of appealing to a person's emotions to get the job done.

Since the art of managing people and controlling their actions and reactions is so dependent on communication, Chapter 4 gives you the *Master Formula for Powerful and Persuasive Writing.* You'll learn how to write powerful letters, directives, and reports. I'll also give you the most effective format I've ever used for a persuasive letter. You'll discover how using the *4-S Formula* can help make you a successful writer. I'll also give you some easy methods you can use to improve your writing style 100 percent overnight, as well as a number of other techniques to help you improve your written communications.

Chapter 5, *Why Top Managers Are Always Masters of the Art of Oral Communication,* shows you how to manage people and control their actions through the spoken word. It shows you how to orally dominate and take full control of any situation. You'll learn certain positive words that stimulate people to do what you want. You'll also discover a list of negative words that turn people off. This chapter will reveal how you can use the "silent skill" to get the results you want.

Chapter 6, *How Successful Managers Always Get the Job Done No Matter What,* offers a variety of techniques you can use to make sure your orders and directives are carried out properly and efficiently. It also gives you a master method you can use to measure your total success as a manager of people.

Chapter 7, *Foolproof Methods Ingenious Managers Use to Encourage Initiative and Ingenuity,* shows you how to use mission-type orders to challenge a person's ingenuity. It also gives you ten infallible guidelines you can use to develop initiative in people. You'll learn how to use the management problem solving process. And you'll see how delegating responsibility is one of the best ways to get a person to think and use his creative abilities for you.

Chapter 8, *The Fine Art of Getting People to Cooperate and*

Work Together as a Team, gives you the most important, effective, and productive methods you can use to get people to go all out for you. You'll learn the key secrets of teamwork and cooperation, including one particular method that's guaranteed to work 100 percent to get people to do what you want them to do. And you'll meet a millionaire, Earl E. Bakken, who says he got where he is today by inspiring people to work together as a team toward a common goal.

Chapter 9, *How Successful Managers Make Those Tough Decisions*, at first glance might not seem to have anything to do with the management of people. It is included in my book for at least two major reasons.

First, as a manager, every decision you make affects every person in your organization in some way. Second, over the years I have found that making a decision is one of the toughest jobs a manager has. Those with the courage to make a decision and accept the responsibility for it will always be found at the top levels of management or on the way up. The person who procrastinates and farms out problems to a committee for further study simply to avoid making decisions will never go far as a manager. If I can help one person conquer that fear of making decisions, this chapter will have well earned its place here.

Chapter 10, *How Many Top Executives Select and Develop Their Key Personnel*, is one of the major keys to management success. A top level manager needs key people under him to hold him up in his position. He cannot survive solely on his own. This chapter shows you how to develop a reliable selection process for the placement and development of your key personnel. It also gives specific tested management guidelines to measure the progress and performance of your key management people.

Chapter 11, *Master Methods Wise Managers Use for Controlling Problem People*, gives you the procedures I've developed and the methods I use for pinpointing the problem person and helping him solve his problems. You'll learn the primary causes of job dissatisfaction. I'll give you the three criteria to use that will establish beyond doubt whether a person is or is not an actual problem to you. Problem people may make up only five percent of your work force, but they cause 95 percent of your people-management problems. This chapter specifically answers your questions about how to handle them.

Chapter 12 reveals the *Secrets Top-Notch Managers Use to Make the Most of Their Time.* As with Chapter 9, this may not at first glance seem to have much to do with the management of people. However, if you will review a few of your own working days, I know you will find, just as I have, that most of the wasted time was caused by people. I'll show you how to use the master key to make your time more effective. I'll give you specific techniques on how to use your time more effectively and a daily checklist to measure your own progress in saving time.

These 12 chapters, then, make up my *Master Guide for Managers.* Each chapter is based on one of my *Master Keys to Management Success.* You'll soon see that I've done away with all abstract and vague generalities. My book is based on more than 35 years of managing real, live people. It was not written in some sequestered and cloistered college sanctuary, but in the active arena of management. That's why it has no hypotheses—no theories . . . it's all raw meat. You'll find no textbook answers about how people ought to act or what they ought to want. I am always amazed at so-called experts in human relations who try to tell people what they want or what's good for them. *You can't tell people what they want. You have to ask them.*

Now then, before we get into the first chapter, I would like to answer a few questions for you before you ask them. You might be wondering why I didn't include material on being technically qualified . . . setting the example . . . knowing yourself and seeking self-improvement . . . developing responsibility for your own actions, and the like. Many of these subjects did cross my mind as possibilities, but I rejected all of them. I felt you would already be far above that particular level of management. Besides, I wanted to give you the most productive key methods and techniques I've learned over the years. I wanted to give you the cream of the crop, not the entire harvest.

The next point I want to make clear is this: *An old idea is still new if you've never tried it.* I do not say that everything in my book is my original thinking; it is not. But I do say that *each technique in the book works.* I know that from personal experience. *If it did not work, it would not be included.* I know you will encounter many ideas you've heard about before, but have never used. Perhaps you've thought they wouldn't work or they weren't really worth while, so you've never tried them. I've made that same mistake in the past. Let me tell you now about one such error.

Years and years ago, I read how Charles Schwab—the man who was paid a million dollars a year by Andrew Carnegie because of his ability to manage people—was able to increase production in a steel mill by *throwing down a challenge.* This mill was not producing its quota. The manager told Schwab he'd coaxed the men, pushed them, cussed them, threatened them . . . but nothing worked. It was the end of the day just before the night shift came on duty.

"Give me a piece of chalk," Schwab said. He turned to the nearest employee and asked, "How many heats did your shift turn out today?"

"Six," was the answer.

Schwab said nothing, but he chalked a big figure "6" on the floor and walked away.

When the night shift arrived, they saw the 6 on the floor. "What does that mean? What's it for?" they asked.

"The big man was here today," the day crew said. "He wanted to know how many heats we made. When we told him, he chalked it there on the floor. And you can't beat it either!"

The next morning Schwab went through the mill again. The 6 was gone. The night shift had rubbed it out and replaced it with a big 7. When the day shift left that afternoon, the 7 was erased. It had been replaced with a huge 10.

Before long this mill, the one that had been running behind all other steel mills in production, was turning out more work than any other in the Carnegie empire. The technique Charles Schwab had used was this: *When all else fails, throw down a challenge.*

I've given you this example for this reason. You see, I read about this technique nearly 25 years before I ever tried it because I thought it was a lot of baloney and wouldn't work. When I finally did use it, I found it worked like magic. I was absolutely astounded at the amazing results it produced. Why does it work? Here's why: When you throw down a challenge and a man beats it, he's fulfilled one of his most basic desires: *the desire to win . . . to be first . . . the desire to excel.* I told the whole story of my first experiment with this technique in a previous book of mine, *Guide to Managing People.*[1]

A Kansas City, Missouri, reader of another book of mine, *Power with People*,[2] also suffered with this same problem of doubt and procrastination that I had. He wrote me to say that he decided to put some of my ideas to work. "I'd read about some of your methods before," he said, "but I doubted their effectiveness. However, when you gave such concrete examples of successful application in your book, I decided to try some of your techniques. Wow! Do they ever work. The results were really fantastic and even better than you said."

My point here is simply this. *An idea will never work for you if you don't try it.* You must give more than lip service to an idea if you want to get results. So really use these techniques you find in my book. You, too, will be amazed at the results you get and the benefits that will be yours.

The last question I want to answer before you ask it is addressed to female readers and has to do with sex. I am not a male chauvinist just because I use the words *he* and *him* rather than *she* and *her* most of the time. It is a customary way of writing, and I did not want to make my sentences awkward and clumsy by saying *he/she or him/her.* Nor did I want to use the word *person* all the time either, although I think I have subconsciously used the words *person* and *people* more often than I usually do simply to avoid criticism from my female readers. I hope you will understand and not take offense for none is intended. I am fully aware of a woman's intelligence and capabilities and I know she is entitled to the same pay, privileges, and benefits as a man when she does the same work.

Let me close this introduction by quoting what President Harry Truman once said about leadership. He said, "Leadership is the ability to get men to do what they don't want to do and like it." Since the objectives of good management and good leadership are

---

[1]James K. Van Fleet, *Guide to Managing People.* (West Nyack, New York, Parker Publishing Company, Inc., 1968).

[2]James K. Van Fleet, *Power with People.* (West Nyack, New York, Parker Publishing Company, Inc., 1970).

identical, and since the roles of the manager and the leader are inseparable, I'd like to give you a slightly different version of President Truman's statement.

From a manager's point of view, *management is the ability to get a person to WANT to do what you want him to do*. When a man *wants* to do something, he'll *like* doing it, and that's for sure. When you can get every person who works for you in that frame of mind, you'll be able to solve most of your people-management problems before they ever happen.

James K. Van Fleet

CONTENTS

Why You as Manager Need to Understand People's Behavior Patterns ● The Higher Your Management Position, the Greater Your Communications Problems Will Be ● Understanding the Roots of Human Behavior ● The Master Key that Controls Human Behavior ● Find Out What People Want and Help Them Get It ● Specific Techniques Successful Managers Use to Motivate People ● Offering a Person the Opportunity for Financial Gain ● Satisfying a Person's Needs for Creative Expression ● Fulfilling a Person's Need to Accomplish Something Worthwhile ● Techniques that Give a Person the Feeling He Belongs ● Fulfilling a Person's Desire for Liberty and Freedom ● Giving a Person a Sense of Emotional Security ● Recognizing a Person's Efforts ● Fulfilling a Person's Desires for New Experiences ● The Best Way to Offer a Person Dignity and Respect ● More Methods Managers Use to Motivate their People ● Initiating Your Own Program to Fulfill a Person's Needs and Desires ● Understanding a Person's Frustrations ● Your Specific Role as a Manager of People

Why a Person Needs a Feeling of Importance ● Worthwhile Benefits ● Techniques You Can Use to Gain These Benefits

2. The Master Power Play that Never Fails ... and Why Smart Executives Use It (cont.)

• An Old-Fashioned Technique that Will Never Go Out of Style • Five Small Words to Make a Person Feel Important • A Psychological Study to Prove the Value of This Technique • Why the Praise Technique Works So Well • Other Basic Desires that Are Automatically Fulfilled by This Technique • Praising Every Single Improvement • Sincere Praise Instead of Flattery • How You Can Use Praise to Correct Mistakes • Asking a Person for His Opinion, His Advice, and His Help • Making a Personnel Problem a "Personal" Problem • Making the Other Person a Real VIP

Why Fear, Force, Threats, or Intimidation Are Not Effective Persuaders • Winning People to Your Way of Thinking as if by Magic • Making It Easy for the Person to Change His Way of Thinking • Changing a Person's Mind by Plugging the Benefits He'll Gain • Asking Him Questions to Overcome His Resistance • Other Benefits from Asking Questions • Exploring the Other Person's Position for Weaknesses • Knowing When a Person Is Ready to Accept a New Idea • Letting the Other Person Feel the Idea Is His • Using Suggestions Rather than Giving Direct Orders • The Secret of Appealing to a Person's Emotions to Get the Job Done

The Primary Purpose of Business Writing • Even Big-City Editors Make Mistakes Sometimes • How to Select the Right Words and Use Them Properly • The Best Way to

Give Them Your Cooperation and Teamwork First • Gain Worthwhile Benefits • The 100 Percent Guaranteed Method of Getting Cooperation from People • Getting Cooperation Between Labor and Management • It Takes More than Money to Get Cooperation • Earl E. Bakken's Success Formula • Getting People to Go All Out for You • The Importance of Equalizing the Benefits • Establishing an Emotional Rallying Point • Getting the Group's Key People to Cooperate First • Kinds of Key People to Watch For • Ways People Can Participate in Management •

Specific Benefits You'll Gain • Techniques to Gain These Benefits • Developing Your Powers of Decision • Learning to Concentrate on the Essentials to Establish Priorities • Developing the Ability to Plan and Order • How to Make an Operation Plan to Implement Your Decision • Format for an Operation Plan or Order • Having the Courage to Act • Do the Thing You Fear to Do and You'll Have the Power to Do It • Five Examples • Guidelines to Help You Make Those Tough Decisions • Five Common Obstacles to Overcome in Making Your Decisions • How to Develop a Sense of Judgment in Your Subordinate Managers

"What I Look For When Selecting a Key Manager . . ." • Character Traits Most Executives Consider Important • Short-Range Objectives to Consider • Long-Range Objectives • Drawing a Person Out in an Interview • Six Keys to

Chapter **1**

Understanding, Predicting, and

Controlling People's Behavior:

The First Master Key to

Management Success

Even though today we live in a scientific age—the age of computer technology—almost everything you and I do as managers is still accomplished through people. True enough, computers are outstanding work-saving devices, but they are programmed, operated, and repaired by people. That's why the ability to lead, manage, control, and direct other people and their actions is so important to you. Wherever people work, managers will always be needed to make decisions, issue orders, supervise the execution of those orders, correct mistakes, and assume the responsibility of solving problems when they arise. Problems caused by people will always come up. Computers may make mistakes, perhaps, but more often than not, these errors can be traced back to a human being.

For example, during my wife's hospitalization recently, the hospital's computer records had her listed as Behua instead of Belva Van Fleet. Her insurance identification number was also incorrectly recorded. When I called the attention of the hospital's finance manager to these errors, her immediate reaction was that the computer had somehow made a mistake.

"But how could such erroneous information get into the computer unless someone put it there?" I asked.

After some embarrassed hedging, she finally conceded some hospital admissions clerk had evidently typed up the wrong data for the computer when my wife entered the hospital. When it comes to computers, the old cliche of "Garbage in . . . Garbage out" still holds true.

Computers cannot be blamed for human errors although many people try to do so to evade responsibility for their own mistakes. Managers will always be required to manage, control, and correct the actions of the persons they supervise. No doubt about it . . . people are here to stay.

This being true, then, the wise manager will learn everything he can about the people who work for him. He'll want to be able to understand, predict, and control each person's behavior. This capability is truly the first master key to the successful management of people.

Why You as a Manager Need to Understand
People's Behavior Patterns

If you want to use the correct psychological stimulus on the right individual at the proper time, you must understand each person who works for you.

The ability to influence and direct the actions of other people so they will do what you want them to do—the fine art of management—depends on your first understanding their behavior. You'll be able to do your job thoroughly as a manager only when you make a continuing effort to fully understand both yourself and the people with whom you work.

You need not be a psychologist or have a college degree to figure other people out. But you should have a complete knowledge of basic human behavior patterns so you can really know what a person wants, what makes him tick, what turns him on. Only then will you be able to gain the maximum effectiveness from all your organization's members.

As a manager, you will find no two people ever respond exactly alike to your actions and orders. You must determine how to best motivate each person to do his utmost for you.

As an observant manager, you'll quickly discover that your actions and orders have a different effect on each one of your people.

Each person will respond somewhat differently to the same order. When you know what each person's response is going to be, you'll know how to best inspire that person to do exactly what you want him to do.

When you understand each person's behavior, you'll be able to mold the entire group into a more effective and efficient team.

The various reactions from the persons you manage will result in a total group attitude toward you and any task assigned by you. If you can obtain favorable results from the individuals under your direction, you can also expect to get a favorable response from the entire group. This will let you mold your group into a reliable and productive team.

The Higher Your Management Position, the Greater Your Communication Problems Will Be

The higher you go in management, the more important it is for you to understand people's behavior patterns. Yet this problem becomes even more difficult for you to solve, simply because of your isolation from the majority of people. It is all too easy to lose the human touch when you're at the top of the pyramid.

Normally, a manager in a top level management position will keep close personal contact with only a relatively small group of persons, no matter how many people are ultimately controlled by him. If this is your situation, you must depend on that small group of trusted subordinates to make your will known, to execute your orders and carry out your directives, and to keep you informed of any personnel problems, just as Jack Reed, a plant manager for Cornwall Industries, does.

"One of my biggest problems is communication, making sure my orders and directives are carried out and keeping in touch with all the people in the plant so I can understand their problems," Jack says. "As plant manager, I'm actually in close personal contact with only a small group of people, even though we employ nearly 2,000 persons here in Springfield alone. I couldn't possibly transmit my orders to each employee individually. I must depend on that small group of persons to make my will known and carry out my purposes.

"I also rely on that same small group to keep me informed about the plant morale as well as what problems people have. However, I still try to visit at least a dozen employees each day to find out if anything's bothering them. If I don't know what people want, if I don't understand their problems, I can't help them. When I can keep people happy and satisfied, I know they will do their best for me."

The final success of your organization, no matter how large, will depend on your ability to promote effective cordial working relationships between yourself, the group, and individuals in the group. Regardless of how high your management position is, or how few people you deal with directly, you must still understand human behavior so you can help people solve their problems and keep them happy. Only then will you be able to develop a healthy atmosphere of cooperation that will result in highly motivated groups and individuals, working together as a team, with mutual confidence and respect.

Understanding the Roots of Human Behavior

It is easy to understand the roots of human behavior when you realize that *people do the things they do because they have certain basic needs and desires that must be met.* Everything a person does is directed at achieving those needs and desires. Some of these are purely physical. Others are acquired through the learning processes as an individual goes through life.

Physical Needs. The satisfaction of a physical need can become a specific goal that motivates an individual to behave in a certain way. The basic physical needs are those pertaining to one's existence and survival: food, drink, sleep, clothing, shelter, and normal body functions.

A manager or an employer seldom has the opportunity to use a person's physical needs as goals to motivate him except in the specific instance where his basic need has become a want because of greed.

I know greed is a harsh word, but I see no use of using some euphemism to describe a drive most of us have, but don't like to admit. To be brutally frank, I've found that *when all other human motives fail, you can always depend on greed.* That's why the flim-flam man and the con artist still survive today.

Greed will make a man want a larger house, a bigger car, better food to eat, more expensive clothes, more money than he needs. Let me give you some specific examples of that. A house with one bathroom could be thought of by most people as a basic need; one with three or four bathrooms would be a desire to many of us. Heat in the winter is a necessity; until the energy shortage, a fireplace for the majority was a luxury. A woman's cloth coat in cold weather would be a requirement; a mink coat would be a desire.

When a person's need becomes a want, it is often because he is driven by a deep desire for ego-gratification—a feeling of importance or pride—plus a desire for more money and the things money will buy. We all want to feel important whether we'll come right out and admit that or not. For instance, would you rather drive a Ford or a Lincoln Continental? Both are transportation. You'd rather have the Lincoln, right? Why? Because you need it or because it makes you feel more important? Of course, everything is relative. The real feeling of importance comes from being more important than someone else. You can enjoy your Lincoln even more when your neighbor owns a Ford.

PS: I'm not immune; I'd rather have the Lincoln, too!

What's my point in all this? I'm not trying to embarrass anyone. I'm as guilty as the next person. I drive a car too big for my needs, live in a house too large for my requirements, and have more suits and shoes than I can wear in a couple of weeks. I eat more and better food than I should; the scales prove that. All I'm trying to bring out is what makes people tick, what turns them on, what makes them do the things they do. I simply want you to understand the nuts and bolts of human behavior.

Learned Needs (Desires). Learned needs are acquired by the individual throughout his life as he learns what is valued by other people and the importance of social attitudes. Psychological needs such as the desire for security, social approval, and recognition can be as strong as the more basic physical ones. People will do anything necessary to achieve them.

As a manager, you can use a man's psychological needs or desires as goals to motivate him far better than you can use his physical needs (except as I previously indicated) to get the action you want from him. The basic needs and desires—primarily learned— every normal person has are these:

1. Financial success: money and the things money will buy.

2. Recognition of efforts, reassurance of worth.

3. Social or group approval; acceptance by one's peers.

4. Ego-gratification, a feeling of importance.

5. The desire to win . . . the desire to be first . . . the desire to excel.

6. A sense of roots; belonging somewhere.

7. The opportunity for creative expression.

8. The accomplishment or achievement of something worth while.

9. New experiences.

10. A sense of personal power.

11. Good health; freedom from sickness and disease; physical comfort.

12. Liberty and freedom.

13. A sense of self-respect, dignity, and self-esteem.

14. Love in all its forms.

15. Emotional security.

I have not listed these basic needs and desires in any particular order of importance. The point is, a person cannot be completely happy and satisfied if any single one of them is not fulfilled in his life. If you don't remember anything else about human nature, please keep these basic desires every person has in your mind, remembering that everything he does is directed toward their fulfillment. His every thought, word, and deed are aimed at achieving those goals. Help him gain them and he'll do whatever you ask him to do.

Some authorities consider the desire to win, to be first, or to excel as a part of the desire for a feeling of importance or the desire to accomplish or achieve something worth while. That may be true to some extent, but I feel the desire to win is important enough to be categorized individually.

There is one other basic desire a person can have. I have not mentioned it because it seldom can be used by a manager to motivate his people. Not only that, it is a motive that is more commonly encountered in abnormal people rather than normal people, although all of us will have the desire at one time or another in our lives. That motivating force is the *desire for vengeance or revenge, the desire to get even with someone.* It is a motive often used in western stories where the hero devotes his entire life to getting even with the person who has wronged him or his family in some way. In a normal person the desire for vengeance is usually short-lived; in the abnormal individual it will become an obsession.

How Sam Cook Uses His Knowledge of
Human Behavior to Get Results

"When I went to work for the Crown Corporation years ago, I was a shift supervisor," Sam says. "My boss, a crusty old foreman, believed in pushing people around and using threats to get the job done. He ran the department like a tough army drill sergeant. People were scared to death of him and hated him as well. They covered up their mistakes. Morale was bad . . . production was low . . . quality was terrible. I vowed then if ever I attained a position of authority, I would do the exact opposite of everything Bill did.

"Finally he left and I became department foreman. I changed procedures immediately. Instead of yelling at people when they made mistakes, I showed them how to do the job properly. Rather than use harsh criticism, I praised a person for his efforts. Instead of threatening a person with the loss of his job, I helped him improve his work methods so he could speed up production and make more money. My supervisors followed my lead. That department changed almost overnight. Where before people fought to stay out of it, they now begged to get in.

"That was a long time ago. I've been rewarded handsomely over the years for my work. I know I would never have attained my position as president of the corporation had I not made the effort to understand people and help them solve their problems. Actually, I should say my people helped me get where I am today because I helped them get what they wanted. I've never forgotten that lesson. I still follow the same principles in dealing with people today."

As a manager, you should analyze your own operation to determine how you can best satisfy the basic needs and wants of your own people, too. When you do this, I know you will find, just as I have, that *whatever a person is lacking at the moment, he has the greatest need and desire for*. It will be your responsibility to find out which specific need or desire is most important to a person at that particular moment.

You will need to keep in mind that each person's needs and desires change constantly. They are never static. What he needed most of all yesterday may not be what he needs today. That's why you'll want to keep up-to-date and fully informed on your people's needs and desires at all times.

At this point you might be saying to yourself, "What's so important about making sure all those people get what they want? What about me? What about what I want? Don't I count, too?"

You sure do, so let me tell you this. I learned a long time ago that *when the person who worked for me got what he wanted, then I always got what I wanted, too*. When I fulfilled his basic needs and desires, he gave me better quality production with less waste. He cooperated with me whole-heartedly to get the job done. You'll find the same thing will hold true for you.

You see, when you give the person who works for you what he wants, then he'll give you what you want. The reverse of this idea is also true. *You'll never get what you want unless he gets what he wants first*. This thought brings us quite logically to the next subject:

The Master Key that Controls Human Behavior

This master key controls *all* human behavior. It is the most important principle in the conduct of all human relations. This master key is even more than a principle; it is a law governing all human conduct. It is the "number one rule" that you can depend on in dealing with people. If you want to be successful in management—or salesmanship or any other profession or human endeavor for that matter—then

FIND OUT WHAT PEOPLE WANT AND HELP THEM GET IT

Does this seem too simple to be the number one rule in all human relations? Think about it for a while. If you follow this rule, it will even solve your family problems for you, too. It can be used in any sort of activity in which people are engaged. There's only one sure way to get anyone to do what you want him to do every time. That's to find out what he wants and then to make sure he gets it when he does as you ask him to do.

For instance, does he want recognition for a job well done? Then make sure he gets it . . . praise his work. Does he want to feel important? Pay attention to him . . . make him important. Does he want a chance to do something really worth while? Offer him that opportunity; give him a challenging job to do. Does he want to feel secure in his job? Offer him that security. Don't use force or fear or threaten to fire him for every little mistake. When a person fears you, he will eventually hate you. I guarantee it.

When you find out what a person wants and show him how he can get it by doing as you ask, you can rest assured of one thing: he will do exactly as you desire when he knows for sure he will get what he wants. In fact, he will do everything necessary to get what he wants, even if he has to move heaven and earth to get it.

That being so, you will know exactly what his actions and reactions to your orders and directives are going to be. As long as you make sure he gets what he wants by following your orders, you can accurately predict every single time what he's going to do. You can forecast his response to the letter.

Finding Out What He Really Wants

You have only one sure way to find out what a person wants,

and that's to ask him questions. Of course, you don't have to be blunt; you can use a bit of finesse and be subtle about it. You can use either formal interviews in your office or informal chats as you go through your organization on routine inspections or supervisory walks.

I've always found informal visits to be better than formal interviews for getting worthwhile information. A person tends to be on guard in a formal interview. He's likely to give you the answer he thinks you want to hear when he's in your office. He will be more candid during an informal chat that "just happens" to take place.

Whichever method you decide on, use your ears, your eyes, and common sense. You'll learn a lot. I use the following guidelines in my interviews and my visits to draw a man out and get him to talk about himself and what he wants out of life.

1. I act genuinely interested in people and their problems.
2. I try always to be a good listener. I listen to what he doesn't say as well as to what he does. I've found patience is required at all times to be a good listener.
3. I encourage him to talk about himself. I ask him questions to help get him started.
4. I talk in terms of the other person's interests so I can find out what he wants. I never tell him what I want; he could care less about that.
5. I make the other person feel important. I feed his ego and I do it sincerely.

I always use the *Five W's* to get specific answers to my questions. This forces me to be precise so I can bring out the answers I need. The Five W's I use are *Who? What? When? Where? Why?* I also use *How?* to get additional information. By asking a person questions, I gain these benefits:

1. Questions help my listener crystallize his thinking and concentrate his attention where I want it.
2. Questions make a person feel important. When I ask a person for his opinion or his idea on anything, I feed his ego—I give him a sense of importance.

3. When I ask questions, I keep from talking too much. My listener has the opportunity to tell me what he thinks and what he wants. My purpose is to get information, not give it away.

4. Questions keep me out of arguments. By asking questions, I get his idea first. If I disagree with him, I don't have to say so. He'll never know what I was actually thinking.

5. When I ask questions, I can find out exactly what a person's desires are. A question is the quickest, most reliable way to find out what a person really wants.

Summing It Up. . . .

This, now, is the end of your "formal classroom style training" in applied psychology and human behavior. The rest of my book consists of techniques you can use every day to help people gain their basic needs and desires so you can get them to do what you want them to do. You'll see how you can use this information to quickly solve your people-management problems in every possible situation. Getting people to do what you want them to do is really the crux of the management of people. Summed up in one sentence, the most important point to remember about people is this:

Every normal person wants to know how to be loved, how to win money, fame and fortune, power, and how to stay healthy.

If you will always keep that one thought in mind in all your dealings with people, you'll never have the slightest bit of trouble in getting them to do what you want them to do. So find out what people want and help them get it. Give your complete assistance to every one of your employees from the lowest paid laborer to your highest paid manager so they can gain their needs and desires.

Help your people attain their goals and you'll become so successful in dealing with them you'll soon have the psychologists coming to you for help. You'll be a lot further along the path to the understanding of the complexities of human nature and human behavior than the average student of psychology ever will be.

Before I get into the specific techniques successful managers use to motivate people, I'd like to ask you to do me one favor. I want you to type on a 5-by-8 card the sentence I gave you just a moment ago about every normal person wanting to be loved and the basic needs and desires I listed back on page 32.

Please keep that card handy at your elbow or under your desk glass so you can refer to it at all times. It will be useful to you as you go through the specific techniques successful managers use to motivate people. Not only that, every time one of your own people does something, you can refer to your card and figure out which desire he's trying to gain for himself.

Before long you'll become an absolute expert in evaluating the behavior of people for you'll know what they want and what they are going to do every time. Others will look at you as an authority in human relations and applied psychology, and to tell the truth, you'll really be one.

SPECIFIC TECHNIQUES SUCCESSFUL MANAGERS
USE TO MOTIVATE PEOPLE

You might ask now if the executives and managers in highly successful companies and corporations use a person's basic needs and desires to get the results they want. The answer is definitely *Yes*. I don't want you to accept my word alone for how well these methods work, so I'm going to bring some of them on as my witnesses. In the next several pages I'll give you specific examples of how they do that.

I will not cover every one of the basic needs or desires I listed. I will take up those that successful managers seem to find most useful in getting the job done. You'll notice something else interesting as you study these examples. When one of a person's basic desires is fulfilled, others are often taken care of at the same time. This is quite apparent in the first example.

Offering a Person the Opportunity
for Financial Gain

In this particular example, you will see how a company's plan helped all its employees financially. You will also discover that the specific method used satisfied almost every other basic desire at the same time for its employees.

As will happen sometimes, this company got into the business of using precise techniques to motivate people through the back door because of necessity. In other words, the company was forced to go to its employees for help because of adverse financial circumstances. But when the financial position of the company improved, the president was wise enough to see the advantages of retaining the system.

One of the biggest Detroit customers of the Donnelly Mirror Company in Holland, Michigan, had put it on the line with the company. Either it would reduce its prices or the buyer would go elsewhere to find a new supplier of car mirrors.

One of the machine operators on the assembly line knew a method that would reduce his crew of five people down to four and help save money. But he hesitated to offer his idea to the company when they asked their employees for help in reducing costs. After all, he might be the one the company let go.

So he approached the management this way. He would give his idea of cutting costs to the company if they would promise that no one would lose his job as a result. The company agreed to his condition. They also extended the same guarantee to any employee who could come up with suggestions to reduce production costs. Let me tell you now about some of the benefits everyone gained.

1. Every Donnelly employee, from the president down to the janitor, can have as big a pay raise each year as his cost-cutting ideas will pay for.
2. Every employee gets monthly bonus checks that can go as high as 20 percent of his base pay.
3. The company is prospering. Employment has almost doubled since the new program was initiated.
4. The company's main product sells for 15 percent less than it used to, a remarkable feat considering inflation.

Donnelly employees are happy and satisfied. They have learned, and so has management, that everyone gains when they all cooperate and work as a team toward a common goal. The benefits of working together are enormous. Workers have bigger paychecks; stockholders enjoy greater dividends; customers can expect stable and honest prices.

Initially, the main aim was to save the company financially. The end result was financial success, not only for the company, but also for all its employees as well. This satisfied one of the basic desires all people have: *money and the things money will buy*. A quick analysis of this example will show that almost all the rest of the basic desires every person has were satisfied at the same time:

1. *Recognition of their efforts* by management and their fellow employees for submitting cost-cutting ideas.

2. *Group approval* for their efforts by fellow employees and by management as well.

3. *Ego-gratification, a feeling of importance* for having contributed to the company in its time of need.

4. *A sense of roots or belonging* to the organization. Hardship creates fellowship.

5. *The opportunity for creative expression* when asked for new ideas and suggestions by management.

6. *The accomplishment or achievement of something worth while.*

7. *The desire for new experiences* was realized as original ideas were put into practical application by the company.

8. *A sense of personal power* was gained as each employee realized how much the company depended on him.

9. *Liberty and freedom* to offer new ideas to management. Some companies do not offer employees this opportunity.

10. *A sense of self-respect, dignity, and self-esteem* was heightened when employees' ideas were accepted.

11. *Emotional security,* which is based on many factors, including job security, freedom from worry, anxiety, and fear was achieved by the employees.

Is a system that fulfills an employee's basic needs and desires while benefiting the company and management all at the same time worth the effort? Executives and managers from many other companies think so. In one year alone, 460 companies sent 1,800 executives and managers to the Donnelly Company to learn their methods and see how their system works. That's exactly how worthwhile it is.

Satisfying a Person's Needs for Creative Expression

A company interested in an employee's new ideas encourages his initiative and ingenuity. This helps satisfy a person's need for creative expression and also offers him the opportunity to accomplish something worth while. Such a company is IBM. IBM has an open door policy that allows any employee to take his idea or suggestion clear to the top, even to the chairman of the board, if necessary.

Eastman Kodak is another company that recognizes initiative and a person's desire for creative expression. At Eastman, people are encouraged to think and use their brains. Kodak employees' ingenuity and creativity have led to the Instamatic camera, sound in home movies, the XL low-light movie camera, and many other innovations.

Fulfilling a Person's Need to Accomplish
Something Worthwhile

All of us want to achieve something worthwhile. Many times, we do not have the opportunity to do so in our private lives. Our only chance, then, lies in being associated with some organization with that same goal.

Procter and Gamble is such an organization. It refuses to be second in anything. It holds first place in the manufacture and sale of these products: detergents (Tide), toothpaste (Crest), shortening (Crisco), diapers (Pampers), toilet paper (Charmin), and even advertising of its products ($375 million a year).

The people making Procter and Gamble products believe they are engaged in a worthwhile endeavor. They feel strongly theirs are the best products on the market. Procter and Gamble salesmen feel the same way; their enthusiasm for P & G products is legendary in the sales profession.

Techniques that Give a Person the Feeling He Belongs

Many companies do this and do it well. IBM, for instance, wants to keep its employees, almost at all costs. It just doesn't believe in letting them go. The company feels once an IBM employee, always an IBM employee. One of their boasts is no one has ever been let go for economic reasons in the last 35 years. Management always finds new jobs for their displaced personnel, retraining them when necessary. In just one year, for instance, 1,700 employees were retrained so they could stay with IBM.

Eastman Kodak also makes their people feel they belong. Very few people ever leave the company to work elsewhere. J. C. Penney excels in this area, too. They never hire "employees." Instead, they take on "associates." Penney's people seldom leave, although other companies try to lure them away. Du Pont is another company that retains its people. As one senior management official at Du Pont said, "Transients don't come to work for us. Our people come to stay. They expect to be with us until they retire."

Many of us could take lessons from the Japanese on how to make a person feel he belongs. Management always takes a deep personal interest in their personnel. As a result, Japanese employees have a deep loyalty to their companies. Takeshi Hirano, president of one of Japan's largest electronic firms, says he attends ten or more employee weddings every month. Members of his board go to many more.

A Japanese worker will stay with his company until he retires or dies. He feels he belongs to the company body and soul, not as a slave, but as a vital contributing member. Ask a Japanese worker what his job is, and he will say with great pride, "I am with Mitsubishi," regardless of whether he works on the assembly line, drives a truck, or is vice-president of the corporation.

Fulfilling a Person's Desire for Liberty and Freedom

This desire is difficult for some organizations to fulfill. General Electric does it by allowing its employees to bypass the chain of management authority to get the job done. A spokesman for G. E. told me this: "Here at General Electric, if you have a piece of work to do, you determine who you have to work with to get the job done. Then you go wherever you need to go to do it. The only requirement is to keep the right people informed about what you're doing. We think results are more important than rules."

Weyerhaeuser, America's biggest wood products company, offers a person the freedom most people would like to have in their jobs. I asked one of their forest engineers what he liked so much about Wyerhaeuser, and he said, "I have the freedom to make decisions on my own and I really like that. I get a chance to use my head. The company I worked for before I came here wouldn't let me do anything on my own. They said I wasn't getting paid to think, but just to carry out orders. What a difference working here!"

Executives at Weyerhaeuser have the freedom to work in sports or leisure clothes. They can also set their own office hours.

Giving a Person a Sense of Emotional Security

One of a person's greatest fears or worries in life is that some catastrophic illness will completely wipe him out financially. Xerox fulfills two of a person's basic desires—emotional security and the freedom from sickness or disease—by having an outstanding health benefits plan that pays all hospital costs for an employee and his family. There is absolutely no limit. Xerox also pays all dental expenses for those who visit their dentists regularly for two years and follow their advice.

The J. C. Penney chain also offers a person a sense of security, but in a different way. One of their buyers of boys' clothing told me this: "J. C. Penney takes care of its own. I have to make a lot of fast buying decisions that could cost the company a lot of money if I'm wrong. But I know the company will back me if my reasoning is sound. It's a good feeling to know you're not going to get the axe for an honest mistake."

Recognizing a Person's Efforts

Eastman Kodak's policy is to recognize a person's efforts by promoting the right people. The good people get ahead at Eastman Kodak. Politics has little to do with promotion and advancement. Kodak prefers to promote from within rather than going outside for its top management people.

The 3M company's management also recognizes a person's efforts and rewards him for what he does. It has been decades since Minnesota Mining and Manufacturing has put an outsider in a top management job. As one top executive told me, "3M offers every possible opportunity to a person to get ahead. If you want a piece of the pie, all you need do is cut yourself as big a slice as you can handle."

General Electric recognizes a person's efforts, too. Management policy is to promote the people who can do the job, regardless of sex or race. G. E. puts its money where its mouth is. It has hired and promoted more blacks and women than other firms of a comparable size.

Fulfilling a Person's Desires for New Experiences

Although many companies try to do this, the Cummins Engine Corporation is a top leader here. Company policy is to give a young person as much responsibility as he can handle. Then, just when he thinks he really knows his job, they move him along to something new. People move back and forth between line and staff assignments so they never become stale. Each job is a challenge and a brand-new experience to look forward to.

The Best Way to Offer a Person Dignity and Respect

You can see from these examples that such companies as IBM, G.E., Eastman Kodak, Procter and Gamble, J. C. Penney, Xerox, 3M, and Weyerhaeuser all treat their people with dignity and respect, or they couldn't keep them. No company can last long or be successful it it treats its people improperly.

One time I was called on to help a company suffering from all sorts of personnel problems ranging from simple absenteeism to malicious sabotage in the plant. it took me less than an hour to isolate their *main* problem. When the production foreman said, "Well, let's take a walk through the plant so you can find out what's wrong with these dirty rotten bastards!" I knew immediately what was wrong.

My remedy was simple. "All you need do is treat every man like a gentleman and every woman like a lady," I told the plant manager. "Do that and your problems will disappear almost overnight."

The plant manager was not impressed with my suggestion, but he agreed to do it when I said, "Sincerely try it for a week. If it doesn't work or make things improve, you won't owe me anything."

Ten days later my check arrived along with an extra bonus and a note that said, "Thanks a lot for your help, Jim. You wouldn't recognize the place now; there's a complete new air of harmony and cooperation."

More Methods Managers Use to Motivate Their People

In this sub-section, I'll give you some examples at random so you can figure out for yourself which basic desires are being satisfied. Keep your 5-by-8 card handy for ready reference.

"Although I'm a laborer, I have the freedom to say something about my job," an employee at the Gaines Pet Food plant in Topeka, Kansas, says. "If I get mad about something, I can bring it up at my team meeting in the morning. If I want to make a phone call or go to the bathroom, I don't have to get permission from some supervisor. I just ask someone on the team to cover for me for a few minutes. Here at Gaines I feel like a human being again—not a robot."

Shell Oil Company offers more than four thousand of its Houston, Texas, employees, the option of coming in any time between 7 and 8 in the morning and leaving between 3.45 and 4.45. A spokesman for Shell says it's a good morale factor for it gives people more flexibility. The company isn't running their lives as much as before. Other companies using the same kind of system are Amoco Oil Company in Houston, General Motors headquarters in Detroit, Chrysler's and Ford's offices in Highland Park and Dearborn, Michigan. The Hewlett-Packard factory in Palo Alto, California, for quite a long time now has allowed its employees to come in between 6.30 and 8.30 and leave between 3.15 and 5.15. They beat both the morning and afternoon rush-hour traffic and have more free daylight hours for themselves.

The Social Security Administration's headquarters in Baltimore lets its employees work any 8 ¼ hour period in a 12-hour work day from 6.30 am to 6.30 pm. Workers can also work overtime two hours a day, making it possible to complete their 40 hour week in four days instead of five. The advantages to the employees far outweigh the disadvantages to management, if any.

Indiana Bell Telephone used to assemble its telephone books in 21 steps, each step being performed by a different person. Now the company gives each person the responsibility for assembling the entire book. One result: employee turnover was cut by 50 percent.

Monsanto's employees in the Pensacola, Florida, plant were allowed to reorganize the entire production system. The workers literally became their own managers. In the first year of the new system, waste from bad work dropped to zero. Productivity increased 50 percent.

In Fort Lauderdale, Florida, Motorola's assembly line was used to manufacture radio receivers. Each woman placed approximately ten parts on a printed circuit board, then passed the board to the next worker. Absenteeism was high; so was turnover. The company received numerous complaints about poor quality from customers. "The work was so monotonous," said one employee, "I'd go home ready to scream."

Then the plant manager decided to let each worker build and test her own radio receiver. She would attach a note saying, "Dear Customer, I built this receiver and I'm proud of it. I hope it serves you well. Please tell me if it does not." Then she would sign her name and package the radio herself.

When the new system was introduced, absenteeism and turnover dropped drastically. So did customer complaints. "The key to our success with the new system is employee involvement," the manager says. "Getting rid of the assembly line allowed people to be proud of their own work."

The Travelers Insurance Company in Hartford, Connecticut, had problems with high absenteeism, poor morale, and low productivity. The employees are mainly punch-card computer operators. The original work method had a person handling only one phase of the operation: receipts, collections, or any one of the numerous punch-card functions.

A management consulting firm recommended changing the system so a computer operator would be responsible for the entire operation for a particular corporate or individual customer. This established a firm operator-customer relationship. Each employee at Travelers now has his own group of clients for whom he is responsible. The first year results of the new program were so impressive—a 26 percent increase in productivity and a 24 percent decline in absenteeism—it has now been expanded to eight of the company's branch offices.

At the Corning Glass plant in Medford, Massachusetts, work teams stick around after work to figure out how to increase production. In the Medford plant where hot plates are made, work teams are allowed to set their own production goals and establish their own work schedules. They even decide when they will take some of their holidays. As one worker told me, "I love it here. You start with nothing, and you can make something of yourself if you really want to. It's all up to you."

Initiating Your Own Program to Fulfill a
Person's Needs and Desires

If at the present time you have no actual program going to

fulfill a person's needs and desires, then start one. You can gain some pointers from some of the examples I've just given you. But to help you get an even faster start, let me give you some statistics from a university study that was made to find out what people want most of all from their employers or their managers.

This survey was conducted by a large midwestern university. It covered 5,000 employees in all kinds of industries; electronics, aerospace, airlines, automobiles, coal, railroad, steel, rubber, communications, and so on. Two questions were asked of all these employees.

1. What do you want most of all from your employers?
2. How would you place these wants in their order of importance?

The answers the employees gave are recorded in this chart:

BASIC WANTS LISTED IN ORDER OF THEIR IMPORTANCE BY EMPLOYEES

1. Credit and recognition for the work they do.
2. Interesting and worthwhile work.
3. Fair pay with salary increases.
4. Attention and appreciation.
5. Promotion by merit, not seniority.
6. Counsel on their personal problems.
7. Good physical working conditions.
8. Job security.

Are you surprised at some of these answers? Are you surprised at the importance, or the lack of it, placed on some points by employees? You are not alone. The University also asked the managers of those same 5,000 employees to rate the same items, not in the way they felt about them, *but in the order they thought their employees felt.* The answers management gave are shown below:

EMPLOYEES' BASIC WANTS LISTED IN ORDER OF IMPORTANCE
BY THE <u>MANAGERS</u> OR THEIR <u>EMPLOYERS</u>

1. Fair pay with salary increases.
2. Job security.
3. Interesting and worthwhile work.
4. Promotion by merit, not seniority.
5. Attention and appreciation.
6. Good physical working conditions.
7. Credit and recognition for the work they do.
8. Counsel on their personal problems.

As you can see, managers expected employees to be most interested in *fair pay with salary increases*. But employees gave *credit and recognition for the work they do* number 1 priority. They placed salary down in number 3 position.

Job security was also a most interesting point. Employees put it way down in last place, but employers had it in number 2 position. The conclusions in this survey have been confirmed time and again by countless other studies in all parts of the country.

What can you learn from this study? First of all, money and job security are *not* the main incentives you can use in getting people to do what you want them to do. In fact, *the main incentives that stimulate a person to do his best for you cost you absolutely nothing at all in dollars and cents.*

Second, if you as a manager want to attain efficiency in your organization, if you want people to do their utmost for you, you must *place your emphasis on giving them what they want, not on what you think they ought to want.*

Third, *these eight points make up the main desires most employees have that employers can fulfill,* so you can use this study to start your own job enrichment program. Or you can use a questionnaire similar to this one to check your own employees. Let them indicate the amount of importance they give to each item themselves. The questionnaire should be turned into you without the employee's name unless he insists on signing it.

Understanding a Person's Frustrations

When a person is blocked in his efforts to realize a specific want, he can become frustrated. His energy is blocked and backs up like water behind a dam. To some degree we all experience frustrations, varying from minor annoyances to major irritations. The amount of frustration depends on the value we place on the goal in question.

Outward evidences of being frustrated can take a variety of forms; anger, swearing, nervousness, even crying. Serious frustrations that deny the satisfaction of a person's wants for a long time can cause adverse changes in his behavior. If a person's hard work does not earn him a promotion, or even a word of thanks from his superior, he may develop a hard bitterness that will affect not only him alone, but also other employees as well.

One of the best ways to keep a person from being frustrated is to assign a person to the kind of work for which he is best suited. If a bright individual is given a dull job, he may become bored and resentful. However, if a person is given a task that is beyond his capabilities, he may become discouraged, frustrated, or resentful. A poorly assigned person cannot be expected to make a maximum contribution to the team effort. *You will always gain more from your people if you fit the job to the person rather than fit the person to the job.* Or as the General Foods plant manager in Topeka, Kansas, told me, "We design the work to suit the person—not the other way around. It prevents all kinds of frustrations."

No one can completely avoid being frustrated about something at one time or another. The normal person plans ahead to avoid many of his frustrations. At the same time, he will take the necessary steps to adjust to the situation. He may also alter his methods for attaining specific goals if the ways he has tried have been blocked. Or he may pick different goals that he feels are more attainable.

There is just no way under the sun you can solve everyone's problems and please every person all the time when you are the boss. But the more effort you make to help people achieve their goals and realize their basic needs and desires, the less of a problem will their frustrations be to you.

Your Specific Role as a Manager of People

As a good manager, it is up to you to establish the *proper climate of management* for your entire organization. Or as Willis A. Strauss, chairman of the board and president of Northern Natural Gas Company in Omaha, Nebraska, says, "A chief executive should create an atmosphere that allows people to do their best work." So that's your first job as a manager—to establish the proper atmosphere, the correct climate, where everyone can do his utmost and be happy about doing it.

As a manager you must also understand and be able to recognize individual differences in the people who work for you. Each person has his own personality and each one is affected differently by his environment. You must be able to recognize types and analyze individuals, so that the proper appeal or approach can be selected that will cause the person to respond willingly in the way you desire.

Your understanding of human behavior, of individual differences in people, and of the drive for satisfaction of basic needs and desires provides a good basis for the establishment of good working relationships and the development of desirable group action. As a manager, you are in a position to provide the means for helping people to satisfy their basic desires. By doing so, you will build an attitude of confidence and respect in them for your management abilities. Your subordinates will feel they can depend on you, that you are interested in their welfare. They will do their best for you. The end result will be an efficient properly motivated organization.

You may have noticed that in this chapter I did not cover one of the basic needs every person has: the desire for importance or ego-gratification. That may have surprised you for one of the best ways to motivate people to do what you want them to do is to make them more important—not only to you, but also to themselves.

That is such a big subject, though, that rather than trying to cover it here in one small sub-section, I'm going to use a whole chapter to discuss it with you. I consider this topic so valuable I've called it *The Master Power Play That Never Fails*. It is the second Master Key to Management Success. In the next chapter you'll find out why smart managers and executives use it.

Chapter **2**

The Master Power Play that

Never Fails . . . and

Why Smart Executives Use It

In Chapter 1, I gave you the "Number One Rule" to use in all human relations: *find out what people want and help them get it.* I also said we all have certain basic desires that must be fulfilled to some extent if we are to be completely happy and satisfied. Of these desires, one stands out above all the rest for it is much more than a desire, it is a craving—*the craving to be important.* Psychologists say the desire to be important is the strongest drive in human nature. Mark Twain said it this way: "I have been complimented many times and they always embarrass me; I always feel they have not said enough."

As you may recall, I also said that when you found out what a person wanted and showed him how to get it when he did as you asked, he would follow your orders and carry out your directives every time. That's your primary goal in managing people: to get them to *want* to do what you want them to do. You can do that by helping them fulfill their basic desires.

If you don't know how or where to begin in fulfilling a person's basic desires, here's the place to start. You can always use a person's desire to be important to your advantage. This method will work every time on everyone, with no exceptions. I have yet to meet the person whose actions I cannot influence when I give him that feeling of importance and prestige he needs so much. You can always benefit by helping a person become more important. *That's the Second Master Key to Management Success.*

Why a Person Needs a Feeling of Importance

The desire to be important comes from deep within us. Dr. Sigmund Freud said everything a person does springs from one of two motives: the sex drive and the *desire to be great*. Dr. John Dewey said the deepest urge of all in human nature is the *desire to be important*. Dr. Alfred Adler said man wants most of all *to be significant*. William James went even further. He said, "The deepest principle in human nature is the *craving to be appreciated*." Discounting the sex drive since it is primarily a physical need, it is readily apparent that *the greatest motivating force in us all is the desire to be great, the drive to be important.*

I have no degrees in psychology or philosophy, but I agree with the conclusions of these four learned gentlemen. I know from my own practical experience in working with people that everyone wants attention of some kind. Each person wants to be recognized and to be important, no matter who he is. I have never met anyone who did not want to feel important in some way.

Even the person who says he doesn't have any aspirations to be important demands that you listen to his point of view on the subject. He may not want to be important, so he says, but he insists on being heard; he commands your attention. He reminds me of the preacher who said, "You don't have the slightest idea of what the word 'humble' means until you've heard my sermon on humility. I'm the final authority on that subject!"

Every person wants the attention of other people whether he likes to admit that or not. He wants to be listened to; he wants to be heard. He has a deep burning desire—yes, even an insatiable craving—to be important, to be recognized and appreciated. In short, *everybody wants to be somebody.*

You think that's not true in your case? Tell me now, have you ever told a joke, only to have someone butt in and change the subject right when you were in the middle of your story? How did you feel? You'd probably have liked to strangle him, right? Do you really know why you felt that way? Because he was impolite and interrupted you? No. You felt that way because he deflated your ego; he made you feel small, insignificant, and unimportant. He put himself on center stage and shoved you right out of the spotlight.

Let's say you look at a group picture taken at the annual company picnic. Where do your eyes go first? To yourself, of course. Why? Because you are more interested in yourself than in anyone else. That's not criticism, only a simple statement of fact. We all feel the same way about ourselves. From my point of view, I am the center of everything; the world revolves around me. But from your point of view, you are the center of everything; the world revolves around you. And everyone feels the same way you and I do.

If people cannot be important in their jobs or at their work, they will make themselves important elsewhere. They will become lay leaders in church; they will hold offices in lodges and fraternal organizations; some will be active in PTA, Red Cross, and civic affairs.

I will never forget the janitor in a company I once worked for. He had the most menial job in the plant. His clothes were ragged and dirty. No one paid the slightest bit of attention to him. But when he left the plant at the end of the day, what a metamorphosis. He wore the latest, most fashionable slacks and sports jacket. He was bathed, shaved, and well-groomed. And he drove off in a flashy red foreign sports car!

You would do well, then, to keep the following thoughts in mind when dealing with people.

1. Every person is an egotist. He demands attention, appreciation, and recognition of some sort.

2. Each individual is more interested in himself than in anyone else.

3. Each person's viewpoint is that he is the center of everything. The world revolves around him.

4. Everyone you meet wants to feel important and amount to something.

5. Each man has to be needed in some way by others. He wants to feel indispensable in his job, home, church, or club. He likes to feel others just couldn't get along without him.

6. We all need respect and approval from others before we can have respect for and approval of ourselves.

7. Each person will do everything necessary to gain the attention and recognition he needs so much so he can feel more important.

When you sincerely feed a person's ego and fulfill his desire to be important,

YOU'LL ACHIEVE THESE WORTHWHILE BENEFITS

1. Each person will go all out to help you attain your goals.
2. You'll gain many, many true friends.
3. You'll have no enemies.
4. People will admire you and respect you.
5. Your people will always do what you ask them to do; they'll give you their full support.
6. You'll win your people's hearts as well as their heads.
7. You'll find this master power play works like magic; it literally performs miracles with people.

TECHNIQUES YOU CAN USE TO GAIN THESE BENEFITS

An Old-Fashioned Technique that Will Never Go Out of Style

Do you want a person to give you his unswerving loyalty and full support? Do you expect to receive his complete cooperation and willing obedience? Would you like him to have confidence in you and respect you? Then all you need do is *praise him*, not just once, but all the time, over and over again.

Praise him. Tell him what a magnificent job he's doing for you . . . how much you need him . . . how you can't get along without him . . . how happy you are he's with your organization.

We all hunger for a word of praise. We all need recognition and appreciation. Everybody likes a compliment. No one is immune. As Mark Twain once said, "I could live for two months on one good compliment."

Be generous with your praise. Pass it around freely; the supply is limited only by you. Don't be stingy about passing out bouquets; they cost you nothing. Above all, never act as if you expected something in return for your praise. Don't pay a person a compliment as if you wanted a receipt for it.

Praise is the best way to make a person feel important. Criticism is the quickest way to destroy a person and make him your enemy. If you criticize a person, he will soon hate you. Nothing is more destructive to a person's pride than criticism. listen to Carla Evans, a store manager for Fairfield Fashions in St. Louis, Missouri, as she tells why she uses praise instead of criticism with her employees.

> "Some people say they find it hard to praise a person, but I disagree with that," Carla says. "It's actually quite easy to find something to compliment in a person and make her feel more important. All you need do is look for something good about the individual.
>
> "For instance, you can say, 'You really handled that difficult customer skillfully, Jane . . . That's really a top-notch idea, Fran . . . I sure appreciate your getting that report out ahead of time, Alice . . . Thanks for staying late and getting those letters out yesterday, Mary . . .'
>
> "See how easy it is? It all depends on what you're looking for. If you want to praise a person and make her feel more important, you can always find something to compliment her for. If you want to criticize her, you can always find something wrong, too. But I'd rather praise than criticize. I find it's a much better way to get my employees to do their best for me."

I agree with Carla. I never criticize anyone, either. I have enough character defects of my own to worry about without taking someone else's inventory. I do make helpful suggestions or show a person how to improve his work methods, but I do not use criticism to do that. I always go out of my way to praise a person, but I am extremely reluctant to find fault.

It would be wise to remember that no person ever criticizes himself for anything, no matter how wrong he might be. He will always find some excuse to justify his actions. If a person will not accept criticism even from himself, then I know he will never accept it from me. However, I do not want to mislead you here. Let me quickly point out that my hestitancy to criticize others will not stop me from taking the necessary corrective or disciplinary action when it's required.

Five Small Words You Can Use to Make a Person Feel Important

I Am Proud Of You are five of the most valuable and powerful words in the English language. You can use them any time on your employees, associates, and friends, or your husband, wife, and children. Just tell them how proud you are of something they did. Be generous with your compliments. They cost you nothing . . . they'll pay you rich dividends.

These five little words will work miracles in human relations for you. You can even use them with your boss. If you feel too self-conscious to say "I'm proud of you" to him, change the words and say, "I'm sure proud to work for you." They'll still produce the same good results you're after.

Does this method work? I'll say it does. I'm not the only one to use it either. George Wheeler, executive vice-president and general manager of a radio and television factory in Missouri, uses it, too.

"I've never found any better words to use with my employees than 'I'm proud of you,'" George says. "That's one of the highest compliments you can pay a person.

"When an employee does an exceptionally fine piece of work or turns in a terrific money-saving or cost-cutting idea, just to say 'Thanks' isn't enough. I go to him right out on the production line and in front of all his fellow workers I pat him on the back and say, 'Thanks a lot for what you did, Bill; *I'm really proud of you.*' He'll work even harder for me from then on. So will everyone else. They want some of that sweet syrup, too."

A Psychological Study Proves the Value of
This Priceless Technique

I want to show you exactly why praise is such a valuable procedure to make a person feel important. I'll also show you why criticism is such a useless method. A team of psychologists from the University of Missouri made a detailed study to determine the relative merits of these two techniques. Here's how they conducted their study and the conclusions they reached.

The team of psychologists carried out their tests with army recruits in the reception station at Fort Leonard Wood, Missouri, a basic training center for the United States Army. Three thousand young men, still fresh from all walks in civilian life, were tested in their first 48 hours at the reception center before they were sent down to their training units to be indoctrinated by tough army drill sergeants with army customs and procedures. The team tested 60 men a day for 10 weeks. Here's how they ran their tests.

Each morning 60 volunteers were divided into six squads of 10 men each. The squads were then given the same set of difficult tasks to perform. As each one completed its work, it was judged on its performance. But the results of each squad were reviewed in different ways by the testing team.

Squad number 1 was praised in public before all the rest of the squads. The second squad was also praised, but in private with only its own members present. Squad number 3 was criticized in private; only its own members were present. Number 4 was publicly criticized in front of all the other squads. The fifth squad was ridiculed and made fun of in private with only its own squad there. Squad number 6 was ridiculed and made fun of in front of all 60 volunteers.

The squads were then given the same exact work to do again. Their second performance was checked against the first. The second performance results are shown as follows:

SQUAD #	CRITIQUE METHOD	% SHOWING IMPROVEMENT ON SECOND TEST
1	Public Praise	90 %
2	Private Praise	75 %
3	Private Criticism	49 %
4	Public Criticism	31 %
5	Private Ridicule	19 %
6	Public Ridicule	10 %

The results are quite clear. Praise is a much better tool to use than either criticism or ridicule when you're trying to motivate a person to upgrade his performance. When you praise people in public, nine out of ten will improve, for you've given them the recognition they need so much. You've made them feel more important in front of other people. Praise in private will not do quite as well as public praise, but three out of four will still respond favorably.

However, if you criticize people hoping to get improvement, you will always fail. Even when you criticize in private, only about half the people will improve and do a better job for you. If you criticize people publicly in front of others, less than one-third will show any sign of doing better. No one wants to be disapproved of or have his faults criticized, including me.

If one of your people asks you to look at his work and let him know where he's making his mistakes, don't be misled. That isn't what he wants at all. He wants you to tell him how well he's doing. He wants you to pat him on the back and tell him he's not making any mistakes. He wants to be praised, not criticized. Read between the lines; listen to what he really said. Remember those basic desires every person has. *To be critized is not one of them.*

Criticism causes the criticized person to do worse; it destroys his incentive to improve. Most people can't criticize without hurting the other person's feelings. They usually do more harm than good. As Josh Billings, the American humorist, said, "To be a critic demands more brains than most people have." You can't criticize another person without deflating his ego and destroying his feeling of importance. Criticism maims and cripples people psychologically. *The best thing to remember about criticism is to forget it.*

Ridicule, either public or private, is a complete waste of time as you can see from the last two figures on the chart. However, I want to take some time here to tell you exactly why ridicule is so useless. You'll be better able to understand one basic desire when I do.

You see, a man will tolerate almost any insult, defeat, or injury, and accept it with some semblance of good grace. You can steal his wife, his job, his money, and although he won't like you for it, he'll probably tolerate it up to a point and still treat you like a civilized human being.

But if you make fun of a man, if you belittle and ridicule him, or if you make a fool of him—especially in front of others—you'll have made an enemy for the rest of your life. He'll never forget and he'll never forgive, for you've absolutely devastated his sense of self-respect, dignity, and self-esteem as well as deflated his ego and injured his pride. Besides these two, you've also destroyed his opportunity to fulfill no less than four more of his basic desires. You've taken away the possibility of being recognized for his efforts by ridiculing him instead of praising him . . . you've destroyed him in front of his peers and prevented the group from approving of him . . . you've ruined his desire to accomplish something worth while . . . you've taken away his feeling of emotional security. Can you blame him now for despising you? Look at the amount of harm you've done to him just by ridiculing and making fun of him.

So if you do ridicule someone and make fun of him, better load your shotgun, bolt the doors, and place a guard at every window. He'll come after you for sure. The basic desire for revenge, vengeance, an eye for an eye and a tooth for a tooth can be a greater driving force than even the desire for importance or the desire for sex.

Why This Powerful Praise Technique
Works So Well

This study by the University of Missouri psychologists confirms something I have known and practiced for many years. *Public praise is the most powerful technique you can use to feed a person's ego and make him feel more important.* Let's dig a little deeper into this technique and find out exactly why praise works so well.

Praise Releases Energy; Praise Acts as an Energizer. That's exactly why it works so well. To praise means to honor, compliment, pay recognition to, express approval of. If you are praised, what is your reaction? Probably the same as mine. You feel thrilled and excited. You're happy you were able to please someone. Praise increases your enthusiasm; it makes you want to do even better. You work harder than before so you can get more of it. So will your people.

Do you see how praise releases energy? Praise makes a person work harder, more efficiently, and with greater enthusiasm. That was proven some time ago by Dr. Henry H. Goddard, an American psychologist.

Dr. Goddard performed his experiments when he was research director at New Jersey's Vineland Training School for Retarded Children. Dr. Goddard used an ergograph to measure energy and fatigue. When tired children were praised and complimented for their work, the ergograph showed an immediate upward surge of new energy. But when they were criticized and reprimanded, the ergograph readings were immediately lowered.

You don't need an ergograph to measure the release of new energy in your employees. Just praise them; you can see the good results. For instance, when you praise your secretary for her typing skills and abilities, you'll find fewer errors than ever in your correspondence. Those letters will also be ready for your signature much sooner than before. Tell your subordinates what good jobs they've done, praise them in front of their fellows, and they'll do even better work for you next time. This technique will work with your wife, husband, children, relatives, friends, anyone. The final proven conclusion is that *praise releases new energy in a person.*

Other Basic Desires that Are Automatically Fulfilled by This Technique

Not only does praise feed a person's ego and fulfill his desire to be important, but it also satisfies such other basic desires as. . . .

1. Recognition of efforts, reassurance of worth.
2. Social or group approval; acceptance by one's peers.
3. A sense of roots, belonging somewhere.
4. The accomplishment of something worth while.
5. A sense of self-esteem, dignity, and self-respect.
6. The desire to win, to be first, to excel.
7. Emotional security.

You can see from this why praise is one of the most powerful techniques you can ever use to get a person to do what you want him to do. You just can't miss when you praise someone for what he's done.

Praising Every Single Improvement

Smart animal trainers know you must praise every single improvement with a kind word of encouragement, a pat on the head, and a bit of food if further progress is to be made. If we know enough to praise animals for every single improvement they make, we ought to be wise enough to use the same technique on people.

Get in the habit of praising even the slightest improvement in your employees. That will inspire them to keep right on improving. Don't wait until someone does something really outstanding or unusual before you praise him. Praise the tiniest bit of progress you can find.

I've been married to my wife for more than 35 years now and she's a wonderful cook. But it wasn't always that way. The first month or so was, well . . . anyway, I haven't had a bad meal since then. Do you know why? Because to this very day I never get up from the table without saying, "Thanks a lot, honey; that was really a terrific meal." That's why I always eat too well.

The words "Thank you" can work magic in human relations when you use them properly. They will always make people glad they did something for you, especially when you use them sincerely. You can soup them up a bit by saying "Thanks very much . . . thanks a million . . . thanks a lot . . . I sure do appreciate it." Look the person right in the eye when you're thanking him. If he's worth being thanked, he's worth being looked at and noticed. Don't be like the checkout clerk in the supermarket who says thank you to the cash register and never sees the customer.

Keep your eyes open and find things to thank people for. Every time you say "Thank you," you're praising the other person. You're giving him credit for having done something you appreciate. When you let people know how grateful you are for what they've done, when you praise every single improvement they make, no matter how small, they will want to do even more for you.

So praise the slightest improvement a person makes and praise every improvement he makes. As Charles Schwab would say, "I am anxious to praise but loath to find fault. If I like anything, I am always hearty in my approbation and lavish in my praise."

Using Sincere Praise Instead of Flattery

To flatter a person means to praise him beyond what is true or to praise him insincerely. The dictionary says flattery is praise that is usually untrue or overstated. In other words, to flatter is simply to lie. To be sincere means to be genuine and honest, free from pretense or deceit.

Flattery is as phony as a three-dollar bill. It's counterfeit and worthless. It avails you nothing. People will spot your phoniness and see through you immediately. You would be far better off to praise a person for some small thing and be sincere about it than to pick out something big and lie about it.

Why do people use flattery when it's so worthless? Usually because the individual who flatters another is too lazy to look for something good and worthwhile the other individual has done.

There's a quick and easy way to know whether you're praising a person or flattering him. Flattery praises a person for what he *is*, not what he does. When you use sincere praise, you do just the opposite. You praise a person for what he *does*, not what he is. Look at the following examples. You'll see exactly what I mean.

FLATTERY: Tom, you're the best salesman in the whole outfit.

PRAISE: Congratulations, Tom. You had the most sales in the entire district last month. That's an outstanding record. Thanks a lot for your excellent work. I sure do appreciate it.

FLATTERY: Miss Jones, you are really the most beautiful typist in the whole world.

PRAISE: Miss Jones, your typing is absolutely superb. I have no hesitancy at all about signing my correspondence now. I really do appreciate your excellent work. Thanks a lot.

FLATTERY: George, you're the smartest worker in the whole plant.

PRAISE: George, that suggestion of yours was a brilliant idea. It's going to save us a lot of unnecessary steps. Thanks a million for your help.

See the difference here? Flattery is vague, ill-defined, indefinite, and usually confusing. It leaves the flattered person wondering *Why? How? In What Way?* He doesn't know what he's actually done to deserve the praise, so he's in no position to repeat his performance. Flattery does nothing at all to help the person improve his work methods. It's really the lazy man's way of doing things, for nothing at all is said about what the person does, only about what he *is*. That requires no effort at all; anyone can do that.

When you praise a person for what he *does*, not for what he is, you are forced to find something to praise him for. Genuine praise requires thought, energy, and effort on your part, but it's well worth it in the long run.

Praising a person for what he does helps in many other ways, too. First, the individual being praised knows exactly what he's being praised for. Second, when you praise a person for a certain act, you are forced to be sincere. Third, praising the act instead of the person helps you avoid charges of favoritism or prejudice.

Praising a person for what he does also saves him embarrassment. People tend to feel awkward and ill at ease if you say they're the greatest of all or they're better than anyone else. When you pick out something specific he's done and congratulate him for it, he feels good about it. There's nothing for him to be embarrassed about.

Some managers don't use praise often enough. They say praise makes people egotistical, conceited, and swell-headed. They think too much praise makes it ordinary and commonplace like turning diamonds into sand. Then they bend too far the other way and become too stingy with their compliments. I can say without hesitation that managers who feel this way have never learned to praise a person properly. They are using flattery—not sincere praise.

So remember to praise a person for what he *does*, not what he is. Praise him for his good work; he'll do his job even better and faster for you than before. As long as you praise the act and not the person, you'll have no trouble. That's the big difference between sincere praise and phony flattery.

How You Can Use Praise to Correct Mistakes

I'll have more to say about constructive criticism later on. Here I want to show you how to use praise to correct a person's mistakes gracefully so there'll be no hard feelings whatever.

The key to this is to *praise a person at the same time you're pointing out his error.* Here are some examples of both the right and the wrong way to correct a person's mistakes.

RIGHT: Miss Jones, your typing is outstanding. You make very few errors and your work is clean and neat. Your spelling is exceptionally accurate. However, I did find one small mistake in this letter. It's not a big one, but unfortunately, it does change the exact meaning of what I wanted to say. . . .

WRONG: Miss Jones, you are without a doubt the worst typist I've ever had in this office. I'm sick and tired of your stupid mistakes. Now do this letter over and get it right this time!

RIGHT: Joe, you did outstanding work on this difficult project on such short notice. I know you were under a lot of pressure, but I've found one thing here I don't seem to understand. I wonder if you'd mind checking this measurement again for accuracy. It seems to me to be a little off. If it is, I'm afraid the whole thing could be thrown out of whack.

WRONG: What the hell is wrong with you, Joe? These measurements of yours are all screwed up again. Of all the idiotic, stupid people I have to work with, I swear you're the worst. Now do it over and get it right this time or else!

RIGHT: Tim, your report card really looks terrific this time. I'm really proud of your work. Your history grade is the only one that's off a little, but I know you can bring that up, too, when I see how well you've done in your other subjects.

WRONG: Why do you get such stupid low grades in history, dummy? You're either too lazy or too stupid to learn. Which one is it? What's wrong with you? You'd better shape up quick!

Whenever you correct the person instead of the act, you get angry. You automatically use sarcasm and ridicule. Words like *stupid, lazy, dumb,* and *idiot* creep into the conversation. Remember when the team of psychologists from the University of Missouri used ridicule on the trainees at Fort Leonard Wood, improvement fell to as low as 10 percent on the second performance.

If you think the language of these wrong statements in the examples I've given you is too strong, let me tell you I've heard much worse four-letter words used by managers and supervisors, even by top-level executives. I've heard every cuss word or obscenity that's ever been invented by man to criticize and castigate another human being. I've heard everything from "Damn you" to words questioning a man's legitimacy at birth and some derogatory terms about his mother's status.

So always correct a person's mistakes by using praise. That way, you don't destroy a person's dignity and self-respect. You've let him save face. It takes time, patience, and understanding to use this method, but the end results are well worth the efforts expended.

As you can plainly see, I'm definitely high on praise, for I've found it to be an absolutely outstanding technique to use to make a person feel more important. I know from experience it works wonders with people. However, you can use a few other techniques to make a person feel important. I'd like to discuss several of them with you right now.

Asking a Person for His Opinion,
His Advice, and His Help

One of the quickest ways to make a person feel more important is simply to ask him for his help or his advice. All you need say is "What's your opinion on this?" You'll send even the janitor home bragging to his wife that the company president had to come to him for help in solving a problem.

A note of caution here. When you do ask for someone's opinion, listen courteously to what he says. I don't care how outlandish his idea sounds to you, listen to him carefully. Hear him out to the end. Don't disagree with him as soon as he's finished. Even though you might know his idea won't work, don't tell him so. You'll injure his pride, deflate his ego, and spoil everything if you do.

When he's finished, thank him sincerely for his help and advice. Tell him you'll give every possible consideration to his idea. You'll find when you do listen to your employee's opinions, they'll go all out to think up new and better ways of doing things. This can be extremely profitable and beneficial for you. Listening to people for new ideas is a lot like panning gold. You see a lot more sand than gold, but when you do find a nugget, it can really be exciting.

Frankly speaking, I do not like a suggestion box. Nor does Paul King, Director of Research and Development for Suncoast Solar Energy Technologies, in Miami, Florida.

"I know most companies use suggestion boxes to get new ideas from employees," Paul says. "We used to have one, but we got rid of it. It was just too impersonal. Besides, a person never knew whether his suggestion was actually read or thrown away in the trash at the end of the day.

"I keep my office door open all the time. Any employee can come in whenever he feels he has a worthwhile idea to contribute. If it's complicated requiring a lot of sketches or narrative description, he gets every bit of assistance he needs from our office staff. When we first started this program, we got a lot of ideas we couldn't utilize, but our people soon settled down. Now when someone comes in my office, chances are good he has something we can really use."

I've seen Paul's office and when he says he keeps an open door at all times, he really means it. The door has been completely removed and taken away! John De Butts, chairman of the board for AT&T, keeps an open door, too. He says it has been a major factor in his successful business career.

Keeping an open door is an excellent way to make people feel important. Such a policy lets your employees know you're really interested in them and in what they have to offer you. They feel they have access to you, that they can bring you their ideas and their problems, and that you'll listen to them. An open door says a lot to your employees about the kind of person you are.

Making a Personnel Problem a "Personal" Problem

A sign on Al Miller's desk reads: MAKE PERSONNEL ACTIONS PERSONAL TRANSACTIONS. Al is personnel manager for a firm in Birmingham, Alabama. He believes sincerely you cannot be a good personnel worker if you don't have a deep compassion for people and their personal problems.

"Everyone wants to be treated as an important person," Al says. "No one wants to be just another number—some nameless anonymity. Every person wants to retain his own individual identity. Unfortunately, in today's automated and mechanized world, a person often becomes just like another piece of office equipment or an extension of some part of the machinery. Here at Hamilton Industries, we do everything we can to keep that from happening. We want to treat every employee as a very important person—a real VIP. We follow a set of specific guidelines to insure that every personnel action is a personal transaction."

Al was good enough to let me use those guidelines. I'm sure you will find them useful. I know that I did.

HOW TO MAKE EVERY PERSONNEL ACTION
A "PERSONAL" TRANSACTION

Special Instructions: Before you complete any personnel action, answer the following questions, sign your name, and attach this questionnaire as a cover sheet to the individual's personnel action file.

1. Have you treated the other person as you'd like to be treated if the situation were reversed?
2. Did you handle this piece of paper with a name on it as a person—or just another piece of paper?
3. Did you really answer all the individual's questions, or did you leave him in doubt about some of your answers?
4. When you weren't sure, did you get help from someone else? Whose assistance did you ask for?
5. Did you weigh each case on its own individual merits without bias or prejudice?
6. When you gave your answer, were you justly proud of the understanding and tolerance you showed in your decision?
7. If you couldn't go along with the person's request, did you tell him why?
8. Did you do everything you could do to help the person solve his problem?
9. Are you truly proud of what you said to the person and how you said it?
10. Can you sign your name willingly to this personnel action without any reservation or hesitation of any sort?

Making the Other Person a Real VIP

As Al Miller said, it's hard in today's automated and mechanized world to keep from being regarded as another piece of office equipment or an extension of some part of the machinery. Even off the job, a person tends to become a nonentity more than ever before since computers depend on numbers rather than names for credit, identification, and billing purposes. Today, people just don't seem to be as important as individuals as they used to be, and that makes them hungrier than ever for attention and a feeling of importance.

You might be Sam Sloditski or Susie Carmichael to some people, but to the electric company you're just account number 334-

40-89085. Trying to win an argument with a computer over how much you owe on your revolving charge account can be one of the most frustrating and nerve-wracking situations you'll ever get into. It can really make you feel small and insignificant when you have to stoop to the point of doing battle with a machine. Of course, the final insult comes when you lose the fight.

A person will go to great extremes to be heard and noticed and gain attention from others simply from the fear of being ignored and not listened to. The social bore who talks only about himself and his own achievements and the neighborhood bully down the street both suffer from this same fear although the outward symptoms seem so much different on the surface.

The desire to be important and the fear of not succeeding at it is such a driving force in everyone you can readily use that fact to your own advantage. Make every one of your employees a very important person and he'll do whatever you ask him to do. You can make each individual in your organization a VIP when you use the following techniques:

1. Give your whole-hearted attention to the other person. Rejection hurts; attention heals. It's just that simple.
2. Encourage him to talk about himself and his own interests. That shows him how important he is to you.
3. Give each individual the special identity he desires by letting him know he's both wanted and needed by you.
4. Remember a person's name. Never degrade it or make fun of it with ethnic jokes; it's his most important and valuable possession.
5. Never take another person for granted. It's one of the quickest ways to reject a person and make him your enemy.
6. Get your mind off yourself and what you want. You'll get what you want when you give him what he wants—your attention.

Now it's time to move on to the *Third Master Key to Management Success*, where you'll learn the dynamic techniques master managers use to win people to their way of thinking as if by magic. Chapter 3 will demonstrate power psychology at its best and show you how to use it.

Chapter **3**

Power Psychology at Its Best: Dynamic Techniques Master Managers Use to Win People to Their Way of Thinking

---

I have met one manager after another who has told me he knew better than to use threats, force, fear, or intimidation to get the job done. Yet, time after time he has found himself threatening people with demotion, dismissal, transfer to the boondocks, suspension, and loss of privileges simply because he was at wit's end as to what else to do.

As one industrial manager from Dayton, Ohio, told me, "I know I shouldn't use threats or try to instill fear in a person, but sometimes, so help me, I get so mad and frustrated, I reach the end of the line. I find myself barking and yelling at people. I realize that's no good, but I'm under so much pressure I run out of patience. I just don't know anything else to do."

Why does an experienced manager like this use threats trying to scare people into doing a better job? Because of frustration, anger, worry, impatience, lack of time, harassment, pressure. Besides, managers can have certain fears, too. They're human beings like anyone else.

Why Fear, Force, Threats, or Intimidation
Are Not Effective Persuaders

I want you to know why none of these methods will work or get the lasting results you want. For instance, take the manager who tries to scare a person into doing what he wants him to do by threatening him with the loss of his job, demotion, a fine, suspension, transfer, or loss of privileges. What will his results be? I can guarantee you he'll soon find himself running scared, too. That manager will have problems of low morale, insubordination, absenteeism, inferior quality, low production, increased waste, pilferage, perhaps even sabotage, for this reason:

The use of threats, fear, or force leads to more problems than most managers can handle because *fear always leads to hate.* The person who is afraid of the boss soon hates him and will do everything possible to discredit or destroy him.

If you think that doesn't happen, listen to what Larry Brooks, a Kansas City, Missouri, management consultant, has to say about fear and hate.

> "I personally saw a factory in Springfield, Missouri, the heart of the Ozarks country, nearly go bankrupt and out of business because the plant manager, production superintendent, department foremen, and shift supervisors all tried to control the labor force by using threats and attempting to fill people with fear.
>
> "But Ozark mountain people are just as stubborn as our famous Missouri mules. Lead them and they'll follow you wherever you go; they'll do whatever you ask. Mistreat them. threaten them, use force, and they'll balk every time. You can't drive them anywhere. That plant, which employed 1,500 people, survived only because of a wholesale dismissal of management personnel from the top to the bottom by the corporation's Chicago headquarters, and a complete change of company policy and procedure."

Please don't make the same mistake of using fear or force to manage people. You'll always fail in the long run. Human nature is much the same the world over. Lead people and they'll follow you gladly. Push them—they'll strike back. Only slaves or prisoners can be ruled by fear or force, and they will rebel at the first opportunity.

If you've been using force or threats hoping to get the job done, this chapter will help you. It is my *Third Master Key to Management Success.* I know you'll find it will work much better for you than fear, threats, force, or intimidation. When you use the dynamic techniques that the master managers use to win people to their way of thinking —

YOU'LL GAIN THESE WORTHWHILE BENEFITS

1. You'll no longer need to use fear or threats vainly trying to get the job done.
2. You'll not waste your time in fruitless arguments.
3. You'll greatly strengthen your powers of persuasion.
4. People will do as you ask. They'll carry out your orders and directives with conviction and enthusiasm.
5. You'll be better able to achieve your goals and purposes.
6. You'll gain a new feeling of self-confidence and personal power.

WINNING PEOPLE TO YOUR WAY OF THINKING
AS IF BY MAGIC

I have selected eight techniques I recommend for winning people to your way of thinking as if by magic. Each one follows the other in logical sequence. I know there are other techniques you could use, but from long experience I have found these eight the best ones to get the results I know you want.

Making It Easy for the Person to
Change His Way of Thinking

The first thing to keep in mind about a person whose ideas or work methods you want to change is that every human being is a creature of habit. He doesn't like to change. He prefers things exactly as they are. He's used to them that way and he's comfortable with them. A person doesn't want his regular routine upset. You'll always encounter resistance to new ideas, novel methods, and different ways of doing things. To reduce that resistance, *make it easy for the person to change.*

Why do people do things a certain way or follow a certain set routine? For two main reasons: First, because it's a habit. Second, *because they feel it is beneficial to them to do it that way*. Whether the advantages gained are imaginary or real makes no difference. As long as a person thinks he'll benefit by doing things a certain way, that's the way he'll do them. If a person believes raw cabbage juice will cure his ulcers, he'll drink raw cabbage juice, no matter how horrible it tastes.

Or take my own father, for instance. For years he suffered with chronic indigestion. He always took two teaspoons of bicarbonate of soda after every meal to help his heartburn, never realizing he was making his gastric juices too alkaline and thus causing his own bad digestion. Nothing his doctor could say would convince my father otherwise, because he was so sure baking soda benefited him. It was not until we took a three-week fishing trip to Canada and he forgot to pack his baking soda that he found he was better off without it. Why did the doctor fail to convince my father? Because, in spite of all his vast professional medical knowledge, he didn't understand human nature well enough. He failed to offer my father a bigger and better benefit than the soda did.

That's what you must do if you want a person to change his way of thinking and improve his work habits. *Offer him a bigger and better benefit than the one he's now receiving, when he makes the change you're asking him to make.* Let him know how he'll gain one or more of his basic desires when he does as you ask. For instance, show him how this change will increase his production . . . how a greater output will mean more money for him. Let him see how his increased production will give him a feeling of accomplishment. Achievement of this desire makes him feel proud . . . it gives him a feeling of being more important. Three big benefits to be gained from one small change.

"I used to try and drive my men to greater efforts by threatening them," says Keith Loring, manager of a Fort Dodge, Iowa, gympsum plant. "For example, if John was holding up production on the assembly line because he was too slow, I'd argue with him. I'd yell at him and threaten him with dismissal for inefficiency, but that never helped one bit. If anything, it slowed him down even more.

"Now I use a completely different approach, Jim. After I read your book, *The 22 Biggest Mistakes Managers Make and How to Correct Them,** especially Chapter 18, I saw what I was doing wrong. Now I would say, 'John, if you do it this way, you can make more money for yourself by increasing your production.' He'll make that change immediately, for *I've shown him how to get what he wants: more money.* That incentive alone will motivate him to change faster than all my threats could ever do."

That's for sure the quickest surest way of getting a person to change. *Show him how he'll benefit when he does as you ask.* If you can't come up with any benefits for him, keep digging until you can. Don't ask him to change anything until you do.

When you're asking a person to alter some improper work method or correct some bad habit, the implication is that he's wrong and you're right. Don't stress that point. Don't make him lose face or feel embarrassed. Let him retain his dignity and self-respect. He'll be able to do that as long as you stress the benefits he's going to gain rather than the wrong methods he has to correct. That makes it easy for him to change his way of thinking and do as you ask.

Changing a Person's Mind by Plugging the Benefits He'll Gain

Ever see a TV commercial that says, "*Our goal* is to sell umpteen cars this month. Come in and see *us* today. Help *us* make *our goal. We want* to sell you a car." What's your reaction to this? Same as mine, I'm sure. I'm not the least bit interested in how many cars that dealer sells. I don't give a continental hoot how many sales records he beats. I could care less about his goals. It doesn't matter to me what he wants. *I want him to tell me how I'll benefit* by buying one of his cars. *I want to know what's in it for me. I'm only interested in what I want* . . . not what he wants.

To get the best results from your people, you must be a salesman as well as a manager. What are you selling? You're selling yourself, your ideas, methods, and procedures. If you want your employees to discard their old ideas for your new ones, don't use the

---

*James K. Van Fleet, *The 22 Biggest Mistakes Managers Make and How to Correct Them* (West Nyack, New York, Parker Publishing Company, 1973).

style of that TV commercial. Your people don't give a hang about what you want, what your goals are, what records you want to beat either. They want to know what's in it for them. Show them how they'll benefit by accepting your ideas. People don't like to give up their old ideas unless they're sure they'll be better off by doing so.

Use the Sears Roebuck sales approach. *Sell the benefits—not features* of your new method. Sears always plugs the benefits the prospective customer will gain, over and over again. They never sell features or tell the customer what Sears wants. What's the difference between a benefit and a feature? Simple. The squelch control on a CB radio is a *feature*. Since it gets rid of static and background noise so you can hear the other party better, that's a *benefit*.

Features Are Used Only to Sell Benefits. Sears teaches its salesmen to offer the customer such benefits as comfort and convenience, safety and security, a feeling of importance and pride of ownership, good health and freedom from pain, a material gain or a savings of money, time, and effort. Before a salesman can offer any benefit, he has to know which feature offers that specific benefit. That's why a Sears salesman has to know his product inside out. He must know everything there is to know about it. If he doesn't, he won't be working for Sears for very long. Sears must be doing something right: they're the biggest, most successful retailer in the entire world.

You have a fistful of benefits you can sell, too: the attainment of those basic desires every person has that I told you about in Chapter 1. Look at your 5-by-8 card; you'll see what I mean. Show a person how he can gain those basic desires by accepting your ideas; you'll win him over to your way of thinking with no trouble at all. He'll do what you want him to do every single time.

Everybody's Interested in What's In It for Them. That's always their first primary concern. Every person wants to know what he's going to get when he does as the boss asks him to do. Many years ago, Buck Owens, the now famous and well-known country and western star, was playing guitar with a group in a little bar in California. One night the owner said, "Buck, I want you to sing, too. We need more voices. I think it'll improve the music." Immediately Buck said, "But you're paying me just to play the guitar. What do I get if I sing?" The boss quickly replied, "You get to keep your job!"

At that time in Buck's career, keeping his job was a mighty big benefit. Today, his boss would have to offer him a lot more than that. My point is you should make sure the person needs the specific benefit you're offering. If he doesn't need it at that particular time, your efforts will be wasted. As Elmer Wheeler, one of America's greatest salesmen of all time, would say, "Don't try to sell a person an empty box." If you're offering a benefit he doesn't need right then, you're doing that; you're offering him an empty box. He won't be interested. You must offer him something worthwhile that he really wants at that point in time.

Let me tell you about one benefit you can consider that I haven't discussed before. You can always appeal to a person's sense of *laziness*. Now you don't call it that right to his face. Like those top-notch Sears salesmen, you disguise it and call it comfort, convenience, saving of effort, time, and energy, efficiency, or any other appropriate euphemism that fits. But you can be sure of this: *Every single person is as lazy as he dares to be and still get by.* Appeal to that sense of laziness in your employee, but call it something else to disguise it. If it saves him time, energy, and effort, he'll buy your idea at once for he wants to do his job the easiest way possible. I'll admit that I'm susceptible, too. I don't believe in standing up if I can sit down or sitting down if I can lie down. How about you?

Asking Him Questions to Overcome His Resistance

When a person offers resistance and objects to your idea, don't get angry about it. You can't change his mind by talking louder or faster or using threats just because he doesn't happen to see things your way immediately.

To overcome his resistance, find out exactly why he doesn't agree with you. Smoke his objection out into the open. You can't overcome it until you know exactly what it is. The information you need to win him to your way of thinking is locked up tight in his head. The only way you'll ever get it out is to ask him questions.

Start With Questions that Are Easy to Answer. Always start out with questions that are easy to answer. Then your listener will relax and feel completely at ease when he talks with you. People enjoy giving answers they are sure of for it builds their confidence. It gives them the chance to show you how much they really know. That makes them feel more important.

If you begin with hard questions your listener can't answer, you make him feel ill at ease. He'll become nervous and withdrawn. You've injured his pride by exposing his ignorance. When you press even harder to get an answer, he'll become sullen and morose. He'll withdraw completely into a hard shell of silence. You'll get no agreement or understanding, whatever, between the two of you that way.

Start with easy questions to answer. You'll find his nervousness and fear will soon be gone. He'll answer you with confidence. He relaxes even more. Soon you're engaged in a pleasant and profitable conversational exchange.

Not only should your questions be easy to answer, but they should also be phrased properly to let you retain control of the situation. Poorly worded questions actually discourage answers. They can confuse, even antagonize, your listener. To correctly phrase your questions, I recommend following these basic guidelines. I have found them to be extremely helpful to me.

Your Question Should Have a Specific Purpose. Your goal is to get your listener to accept your new proposition or point of view. Ask questions that will lead him straight toward your goal. You can use a variety of questions to do that. For instance, one question might be used to arouse your listener's interest and make him more alert and attentive. Another one, to stimulate thought. Still another, to emphasize a major point. You can also use a question to check your listener's immediate understanding while a similar one can be used later on to check his retention.

Your Question Should Be Easily Understood A question that's easily understood is not necessarily the same as a question that's easy to answer. A hard question can be made much easier to answer if you keep it short and simple. Don't ask complicated or long-winded questions that require a lot of explanation and clarification. You'll only confuse the issue. By the same token, avoid vague abstract language and government-style gobbledegook. Instead, use clear, concise, plain, and simple one-and two-syllable words so your listener will know immediately what you want and exactly what you mean.

A Good Question Emphasizes Only One Point. The best question covers only one point and asks for only one answer. Don't combine two or three questions in one sentence. If your question requires more than one answer, break it down into two or three separate questions.

Ask a Question that Requires a Definite Specific Answer. A vague and indefinite question gives you a vague and indefinite answer. That's no help at all to you. Word your question so a definite and specific answer is required. Don't give up until you get the answer you need.

A Good Question Will Discourage Guessing. Don't ask questions that can be answered "Yes" or "No" unless you follow them up with "Why?" or "Why not?". This kind of question makes your listener explain his answer. You want answers that are based on facts, not guesswork. Of course, there'll be times when you want a person's candid opinion, but his subjective thinking has to be based on objective facts if it's going to do you any good.

When you ask questions, listen carefully to the answers. Don't interrupt; you wound a person's ego and make him feel unimportant when you do. That could cause him to have a mental block to what you say when you present your viewpoint. He will not be willing to pay attention or listen to you if you don't pay attention to him first. If you want to win him over, be courteous enough to listen to his ideas.

In this particular situation you're using questions to obtain a specific benefit for yourself: that's to win the other person to your way of thinking. However, asking questions can gain you a lot of other benefits, too.

Other Benefits You Can Gain by Asking Questions

1. Questions increase your listener's interest.
2. When you ask questions, you make the other person think.

3. A person's real attitude can be revealed by questions.

4. Questions let your listener contribute his own ideas.

5. You can reinforce and emphasize major points with questions.

6. Questions let you know if you're getting your point across.

7. When you ask questions, you can quickly adjust your presentation to your listener's level of understanding.

8. Asking questions is the most reliable way to get accurate information from people.

Exploring the Other Person's Position for Weaknesses

Suppose you want an employee to change the way he does a certain job. You suggest the new method, but your employee doesn't want to change. He feels the old way is better. Since you're the boss, you could put your foot down and tell him to change his work methods or else. If you do it that way, you'll get nothing more than the bare minimum from him from then on. Persuasion is always better than force even when you're the boss. Your benefits will be greater and last a lot longer.

Your goal is to get him to discard his old idea and accept your new one. He won't do that until he's thoroughly convinced that the new methods you want him to use are not only better than the old ones, but that they are also more beneficial to him. To help your employee become more receptive to your idea, lead him on an objective fact-finding survey of his own position so you can pinpoint and expose its weaknesses.

When you find a weakness, use it to persuade him to your point of view. When he sees the weakness in his own argument for himself, he'll become more open and receptive to your proposition. When you want to persuade someone to your point of view, it's better to let him talk first. Let him try to justify his own position. You already know you have a stronger case than he has, so weaknesses are bound to show up as he talks. You can use these to penetrate his defenses, but it's best to let him discover them himself.

How can you get him to discuss his viewpoint? Ask him leading questions to guide his thinking as I showed you a few moments ago. To give you an even better idea of how well this works, let's listen to Mrs. Shirley Bennett, Director of Industrial Relations for a chemical corporation.

"If a new plan or idea of mine meets resistance from an employee, I always go out of my way to hear the person out," Mrs. Bennett says. "What he says will usually give me a hint as to how to proceed for he'll almost always expose the weaknesses in his argument while he's talking. In fact, he'll see them for himself which helps tremendously.

"I ask him to go over his main objections again several times. I seek more information by asking him if there's anything else he wants to add. I ask lots of questions so I can get every possible fact he feels is important and relevant to the issue.

"Before I state my case, I show him I'm deeply interested in his viewpoint. I let him do most of the talking in the beginning, but I never let him take charge of the situation. I retain control by asking questions; he'll eventually exhaust himself from answering them. Then I can take over.

"If you want to make sure of winning him to your way of thinking, let him discover the weaknesses in his own position himself. That way he'll be more willing to accept your point of view."

You can do the same. If you let your employee state his position first, you get his ideas out in the open where you can probe them for weaknesses. The moment he realizes he has some holes in his argument, he'll be much more willing to accept your viewpoint.

If by some strange chance, his old method is better than yours, you can keep the old one and throw your new one away. Either way, you'll still win.

Knowing When a Person Is Ready to Accept a New Idea

The best idea in the world, presented to a person at the wrong time, will fall flat. You need to know when he's ready to accept your new concept. You'll also want to be able to tell when the individual is not ready so you'll not move too rapidly to take your objective. Three red flags warn you when he's *not* ready.

1. He asks unnecessary questions. When a person asks a question, the answer to which was readily apparent in what you just told him, you know he's not yet interested in what you're saying. He's not listening to you carefully. Had he been, his question would have been unnecessary.

2. He returns to a question that has already been answered. This shows he's still at point A while you're way ahead of him at point D. You have no choice but to start over, preferably with a different approach.

3. He changes the subject abruptly or presents ideas completely counter to yours. If he changes the subject abruptly, he may have something so pressing on his mind, he can't wait to tell you about it. If it's a personal problem, bear with him. Hear him out and get back to your subject as soon as you can. If he's presenting ideas completely counter to yours, he may be so ego-hungry he can't wait to show you how smart he is. Let him explain his position thoroughly. Ask him questions about it. As soon as you've exhausted his viewpoint, get back to yours and start over again.

How will you know when he's ready to accept your ideas? One or both of two ways. One signal comes when he makes statements filled with doubt. The other occurs when he shows interest by asking relevant questions himself. Let's take a look at the first clue, expressions of doubt.

"This is the way I look at it, but I could be wrong on a point or two."

"Of course I'm always willing to change if I'm wrong."

"To tell the truth, I've never looked at it that way before."

"Maybe I could be in error on this one small point."

"Well, I'm not alone; we all make mistakes once in a while."

When you hear expressions of doubt like these, you know it's time to launch your attack. Your listener is now receptive to change; he's ready to listen and be persuaded to your point of view.

The second clue can be detected when he asks you logical relevant questions. When you hear the question words *who, when, where, why, what, how,* that's a sure sign the person is interested in what you're saying. You know he's almost ready to change his mind. He's asking for more information so he can make a rational decision that is favorable to you, yet at the same time allow him to save face. Another sure sign that he's ready to change is when he wants to know the benefits he'll gain. If you hear questions similar to these, it's time to move in and consolidate your position.

"*Why* do you want me to do it this way?"

"*Who* will benefit by this new procedure?"

"*What's in it for me* if I do it your new way?"

"*How will I be helped* by your new system?"

"*What benefits do I get* out of this?"

"*Where will I gain* from your new methods?"

Letting the Other Person Feel the Idea Is His

Let's say you want to make certain changes in an individual's work methods or you want him to accept a new idea. But the individual happens to be one of those strong-minded persons who finds it hard to accept any suggestion from others no matter how good it is. He thinks the only worthwhile ideas are his. How do you go about getting this fellow to do things your way or make the changes you want?

You Let Him Think the New Project Was All His Very Own Idea. You plant the seed . . . let *him* harvest the crop. Will it work? I'll say it will. I've used it for years. But don't take my word for it alone. Listen to Kelly Riebold, assistant manager for a large Missouri electronics manufacturer.

"I've found the best way to make any change in work methods or plant procedure is to let the other person think it was all his own idea," Kelly says. "I let him take all the credit for the change. I compliment him on his initiative and foresight. He becomes convinced that he thought it all up in the first place. We both win. He feels more important and secure in his job . . . I get a more efficient operation. I've yet to meet the person who isn't susceptible to this approach.

"Take our production superintendent, for instance. Last Friday I said to him, 'Jack, I believe we could speed up production if we moved the number 3 cutting machine over there and added two more motor winding stations. Wish you'd let me know how you feel about that.'

"Yesterday he came to my office and said, "Kelly, this weekend *I had the most wonderful idea*. If we move the number 3 cutting machine to here and add two more motor winding stations, we can cut down a lot of wasted motion on the assembly line and speed up our motor production by at least 5 to 10 percent. Shall we try it?'

"That's exactly the change I wanted to be made. This way is better than telling an employee what to do. People don't like to be told how to do their jobs. They like to do things their own way. This method works every time. I get what I want. The employee gets the credit for the idea, so we're both happy."

The only special requirement for this technique is time and patience. Take it easy . . . don't rush. Give the person time to absorb your idea so that before long it will become *his*. Remember to plant the seed . . . let *him* harvest the crop. But give it a chance to take root and grow. You benefits will be enormous when you do.

Another highly effective variation of this technique is to *ask a person to show you how to do the job*. Now you know exactly what you want done. You could give him a direct order to do it. But instead of doing that, you ask the person to show you how to do it. That makes him feel more important, for you've asked for his opinion, his help, and his advice.

One area where this works extremely well is in reducing overhead and cutting costs. Let me give you a concrete example of that. Dale Williams is a store manager in Florida for one of the most prominent supermarket chains in the South.

"One of the toughest jobs in the grocery business is cutting costs and reducing overhead," Dale says. "When your net profit is figured in pennies, as it is in the food business, you cut corners every chance you get. You can't do that on food quality, or your customers will go somewhere else. So you have to find other ways to economize.

"I go to my people for help and suggestions on how to reduce our overhead. Most of the time they come up with workable solutions. Then all I do is ask them to put their own suggestions into effect. I do it this way because I've found *people will always support their own ideas.* I've never had a person refuse to help me when I ask him to show me the best way to do it."

I've also used Dale's procedure to cut the monthly utility bills in my own house. With utility costs being what they are today, I use every money-saving suggestion that's made to me. If the rising cost of gas and electricity in your home has put you into orbit, ask your wife and children to show you where the family can cut down. Then ask them to put their own suggestions into effect. You could be pleasantly surprised at the results, just as I was.

Using Suggestions Rather than Giving Direct Orders

No one likes to be told what to do. No one wants to be ordered around. If someone commands me to do something a certain way or else, the back of my neck turns red and starts to burn. The adrenalin flows, my pulse rate speeds up, and I immediately prepare for battle. I start thinking of every possible reason to keep from doing what I was told to do.

But if I'm asked courteously to do the same thing I was ordered to do, if the person says *please* or *will you help me*, I'll hop to it at once, glad that I'm able to be of assistance. I'll bet you react the same way.

The people you manage are no different. They don't like to be ordered around and told what to do either. That's why most of us have a natural antipathy for policemen. We're not really afraid of them, but they represent authority. They can tell us what to do, when and where to do it, and make it stick. We don't like that.

Order a person to do something, *tell* him to do a specific job a certain exact way, and he'll glare at you. He'll respond, perhaps, but only at a snail's pace. *Ask* him to do the job, *suggest* he do it, use "please" in your *request*, and 99 out of 100 people will do what you want them to do quickly, willingly, enthusiastically. That's really the major difference between authoritative and persuasive (I said persuasive—not permissive) management.

Ellen Price, a lieutenant colonel in the Women's Army Corps, is the chief administrative officer at Fort Ord, California. Colonel Price has a great many men and women, both officers and enlisted, under her direct management control. She has both the rank and authority to give commands and issue orders, but she tells me she has seldom had to exercise her prerogatives.

> "I've been in the service nearly 20 years," Colonel Price says, "and in all that time, I can't remember giving anyone a direct order to do anything. I usually phrase my order so it becomes a request or a suggestion. I'll say, 'Would you be kind enough to . . . would you please do . . . I'd appreciate it if you would. . . .' A request or suggestion makes it easier for people to carry out my orders."

I've met some officers who had no hesitation at all about ordering people around. But officers using direct orders and commands were never as successful as those using requests and suggestions. Whether they were male or female made no difference at all. You just don't have to yell at people or boss them around to get the job done.

You see, contrary to what many people might think incentive methods and motivation are as important in the armed services as in business or industry, if not more so. People will always be people, whether in or out of uniform. Using direct orders and telling them what to do, even in the military, will get only the *minimum* results. Asking people or using suggestions to get the same job done will secure the *maximum* benefits you want.

Is there ever a time or place when a direct order is necessary? Of course there is. In an emergency when life or property is at stake, time is of the essence. Then, a direct order or command to get action and get it now is most certainly appropriate. An emergency is not the time to be subtle. But even so, you don't have to be unpleasant or discourteous. Although you may need to raise your voice to make yourself heard, you still don't have to bellow at people unnecessarily.

I learned a long time ago never to yell at a person unless he was so far away I had to shout to make myself heard.

To sum up this idea, let me say it's only human nature to resent orders and commands. We just don't like being told what to do. This is especially true of top-notch people—those with unusual initiative, intelligence and ability—the kind of people you're no doubt used to working with. Far better results can be gained by using suggestions, especially if you explain why you want certain things done a certain way. When you use suggestions or requests, a person is glad to help you. You make it easy for him. You can truly win him over to your way of thinking as if by magic.

The Secret of Appealing to a Person's
Emotions to Get the Job Done

How many times does a girl marry the man her parents did not prefer? Mother had her eye on the young banker or doctor who had money, a promising career, social status and a prominent position in the community. Or maybe Dad had picked out the brilliant young attorney who was headed for the governor's mansion in a few short years. But Daughter married the milkman . . . the farmer . . . the shoe salesman . . . the rock musician . . . the garage mechanic . . . the grocery clerk. Why? Well, Mom and Dad picked their daughter's potential husband with their heads. Daughter picked him out with her heart. The moral of this little story is quite simple. People are guided by emotions more than by logic and reason. This is not to say Daughter was wrong, even though in view of today's divorce rate, you might think so. I'm not saying anyone's right or wrong; I'm only saying how and why people say and do the things they do.

If you want a person to listen to you, if you want to change his thinking so he'll do things your way, then get him emotionally involved. Appeal to his basic emotions until you have him properly hooked. Then make your follow-up pitch to his logic and reason. In short, *go for his heart first—then for his head.*

Check back in your own life and see how many of your own decisions were made on an emotional basis. If you didn't make most of your decisions that way, then you're a lot different from most of us. Almost everything the rest of us do—buying cars, falling in love, moving to a different home, quitting a job—is done on impulse—the way we *feel* about something at a specific moment in time, logic and reason be damned, no matter what the consequences.

You'll never get the best out of a person unless you appeal to his basic emotions. How do you do that? Well, we're right back to the beginning again. First of all find out what he wants; then show him the easy way to get it. Show him the benefits he'll gain when he reaches his goal. It's been proven many times that when a person really wants to succeed, he can, even though before he might have failed.

I've seen students flunk out of college because they were taking courses that held no interest for them. Why were they taking those courses? Because they were trying to become what Mom and Dad wanted, but their hearts weren't in it. Those same students have returned and pulled down straight A's when they finally had their own goals and knew exactly what they wanted to do. It was a matter of Dad's and Mom's heads versus Son's and Daughter's hearts.

I've also seen men and women, who were plodding along in some hum-drum job they hated, simply to make a living, become transformed by changing careers. When a person works at a job he doesn't like, only to exist, earning a living truly gets in the way of enjoying life.

If you want to appeal to a person's emotions to get the job done, if you want to get him deeply involved, remember this one idea:

THE HEAD NEVER HEARS 'TIL THE HEART HAS LISTENED

This final thought succinctly sums up the concept of how to win people to your way of thinking as if by magic. Now let's move on to my *Fourth Master Key to Management Success*—and learn the master formula for powerful and persuasive correspondence.

Chapter 4

The Master Formula for

Powerful and Persuasive Writing

The Primary Purpose of Business Writing

If I said to you, "As a manager and executive, what is the primary purpose of business writing?", you might say, "To make myself understood . . . to transmit my orders and requests to others." I would agree. Yet I would go even further. I would say your primary purpose is not only to make yourself understood, but also to word your orders and directives, your letters and reports, in such a way they cannot possibly be misunderstood. However, there's even more to it than that. Let me give you a specific for-instance:

When my two sons were still home, I can well remember Larry coming to me, saying, "Dad, give me a couple of bucks. Me and Bob are going to the movies." I would flinch inwardly and say, "Larry, '*Me* and Bob are going to the movies,' is the same as '*Us* are going.' You wouldn't say that, would you? Why don't you say 'Bob and I?' That's the correct way."

Larry would grin and say, "But you understood me, didn't you, Dad? What difference does it make whether I say *I* or *me* as long as you understood?"

I had to admit I understood him, but how he said it still made a big difference to me. Happily, time has resolved his incorrect use of the word, *me*, but I still hear it from others. It is a common mistake. I have often heard *I* and *me* improperly used, many times by well-educated managers and executives holding down high-level positions in business and industry. It is a widespread grammatical error.

Even Big-City Editors Make Mistakes Sometimes

As you can see from this example of my son, making yourself understood is not enough. I understood him perfectly well when he said, "Me and Bob are going to the movies." But his choice of words bothered me. You, too, will want to make yourself understood without rubbing people the wrong way with the improper choice of words or careless grammar. You leave yourself wide-open for criticism, even sarcasm and ridicule. People love to snipe at their superiors' mistakes behind their backs. That's an important matter to keep in mind, as Ralph Martin, an executive editor for a California newspaper, points out.

"When I'm composing a letter, article, or report, I concentrate intently on my subject," Ralph says. "I become so interested in what I'm saying, I often forget how I'm saying it. Sometimes I use the wrong word or improper grammar here and there.

"When that happens, I must catch my mistakes and correct them, before I sign the letter or approve the final article or report. Careful writing entitles me to attentive reading. Careless and slipshod writing invites annoyance and irritation, perhaps even scorn and ridicule from my reader. He may become so disgusted he will pay no attention whatever to my message."

If a man as expert as Ralph Martin in the use of the English language admits he makes mistakes in his word choice and grammar once in a while, what about people like you and I (oops, I mean you and me) who aren't newspaper editors? I can't speak for you, but I can for myself. Unfortunately, I still make far too many mistakes.

One last point about your purposes in business writing. Not only is *what* you say important, but also *how* you say it. Your choice of words—positive or negative, active or passive—will greatly influence your reader. Your purpose in writing is to get him to *want* to carry out your orders or do as you request. The correct choice of words can stir his emotions and put him in the right frame of mind. Then he'll want to do as you desire.

To help you reach these goals I've mentioned here, in this chapter I'll give you the master formula for powerful and persuasive writing: my *Fourth Master Key to Management Success*. I'll cover how to best use the basic tools of writing—words, grammar, sentences, and paragraphs—to work for your benefit. Here's why I say that:

Many managers and executives are prisoners of an old-fashioned business correspondence system. They think they should use "formal" English when they write and "informal" English when they talk. Not true. *You should always write the same way you talk.* When you do that, you'll be able to break out of that old rut of saying simple things in extremely complicated ways. In fact, you'll be able to say complicated things in extremely simple ways.

Of the four basic tools of writing, most of my emphasis is on word usage, so let's start with that:

How to Select the Right Words and Use Them Properly

How successful you are in getting your point across to your reader depends on your choice of words and how you put them together. The shorter and simpler the word you choose, the better your chances are he will understand what you wrote.

Not only is the selection of words important, but also how they are strung together in your sentence. For instance, every word in this sentence is simple and easy to understand:

"All racing car drivers do not own their own cars."

Does that sentence actually mean what it says? As written it says not a single racing car driver in the whole world owns his own car. But that's not true. That's not what the writer meant. I know that because the sentence came from an article in a popular nationally-read automobile magazine. The author is a well-known non-fiction sports writer.

What did he really mean to say? He meant to say, *"Not all racing car drivers own their own cars."* The rest of his article made that clear. The word *not* was simply out of order and not in its right place. But its wrong positioning changed the meaning of the entire sentence. So you see it's not enough just to use the correct word. You must also put it in the right place in your sentence.

The Best Way to Build the Proper Vocabulary

Lots of people use the dictionary to find big words to dazzle their readers with their knowledge. Not I. When I run across a big word in someone's letter or report, I look it up only to find out how I can use a smaller word in its place. Then I'll never have to use that big cumbersome word myself. I use the dictionary much differently than many people do. I use it to make little ones out of big ones, for small words let me write with clarity and force.

One of the highest compliments I've ever received about my writing came from a California reader of my book, *Power with People.** Helen Morse, the purchasing manager for a large container corporation, wrote me to say, "Thank you for writing so clearly I was able to understand your book on the first reading. That's more than I can say for other self-improvement books I've read. Although you expressed some deeply profound ideas, you used such plain and simple words I never once had to turn to the dictionary to find out what you meant. Thanks again."

Why You Need to Know and Understand Big Words

It's important to be familiar with pompous and ostentatious words for only one reason: to understand people who use these words when they write or speak to you. An extensive vocabulary of pretentious words is an asset only if you use those words for catching, not for pitching.

You'll be able to grasp quickly the ideas thrown at you, but these words will not help you put your concepts across to others. Keep in mind you're writing to make your thoughts known, not to impress people with your erudition and brilliant scholarship.

Whenever you stop your reader with a word that puzzles him or forces him to the dictionary, you've broken his stream of thought. Do that often enough and you'll lose your reader completely. Your letter or directive will end up in the waste basket.

A minister once complained to me about religious writers

---

*James K. Van Fleet, *Power with People* (West Nyack, New York, Parker Publishing Company, 1970).

using unnecessary complex language and complicated words. The next Sunday he spoke about the unfortunate "dichotomization" of the church in his morning sermon.

My pew neighbor nudged me and whispered, "What does 'dichotomization' mean, Jim?"

"It means to break into two branches or split into two parts, Joe," I whispered back.

"My God!" Joe said aloud, forgetting where he was. "Why didn't he say so!"

I simply feel this way about big words. Most of them are too clumsy, cumbersome, and pompous to use. They bog you down and get in the way of what you want to say. To tell the truth, small words will say everything big words will say, and say them quite well. I never use a word of three or more syllables if a word with one or two will do.

I know in today's highly technical, scientific, and computerized world, a lot of complex and complicated terms exist that must be used. You may understand the meaning of the technical term you're using, but does your reader? If you have any doubt about his level of understanding, define or explain the meaning of that word. Then surround your technical terms with such simple one- and two-syllable words as *make, do, get, give, work, upset,* for better understanding. Even well-educated and highly qualified technical people will be glad for the breather.

How Not to Write

Government writers and federal bureaucrats seem to have a special gift of making simple things complicated and hard to understand. Frankly, I can think of no excuse for using big words if small ones will do the job just as well, but I find that most government writers don't agree with me. Many of them suffer from the disease known as *logorrhea*—a diarrhea of words. But perhaps they should be excused. After all, that's all so many of them have to do with their time.

For instance, take the army writers who said, "Heavy equipment operators must wear *sound attenuators*," when they really meant *ear plugs*. Those same writers went on to say that "Sound attenuators eliminate the heavy equipment operator's ability to detect audible danger signals or apprehend vocalized instructions." You can't correct this kind of writing. The only thing to do with it is throw it away and start over.

Let me give you two more examples of government bureaucratic writing so you can see for yourself how *not* to do it. In only 14 words, my dictionary says a ladder is "a set of rungs or steps fastened to two sidepieces, for use in climbing."

A recent federal Occupational Safety and Health Administration bulletin used *65 pages to define ladders* and to outline government regulations for their safety and use. I will not go into the boring details except to say that to the government writers in OSHA a ladder is not a ladder at all. It is a "walking working surface."

One Michigan Congressman, Representative Marvin L. Esch, was so upset by the OSHA regulation, he said, "This is the most ridiculous government publication ever to cross my desk during my ten years as a congressman. It's a good thing Jacob had his ladder when he did, because it probably would not pass OSHA's standards of today."

Another gem of government gobbledegook is OSHA's definition of an exit. OSHA's writers really went all out on that one. My dictionary simply says an exit is "a way out of an enclosed place."

But OSHA says that "an exit is that portion of a means of egress which is separated from all other spaces of the building or structure by construction or equipment as required in this subpart to provide a protected way of travel to the exit discharge. Exit discharge is that portion of a means of egress between the termination of an exit and a public way." Care to comment on that inanity? And to think our good tax money pays for this nonsense.

Frankly, after reading numerous government publications, I have reached this simple conclusion:

The average government document is an explanation of nothing in great detail.

The Best Way to Get Rid of Big and Useless Words

What big words should you cut out of your writing? *Abstract nouns made out of verbs* ought to be the first ones to go. To keep from sounding like a government writer, don't use words like *enumeration, performance, repetition, preparation, impression, opposition, supposition,* and so on unless you cannot possibly replace them with several smaller ones. Every one of these is an abstract noun made out of a verb. You can easily recognize them by their endings *-ion, -tion, -ance, -ence,* and *-osity.*

How can you get rid of them? Let me show you. Simply use two or three smaller words for the big one like this: "fall apart" for *disintegration* . . . "break through" for *penetration* . . . "look down on" for *condescension* . . . "come between" for *intervention* . . . "talk about" for *discussion.* Whenever you use abstract nouns made out of verbs, you sound like a federal bureaucrat; it's time to clean house and get rid of the trash.

Abstract nouns made out of verbs need weaker passive verbs to support and carry them. A simple sentence like *He decided to go to town* becomes *The decision to go to town was made by him.* The first sentence has six words; the second—ten.

Or take the simple statement: *The policeman questioned the prisoner* (five words). That can be blown up into *The prisoner's interrogation was conducted by the policeman* (eight words). As you can see from this last sentence, it is almost impossible to use a strong powerful one-syllable verb like *make, run, throw, hit,* when you have an abstract noun for your subject.

Abstract nouns are vague and subjective; they usually describe qualities and ideas. Most of the time they can be replaced with concrete nouns. Concrete nouns are best to use for clear and immediate understanding for they are the names of people, places, and things.

If you learn nothing more from this chapter than how to cut out most of the words that end in *-ion* and *-tion* when you write, you'll do wonders for your style. You'll be saying what you want to say with clarity and force.

How Using Small Words Can Improve Your Writing Style 100 percent

Now that you know how to get rid of big words, I want to

show you how to use small ones effectively to completely revamp your writing style. When you write with strong action verbs and specific, concrete nouns, your writing will improve 100 percent. That's the truth; I guarantee it.

How These Simple Action Verbs Make Your
Writing Strong and Powerful

Verbs are the most important words in any language because they give your writing force and bring your sentences to life. The right verb can make your writing strong, powerful, vigorous, and direct. The wrong one will make it weak, passive, vague, and inconclusive.

Watch out for verbs that end in *-ize* like *finalize, utilize, conceptualize, personalize.* Other troublemakers end in *-ate,* for example, *fabricate, consummate, initiate, ameliorate, promulgate, disseminate, alternate,* and *obfuscate,* which is exactly what you'll do to your reader if you use these abstract verbs. These verbs can easily be made into abstract nouns; most good strong action verbs cannot.

To help you get rid of abstract nouns and passive verbs, I've made up a list of simple verbs you can use to describe nearly any action you can think of. When you use these simple but powerful verbs, it is almost impossible to make their subject a vague and abstract noun.

Ache	Call	Dig	Go	Keep	Mark	Press	Shake	Stick	Tie
Act	Can	Do	Happen	Kick	May	Pull	Show	Stir	Touch
Add	Carry	Draw	Handle	Know	Mean	Push	Shut	Stop	Try
Aim	Cast	Drive	Hang	Lay	Mind	Put	Sit	Strike	Turn
Ask	Catch	Drop	Hate	Lean	Move	Raise	Skip	Take	Twist
Bear	Check	Fall	Have	Leave	Owe	Reach	Slip	Talk	Upset
Begin	Claim	Fear	Hear	Let	Pick	Run	Smell	Tear	Use
Bind	Close	Feel	Help	Lie	Pitch	Say	Split	Tell	Walk
Blow	Come	Find	Hide	Like	Pin	See	Stab	Test	Want
Break	Cover	Fix	Hold	Look	Plan	Sell	Stand	Think	Watch
Bring	Crawl	Get	Hunt	Lose	Play	Seem	Start	Throb	Wear
Buy	Cut	Give	Hurt	Make	Poke	Set	Stay	Throw	Whirl
									Work

Don't look at this list as final or all-inclusive. Use it instead as a foundation for your own *verb vocabulary*. Add your own simple one- and two-syllable verbs as you run across them.

When you use these verbs, it is impossible to write abstract sentences. You're forced to be direct, concrete, and to the point whether you like it or not. Try as you may, you can't be vague and abstract with such verbs as *make, do, hit, walk, run, strike*. Your writing will become powerful, strong, and vigorous when you use these simple verbs.

Adverbs and Prepositions You Can

Use Safely with These Verbs

I've selected for you some adverbs and prepositions of time and place that naturally go with these simple verbs. When you use these words together, you can talk about almost any abstract idea without using vague and indefinite language.

About	Ahead	Away	Beneath	Down	In	On	To (toward)
Above	Along	Back	Beside	For	Into	Out	Together
Across	Apart	Before	Between	Forth	Inside	Over	Under
After	Around	Below	Beyond	Forward	Near	Since	Up
Against	Aside	Behind	By	From	Off	Through	Within

Let me show you a few examples of how well these verbs and adverbs or prepositions go together, and the abstract words they replace:

Abandon . . . . .Give up
Acquainted . . . . .To know
Agitate (tion) . . . . .Stir up
Anticipation . . . . .Look forward to
Consideration . . . . .Think about
Contribution . . . . .Give to

Dependence . . . . .Lean on
Discontinuation . . . . .Stop
Facilitate . . . . .Make easy, to help
Initiate (tion) . . . . .To begin, to start
Investigation . . . . .Check up on
Obligation . . . . .To owe

Many other verbs and adverbs or prepositions can be used together to make your writing easy to understand. Words like *black-out, pin-up, line-up, strike out, work slow-down* or *speed-up, touchdown, tryout, stand-in, checkup, sit-down strike* are standard usage in our language. Why use a bigger word to replace them when everybody knows exactly what they mean?

I also want to give you a short list of helping verbs or verb phrases that go naturally with those action verbs I gave you before.

Aim to	Happen to	Mind (ing
Be apt to	Hate to	Need to
Be bound to	Have to	Plan to
Begin to	Help (ing)	Scared to
Be known to	Keep (ing)	Seem to
Be supposed to	Liable to	Stop (ing)
Be sure to	Like to	Try to
Care to	Likely to	Use (d) to
Claim to	Love to	Want to
Get to	Mean to	

When you get rid of abstract nouns made out of verbs and use concrete nouns, along with short, simple verbs, adverbs, and helping verbs, your writing style will take on a sleek, trim look. You'll be able to say what you mean and mean what you say.

Another Method You Can Use to Improve
Your Writing Style Overnight

This final section on word study will help you put the frosting on the cake. It shows you how to get rid of whatever dead and useless words are left in your writing. Dead words are particles, prepositions, prepositional phrases, and conjunctions that add no meaning to your sentence. Actually, they often confuse or muddle your reader.

These dead and useless words make up more than half of all the words you use, so the more of them you get rid of, the clearer your meaning will be. When you use the simple and concise prepositions *so, for, since, because* instead of the long complicated ones like *accordingly, for the purpose of, in the event that, due to the fact that,* your style will improve quickly. You might not become a professional writer, but a lot of people will think you should be one.

One dead word is better than two or three, and a short one is better than a long one. If you can get rid of the dead word altogether, do so. However, words like *a, an, any, few, several, some, the* are necessary. *Dog bit boy* instead of *The dog bit the boy* makes your writing sound like a telegram. That's not what you're after. Don't sacrifice clarity for brevity.

The dead words I *try* to cut from my writing are in the first column. The words I use in place of them follow in parentheses. I say *try* because I miss sometimes, too. After all, I'm not infallible.

Accompanied by	(with)
According to	(by, under) or leave out
Afford an opportunity	(permit, let)
Along the lines of	(like)
As to	(about)
At all times	(always)
At an early date	(soon)
At the present time	(now)
At your earliest convenience	(as soon as you can)
Consequently	(so)
Due to the fact that	(since, because)
Early on	(earlier, before)
For the purpose of	(for)
For the reason that	(since, because)
For this reason	(so)
From the point of view of	(for)
Furthermore	(then)
Hence	(so)
In accordance with	(by, under)

In addition to	(besides, also)
In compliance with your request	(as you asked)
In favor of	(for, to)
In order to	(to)
In the amount of	(for)
In the case of	(if)
In the event that	(if)
In the near future	(soon)
In the nature of	(like)
In terms of	(in, for)
In the neighborhood of	(about)
In view of the fact that	(as, since, because)
In spite of the fact that	(though, although)
Inasmuch as	(since, because)
Incidentally	(by the way)
Indeed	(in fact)
Likewise	(and, also)
More specifically	(for instance, for example)
Moreover	(now, next)
Nevertheless	(but, however)
On the basis of	(by)
On the grounds that	(since, because)
Owing to the fact that	(since, because)
Prior to	(before)
That is to say	(in other words)
The fact that	Do not use, period!
Thus	(so)
To be sure	(of course)
With a view to or a view toward	(to)
With reference to	(about)
With regard to	(about)
With the result that	(so that)

That finishes up our word study. I could cover much more material, but this is a book on management—not English. What I have covered here will make you a better writer of letters, directives, orders, and reports that are such an important part of any manager's job. Now to cover grammar, sentence structure, and paragraphing.

What to Do About Your Grammar When You Write

You do not have to be a grammarian or a professor of English to write a good sentence. The primary reason for all those grammar rules you learned back in school is to help you focus your reader's attention on the meaning you want to convey. If you take care to make your meaning clear, your grammar will usually take care of itself.

When you get right down to it, grammar is simply the arrangement of words together in a way that gives them meaning as a sentence. The rules of grammar are quite flexible; they leave plenty of room for individual style. All those old grammar school rules of *don't split an infinitive . . . never end a sentence with a preposition . . . "none" should always be followed with a singular verb . . . every sentence must contain a subject and a predicate* don't stand up in actual everyday usage.

Only a fanatic insists that these rules can't be broken. As we talk about how your sentences should be constructed, you'll see that grammar becomes a natural subconscious part of your writing so that it's really nothing at all to worry about.

How to Write Strong and Powerful Sentences

I've already given you information on the words to get rid of and the ones to use in their place. That's the first step in writing strong and powerful sentences: concrete nouns, strong verbs of action, and no vague or abstract words. But there's more to it than that.

Not only should you use short and simple words, but you should also use short and simple sentences. You'll find it's hard to make up long and cumbersome sentences when you use the verbs and adverbs I've given you.

You should vary your sentence lengths, however. The best way to determine how long a sentence should be is to use one sentence for one idea. When you come to the end of one thought, stop. Start a new sentence. A lot of conjunctions—*and, but, however*—

should serve as a clear warning that your sentences are too long. Chances are, they contain more than one idea. Let me give you an example: first, the wrong way, then the right.

> There is not enough time available for the average manager to do everything that might be done, and so it is necessary for him to determine wisely the essentials and do them first, then spend the remaining time on things that are "nice to do." (One sentence)

> The average manager doesn't have enough time to do everything that might be done. He must decide what is essential and do that first. Then he can spend his remaining time on things that are "nice to do." (three sentences)

Take a Direct Approach . . . Use the Active Voice

Express your ideas immediately and directly. Unnecessary phrases like *it is, there is,* and *there are* weaken your sentences. They also put part of your sentence in the passive voice. The passive voice means the subject has something done to it by someone: The boy was bitten by the dog. The active voice means someone did something to the object: The dog bit the boy.

When you start a sentence with *it is, there is,* or *there are,* you get passive sentences like these: "*It is* the foreman's recommendation that the report be forwarded immediately to the personnel manager by Smith." This can be easily re-worded to read "The foreman recommended that Smith send the report to the personnel manager at once." "*There are* six men in his department" can be rewritten to read "His department has six men." "*There is* a standing rule in this company" can be written "This company has a standing rule."

Avoid Wandering Sentences

Long, straggling sentences often have a hodgepodge of unrelated ideas. For example, "The foreman, an irritable fellow who had formerly been a truck driver, born and raised in the coal mining regions of West Virginia, strong as an ox and over 6 feet tall, fixed an angry eye on the guilty employee." Don't bring in unrelated facts like this. The meat of this sentence is that the foreman is angry with some guilty employee. The rest of the information is unnecessary.

How and When to Start a New Paragraph

Paragraphs should be no longer than your reader can grasp in *one mind-ful*. Keep them short for clarity and ease of reading. No hard and fast rule can be set down for paragraphing, but from three or four to seven or eight typewritten *lines* (not sentences) is a good rule of thumb to follow in correspondence.

The old school rule—which is still a good one to follow—is to start a new paragraph when you have a new subject or a new group of ideas that belong together. Even when the subject material is still the same, you should start a new paragraph rather than have one that runs on and on and on. A fresh paragraph gives your reader the chance to take a mental breath and come up for air.

How to Write Powerful Letters, Directives, and Reports: Six Guidelines

1. **Establish the Proper Foundation.** Effective and powerful writing is based on proper and adequate preparation: the selection, analysis, and organization of your ideas. You pick your specific objective, marshal your forces, and organize your attack.

The preparation may take only a few moments, or it may require several days. That depends entirely on the size and scope of your project. However, it will actually be the most important phase of your writing effort. Gather together all the facts bearing on your problem. You'll need to think things through carefully and find the answers to *who, what, when, where, why,* and *how* before you write the first word.

"Many people compose weak and ineffective business letters because they write them before they do all their homework," says Sarah Bayles, business office manager and executive secretary for an oil company in Montana. "That's why their letters don't get the results they want. Part of my job is to review all outgoing correspondence. I normally need to re-do about 50 percent of the letters composed by our top management people. Things are looking up, though. When I took over this responsibility, I had to rewrite almost all our company correspondence."

Establish the proper foundation before you start to write. Do your homework first. Think your subject through carefully before you pick up your pen or start dictating to your secretary. Get the answers to the question words—the five W's—first. Then you can begin the actual job of writing.

2. Identify Your Reader. Who will read your correspondence? Is it going to a well-educated individual, an executive or manager with a B.S., an M.A., even a Ph.D. behind his name? Or are you preparing an official announcement for the company bulletin board? Will your directive be read by every single employee or does it go only to your key management people?

You can get your ideas across to your readers when you use words they understand easily. Then, whether they read you "loud and clear," understanding at once everything you say, will depend entirely on their knowledge and education—not on yours.

Writing intended for general company distribution should be drafted with short, simple words and sentences that are easy to grasp without causing your reader to do a double-take. The reading skills of other people are often much less than your own. I do not mean you should write down to your employees. When you use simple, easy-to-understand words and short sentences, you're not. It's only when you use big pompous words and high-faluting phrases that you do.

"You can use technical lingo throughout if all your readers are technical people," says Doctor Donald Middaughs, a biochemist and senior executive with a large chemical corporation. "But why do so if you don't have to? Even well educated people hate big words. But if you are writing for untrained people, you must use simple non-technical language.

"Technical jargon, unfamiliar abbreviations, uncommon words, and long complicated sentences hide the meaning and make reading hard and tedious, even for brilliant persons. We try to make everything as simple and easy to understand as possible. Things are complicated enough already in biochemistry. Why make them more difficult by using unnecessarily complex language?"

Before you start writing, ask yourself this one question: "Who must read and understand this?" Keep that answer in mind while you write. But no matter to whom you're writing, let me say that *even the most abstract idea can be understood when you describe it in simple concrete words.* Your readers will appreciate your doing that.

3. **Know Why You're Writing Your Letter.** Every letter you write should have a definite purpose, or it should not be written. That purpose is worthwhile only when it's important enough to offset the substantial costs of preparing, dictating, typing, proof-reading, recording, copying, filing, and mailing. You may have even more steps in your letter-writing process than these. Writing even the simplest, shortest, one-page letter costs money, time, and effort. Is it really worth it to you? What is your purpose in writing it? Do you need a permanent record or will a phone call do just as well?

Most business letters, directives, and reports are written for three main reasons (1) *to direct or order some action,* (2) *to tell someone something,* (3) *to persuade someone to do something.* All three types have to do with *who, what, when, where, why,* and *how,* but the emphasis will be different. In an order or directive, the main emphasis will be on *what* has to be done. Informative writing will explain primarily *how* something should be done, while persuasive writing will concentrate on *why* you want your reader to do a certain thing.

Whatever your specific objective, know exactly what you're after and stick to that point. Zero in on it. Don't wander aimlessly. A fundamental secret of salesmanship that also applies to good writing is *concentrate on a single point—don't scatter your fire.*

4. **Emphasize Your Main Points.** Determining what to leave out is often harder than deciding what to put in. You should get rid of all ideas or facts that are not needed for your reader's understanding.

Irrelevant details tend only to obscure your main objective and weaken your meaning. Search, research, define, sift, discard until all you have left is one clean, clear objective with the necessary ideas to support or explain it.

5. **The Best Writing Is Done from a "Working" Outline.** A good working outline is more a sketch than a final blueprint. It makes your writing plan easy to see. If a better idea strikes you, you can change your outline. Give every major point in your outline a main heading. For clarity and easy understanding, you can give subheadings to the minor items supporting your major points of emphasis. Your outline is not the finished product. Use it as a working paper to help you keep your thoughts in order, so you can prepare the best final document possible.

6. **Review Your Writing for Objectivity.** All writing is subjective because writing is a personal matter. Your letters reflect you, your viewpoints and ideas, your best thinking. That's the way it should be. Your writing should reflect your personality. It should be you and no one else. At the same time, you cannot let your subjective opinions overrule objective facts. Base your writing on correct information that can be checked for accuracy. Don't let your subjective prejudices and opinions color or cover up the true facts.

No matter what the reason for my writing (to direct or order some action, tell someone how to do something, persuade someone to buy my product or accept my viewpoint), I always make up my outline in terms of *Benefits and Features* or *Benefits and Techniques*.

In other words, someone—including me—must benefit from my writing or it's not worth it. Even when I'm issuing an order or a directive, I point out how the person will *benefit* by carrying out my instructions. If I'm telling him how to do something, I also let him know how my new method is more *advantageous* to him than the old one. If I'm persuading him to my point of view, I give him the *features* to back up the *benefits* I'm offering, or I show him the *techniques* he can use to gain those *benefits*. No matter what you're writing, *your reader must benefit*, or he won't be interested.

The Most Effective Format I've Ever Used
for a Persuasive Letter

Let me show you now the most effective format I've ever found for a persuasive letter. It is simple, yet highly effective. It can be used whether you're selling a product or getting someone to do or see things your way.

Although the time-honored AIDA formula will always hold true (Get his *attention* . . . arouse his *interest* . . . kindle his *desire* . . . incite him to *action*) just knowing the formula is not enough. I've met many people who knew the AIDA formula by heart, but didn't know how to put it to practical use. Let me show you how best to put that formula to work.

First, look at your 5-by-8 card so you can review the 15 basic needs and desires people have and the sentence summing them up that reads:

Every normal person wants to know how to be loved, how to win money, fame and fortune, power, and how to stay healthy.

Know the benefit you have to offer. Tell him all about it *right away* to get his *attention* and *interest*. Kindle his *desire* by ticking off all the good things that will happen when he does what you want him to do. Offer him proof by bringing on your witnesses to vouch for you or your product. Spur him toward your goal by telling him exactly what he must do to gain those benefits. Finally, to get the *action* you want, tell him what will happen if he doesn't do it and do it right now. In an outline form, the best format for a persuasive letter looks like this:

1. **The Opening.** Start out immediately with the benefits your reader will gain. I used to write an opening paragraph to rouse my reader's attention in a variety of ways. I called it the introduction and I waited until the second or even the third paragraph to stress the benefits. Not any more.

Now I get to my point immediately. I tell him at once how he can profit or benefit by doing as I ask. Today, more than ever, people are pressed for time. If you don't grab your reader in your first sentence, you may well have lost him. He won't read the second line. The first ten words are more valuable than the rest of your letter.

Tell your reader right away how he will benefit, how he will save money, time, effort . . . get more pleasure out of life . . . be happier . . . have more leisure hours for himself, and on and on, depending on what you're offering him. I can't stress this point too much so I'll say it again:

Start immediately with the benefits your reader will gain.

2. Now Explain How He'll Gain Those Benefits. Tell him how your product will give him those benefits you promised him. Here you can talk about the *features* that give him the benefits. For example, the new squelch control on the CB radio, the extra wide-range speakers on the stereo set, the ultra-modern battery that never needs water. If you're selling an intangible, a system or an idea, say why your method is better than the one he's now using. *Always sell benefits—not features. Use features to support and prove your benefits.*

3. Offer Proof that What You Say Is True. The best proof you will ever have that your proposition will do what you say it will is *people-proof. The satisfied customer is still your best witness.* Mrs. Jones next door says . . . Mr. Smith down the street has one, ask him . . . Sam Brown, Bill Jones, Sally Black. . . . Use the names of people who've benefited so he can check and see for himself that you're telling the truth.

Medical doctors don't like what they call *anecdotal medicine*, especially in articles or books. That's the kind where people tell about their case histories and how good the doctor's treatment was. But people still make better witnesses than all the laboratory reports in the world.

For instance, in 1976, the swine flu shots were declared safe by scientific laboratory research and government reports. But dead people made far better and more effective witnesses *against* the swine flu shots than all those favorable lab reports and government researchers made *for* it.

4. Tell Him Exactly What to Do to Gain Those Benefits.

This usually comes in the next-to-last paragraph. Here you tell your reader exactly what to do to gain the benefits you're offering him. You give him his exact instructions: Fill out the form . . . send your check or money order . . . don't send cash . . . call this number . . . use the enclosed self-addressed evelope. Tell him precisely what to do. *Make it easy for him to do as you ask.* Don't create any mental stumbling blocks for him. If it's not simple and easy for him to comply with your request, he won't.

5. **Set the Hook.** Every good fisherman knows you can get a lot of nibbles, but you can't land your catch until you set the hook. Writing a persuasive letter without the hook is like going fishing with only a piece of string. No persuasive letter is ever complete without the hook. This is the snapper or penalty you hold over the reader's head.

You hook him and force him to take action by telling him what will happen if he doesn't. Whatever your offer, a time penalty is one of the best ways to get the action you want. *This offer expires in 5 days . . . Good only until April 19th . . . Prices go up next month . . . Limited supply, first come, first served.*

You might think this information is old hat, and maybe to you it is, but I know that to one big corporation and some top-notch advertising companies it isn't. Here's why I know that. In recent months I've seen a TV commercial that says such and such a car has a "wide track." The actor in the commercial then says, "Isn't that interesting?"

No, it's not interesting. A wide track is a feature of the car— not a benefit. Not once in that commercial does the actor ever say what that wide track will do for you. Not once is the benefit of the wide track given to the viewer. He has to guess. All he knows is that wide track "is interesting," but he doesn't know why. This is a classic example of selling a feature instead of a benefit. It is a direct violation of the basic principles of salesmanship.

How Using the 4-S Formula Can Make You a Successful Writer

Throughout this chapter I've taken several good pokes at the bureaucrats in the federal government for their writing style. But I believe in giving credit where it's due, so I must do that now.

The following formula, better known as the *4-S Formula*, can be found in the General Services Administration handbook, *Plain Letters*. The principles of this formula are *shortness, simplicity, strength,* and *sincerity*. But to tell the truth, although the principles are sound, much of the government language in the handbook is still too abstract for me, so I've used my own words to paraphrase some of theirs. These are the rules for using the *4-S Formula*.

How to Insure Shortness in Your Writing

1. Don't repeat what was said in a letter you answer.
2. Leave out unnecessary words and use less information.
3. Shorten your prepositional phrases.
4. Don't use nouns and adjectives made from verbs.
5. Don't qualify your statements with irrelevant "if's."

How to Gain Simplicity in Your Writing

1. Know your subject so well you can talk about it naturally and confidently.
2. Use short words, concise sentences, and compact paragraphs.
3. Keep closely related parts of your sentences together.
4. Tie your thoughts together logically so your reader can follow you without getting lost.

How to Give Your Writing Strength

1. Use concrete and specific words: the names of people, places, and things.
2. Use short active verbs.
3. Give the answer first; then explain if necessary.
4. Don't hedge by being vague and abstract.
5. Get rid of all empty, dead, and useless words.

How to Achieve Sincerity in Your Writing

1. Be yourself . . . not someone else.
2. Always tell the truth.
3. Admit your mistakes.
4. Don't exaggerate.
5. Don't write down to your reader.

A Few Final Thoughts to Help You as You Write

1. Use Personal Words like *I, me, you, we, us.* They make your reader feel more comfortable. Don't say "This writer believes" or "It is the opinion of the undersigned." Say, "*I* believe . . . It is *my* opinion." I've never been able to understand why a TV commentator or a writer will say, "*This reporter* has been told," when all he really means is "*I've* been told."

2. Use Specific Words. Don't say machine if you mean *bulldozer, mimeograph, typewriter.* Why say *personnel* if you mean *John* and *Mary* in the accounting department? If you know who did it or who it is, say so. Don't blame it on *them. They* said or *they* did it has always been one of my pet peeves.

3. Don't Exaggerate. Avoid words or phrases that overstate what you actually did. People know better. Why say you made an *exhaustive search* if you looked through only one file? *Tried but failed* is more believable than *a strenuous effort was made without tangible results.* Most people interpret that last remark to mean nothing at all was done.

4. Don't Use Pointer Words in Your Writing. Pointer words like *herein, herewith, inclosed herewith, hereunder, attached hereto, hereinafter* are unnecessary, old-fashioned, and out-of-date. Why use them?

5. Crutch Words Cripple Your Writing. Crutch words cripple forceful writing. Don't use crutch words like *very, such, same* in these ways: Rather than say it's *very* hot, say *It's hotter than the hinges of Hades*. That says it more expressively than *very*. *Such* is useless in this sentence: Mailmen, *as such*, walk many miles a day. *Same* is awkward in this sentence: The new procedure will not be used until the manager approves *same*. What's wrong with using *it?*

6. Use Informal English: Write as You Talk. Using contractions is a good way to do this. Nothing wrong with *don't* for *do not* and *won't* for *will not*. Reduces your word count by one each time. Use your own language, too. Don't copy someone else. He might be wrong.

Simple active verbs, concrete nouns, short sentences, the precise use of words, clear thinking, and careful construction—all these are the elements that make for clear effective writing that will put your ideas across to people. Admittedly, it is much easier to be lazy and write otherwise, but it is better to write with care for then you can be sure of getting the results you want.

Chapter 5

Why Top Managers Are
Always Masters of the
Art of Oral Communication

Almost everything I said in the last chapter about writing applies to the spoken language. The rules about using small words, short sentences, the direct approach, the active voice, avoiding pretentious words are as important to follow in talking as in writing.

However, a huge amount of brand-new, exciting, and useful information is waiting for you here in this chapter. I want to give you my *Fifth Master Key to Management Success*, so you, too, will become a master of this fascinating art of oral communication.

Solving the Oral Communication Problem in Management

Communication—the ability to clearly transmit orders and directives down to the lowest working level so there will be no possibility of misunderstanding—is one of the biggest problems a top-level manager has to solve.

The average manager spends 75 percent of his time in oral communication. Out of every eight hours on the job, six are spent in talking or listening to others. Most of a typical executive's working day is used to give and get information, issue orders and instructions, orally correct mistakes, and help people solve their problems.

It's hard for a manager to realize he spends three-fourths of his working time in oral communication. If you, too, have a hard time believing this, try working at your job some day without talking or listening to anyone. You'll give up before the first hour is over for you'll accomplish absolutely nothing.

No matter how intelligent you are, or how much you know, unless you can communicate your knowledge to others to get the job done, your managerial wisdom might as well be stored in a bank vault.

How successful is the average manager in his oral communication? How well does he make himself understood by the people who work for him? Listen to a few of the complaints I've heard over the years from both sides and judge for yourself.

MANAGER: I explained it so clearly even an idiot could have understood what I meant; still he fouled it up.

EMPLOYEE: Why doesn't he talk straight and say what he means?

MANAGER: If he didn't understand me, why didn't he say so?

EMPLOYEE: I didn't misunderstand . . . he didn't say it right.

MANAGER: What's wrong with you . . . don't you understand plain English?

EMPLOYEE: Why doesn't he tell me exactly what he wants me to do?

MANAGER: How many times do I have to tell him how to do it?

EMPLOYEE: Why can't he make up his mind instead of always changing things?

Since three-fourths of your management duties consist of oral communication, the sooner you solve your problems in that area, the better off you'll be. The less time you spend in untangling misunderstandings that come from a garbled transmission, the more time you can devote to other managerial activities.

The more capable you become in the ability to express yourself clearly to others, the greater will be your opportunities for becoming successful as a manager. Ninety-nine percent of the time, the person who achieves the most success in business and management will be the one who has mastered the art of oral communication. When you become adept and skilled in this art —

YOU'LL GAIN THESE WORTHWHILE BENEFITS

A winning, positive, out-going personality,

Greater inner security, self-confidence, peace of mind,

The ability to think clearly and express yourself precisely,

The skill to cause others to think of and act favorably toward you,

The power to motivate others to do what you want.

Other people will like you, listen to you, enjoy working with you, and do things for you with a friendly attitude and a cooperative manner.

You'll gain greater results with less mistakes; your superiors will always take note of that.

How to Develop Your Own Distinctive Talking Style

Some years ago, I met a young, up-and-coming insurance salesman, Gary Davis, in his company's regional office in St. Louis. Gary was only 5 feet 4 inches tall. He was a quite common, ordinary looking person except for one thing. He wore a fiery red beard, and this was long before beards were commonplace. "Why?" I asked him.

"To attract attention," Gary said. "I want to make sure people remember me. You wear a mustache for the same reason, don't you?"

I had to admit he was right. People remember me as "that man with the salt and pepper mustache." If it were not for that, most of them wouldn't recall the slightly overweight, rather short, middle-aged fellow with thinning hair who wears glasses. Besides, that description fits most American men over 40. But people do remember the man with the "distinguished looking" mustache.

By the way, that young insurance salesman is now a division manager and vice-president of his company. Somebody topside kept him in mind. He still sports that flaming red beard, too.

My point is you need to be distinctive in some way to be both *noticed* and *remembered*. Generally speaking, a salt and pepper mustache or a crimson beard is not enough. That will help you get *noticed*. But unless you happen to have some of the charisma of Paul Newman or Robert Redford, developing your own distinctive style of talking is one of the best ways to be *remembered*.

It's also one of the most profitable. When I was a boy, the Keokuk Hotel in Sigourney, Iowa, was the most popular spot for miles around with traveling salesmen. They drove out of their way to stay there. Why? Because the owner, "Happy" Weller, was always cheerful and smiling. He had a good word for everybody. I never once heard him say an unkind thing about anyone in all the years I knew him. Hap Weller had his own distinctive style and he became successful and well-to-do because of that.

The style of your talking, the way you converse with others, makes a vital contribution to your reputation and your success. If you talk down to your employees, they will resent you. If you are too deferential to your superiors, they may consider you weak and spineless, incapable of accepting further and higher responsibilities. Your talking style is not only a matter of the words you use, but also your way of using them, as well as your attitude and bearing.

Be Natural, Be Yourself When You Talk

Don't try to imitate someone else or be something you're not. Too often, people try to copy the style of others who are "supposed" to be successful or in the know. (That's why those government writers always go wrong.) It's good to learn from others, but don't try to copy another person's style or manner of talking. People will always know. You'll be like the alcoholic who can't hide his "sins." People can always smell them. The best person you can be when you talk is yourself. Develop a style that is distinctively yours, not someone else's.

For instance, I was born and raised on an Iowa farm. I have made my home in the midwest most of my life. I still have that flat midwestern way of speaking. I've never tried to change it. Why should I? If you have a southern accent, don't try to get rid of it. As long as people understand you, leave it alone. The same goes for the long Texas drawl of the southwest, or the clipped abrupt New England way of speaking.

A friend of mine, Walter Baker, says flatly any success he has is due to his ability to talk with people. Walter, a top-level executive with an Oklahoma oil company, has a distinctive style all his own. He is gentlemanly, cordial, and sincere. He never tries to be anyone except himself and he knows who he is.

As Walter told me, "A lot of people in our company are better geologists than I am. I attribute whatever success I have attained to my ability to put myself and my ideas across to others.

"So many people feel they need to put on an act or wear a false face when they're talking with others. Some try to be overly friendly—sometimes even servile. Others are too dynamic; they come across too strong like a TV commercial. Still others try to act tough. The trouble is, none of these people are ever themselves, so they just don't register.

"But I'm always me. What you see is what you get. Whether you like what I am or not, you'll always know it's the real me talking with you, not some phony. Right or wrong, I'll always be honest with you."

How to Be Forceful, Positive, and
Convincing When You Talk

Force makes your speech positive and convincing. It gives vigor and strength to what you say. Force creates movement; it makes things happen; it brings your words to life.

How can you be forceful when you talk? *Use lots of short active verbs that denote or imply movement.* Remember the one- and two-syllable verbs I gave you back on page 104 in the last chapter? Verbs like *break, cut, drive, drop, kick, pull, push, stir, strike, tear* will bring life to what you say. They impel people to do things,

Another way to be forceful, positive, and convincing is to *be clear and precise when you talk.* Give your listener only one idea at a time to digest. When you come to the end of one idea, stop. Pause. Take a breath. Then go on to your next thought. Don't link one idea to the next with endless connectives like *and, but, for, or, nor.* Too many thoughts at once bewilder and confuse your listener. Even the most difficult technical explanation can be made plain and clear if you present your information one step at a time.

It is impossible to be forceful, positive, and convincing when you use vague and abstract words and long-winded sentences. Try saying this sentence out loud with power and conviction as if you were actually talking to one of your subordinates.

> It is directed that you take immediate appropriate action to accomplish the correction of your financial records, and that you transmit a directive to your branch offices with the view to having them make a similar correction of theirs.

Now say it out loud this way. Note the difference in the positive tone of force you can put in your voice.

> Straighten up your records right now. Tell your branch offices to do the same thing.

Eight guidelines to follow so you can be forceful, positive, and convincing when you talk are these:

1. Use active verbs of motion for *force.*
2. Small easy-to-understand words make your speech *positive.*
3. One idea at a time makes what you say *convincing.* Too many ideas at once confuse and muddle your listener.
4. Specify; use illustrations and examples.
5. Be direct. Don't beat around the bush.
6. If you don't know, say so. Don't bluff.
7. Avoid all pompous and pretentious, vague and abstract words.
8. Don't insult your listener by talking down to him.

Know the Purpose of Your Conversation

Do you remember what I said about good writing in the previous chapter? I said most business letters, directives, and reports are written for one of three main reasons: (1) to direct or order some action, (2) to inform someone of something, (3) to persuade someone to do something. The same principles apply here.

Sometimes, your conversation will have a dual purpose. For instance, if you're talking to a subordinate, you may want to tell him about a mistake he's making and then *direct* him to change his methods. To a superior, your dual purpose might be to *inform* him of some problem and *persuade* him to accept your solution.

Whatever your purpose, know it and stick to it. Ask yourself this question: "What is my specific objective?" If you know precisely what you want to accomplish, your conversation will be exact, clear, and to the point. If you're not sure of what you want, you'll find yourself talking all day long about the weather, the last World Series, politics, and the state of the economy, and then wondering that night why you didn't get any work done.

A top-notch salesman knows better than anyone else how to talk effectively to get results. Such a person is Norman Vance. Norman was making $50,000 a year selling insurance before he was 30 years old. That was nearly 20 years ago when a dollar would buy a lot more than it will today. Today, only Norman and the IRS know his income, but I know you don't buy country estates, a yacht, Cadillacs and Lincolns, and take trips around the world with Monopoly money.

Norman gave me the following seven steps he follows in all his business conversations. I heartily recommend them to you.

1. Lay your foundation by being properly prepared. Know your subject thoroughly, better than anyone else.
2. No matter how much you know, talk at the level of your listener's understanding. Don't try to impress him with your vast knowledge.
3. Determine your specific objective. Know the exact purpose of your conversation and stick to that point. Don't wander around aimlessly or get off on a subject your listener would like to talk about.

4. Emphasize your main points. Come back to them again and again until you're sure they're absolutely clear in your listener's mind. If you don't accomplish the purpose of your conversation, your whole effort has been wasted.

5. Make up a mental outline and follow it. If necessary, write your main points down on a card and refer to them.

6. Don't stray from that outline. When you know your specific objective and know exactly what you want to get done, it's easy to go from point A to E directly without detours.

7. When you've achieved your objective, stop talking. A poor salesman often loses a sale because he keeps blabbering away after the sale has been made. He gives the customer a chance to think and change his mind. Watch your terminal facilities. When you're through, quit.

Know What Your Listener Wants to Hear

No matter what you talk about, your listener always wants to know first off what's in it for him. Let him know right away the reward he's going to get just for listening to you. Even if you're going to tell a person how to correct a mistake he's making, still *use the approach of telling him about the benefits he'll gain when he uses your method.*

A person's primary concern is how he's going to benefit by doing as you ask, so tell him that. Of course, if he's working for you, he may have no other choice than to do exactly as you ask, but without giving him the proper incentive, you'll get only the minimum results.

Show him how he can fulfill his basic needs and desires when he does as you ask. Then you'll always gain the maximum from him. That alone will lift you out of the average manager's class and put you in the superior executive's category. The person who can get the most from his subordinates will always be earmarked for promotion first.

Why I "Try" Not to Talk Too Much

Like most other people, I tend to keep on talking once I get started. Someone asks me a question about a subject that interests me or on which I'm knowledgeable, and I find I'm spinning away like a phonograph record. I become hypnotized by the sound of my own words. When I discover that's happening, I try to turn myself off, for I'm always reminded of what John Carradine, the famous Hollywood and Broadway character actor once said.

"When I was very young, I was auditioning for a part in a Shakespearian play in New York," Mr. Carradine said, in effect. "I was quite impressed with my speaking abilities and got really carried away with myself during the audition. Right at the climax, a deep voice boomed out of the darkened theater seats and said, 'Young man, you're in love with the sound of your own voice.' That really taught me a valuable lesson I've always remembered through all my acting years."

Another point to remember is not to badger and harass your listener with more information than is necessary to get the job done. Don't tell him more than he needs to know. My father taught me this lesson early in life. He was a quiet man who had little use for small talk.

He regarded a sermon as an archaic nuisance and was extremely critical of ministers who kept on preaching long after their sermon was through. He was especially irritated when the service went beyond 12 o'clock.

My dad loved to fish on weekends. Had he had his own way, he would have been sitting on the river bank early on Sunday mornings. However, to keep peace in the family, he took us to church and waited until afternoon to pursue his first love.

One particular Sunday on the way home from church, my mother asked him how he had enjoyed the sermon. It was not the right day to ask. The preacher had been unusually wound up, the service had run until 12.30, and my father was going to be late getting down to the river.

With a quiet patience with which I've never been blessed, he turned to my mother and gently said, "He said more than he had to talk about."

If you want to retain your listener's interest and have him pay close attention to everything you say, I recommend you keep these two points in mind:

1. Don't fall in love with the sound of your own voice.

2. Don't say more than you have to talk about.

Why I Don't Take More Time than My Subject Is Worth

"I don't think I've ever seen a church where people actually wait in line to get inside," I said to Walter Parkhill, pastor of a Presbyterian church in Des Moines, Iowa. "What's your secret? A lot of speakers would give anything to draw the crowds you do."

"Well, I'd like to think people are anxious to hear my message," Walter said. "I would hope that's at least part of the reason. But I also believe one explanation for our large attendance is I don't beat a dead horse to death over and over again from the pulpit. I never take more time than my subject is worth. I leave my congregation anxious to hear more for *I always quit before I'm through.*"

Maybe you can't follow this principle when you're issuing an order to a subordinate or giving detailed instructions on how to do a certain job. Other than that, though, this rule is good to follow at all times I can think of. Besides, most orders and directives, rules and regulations always use more words than are necessary to get the job done.

Don't muddle and confuse your listener with information he doesn't need. Don't drown him in details. Unnecessary trivia can cause confusion, loss of attention, and misunderstanding. *Attention is always lost when understanding is gone.*

To keep the full attention and interest of your listener, and to gain his complete understanding, don't talk too much. Make your sentences short. Don't use unnecessary words. Stay on course. Stick to your point. Let me give you a classic example of this principle.

Nearly 2,000 years ago, a man who walked by the Sea of Galilee understood this precept of simplicity well. Everything in His life was plain and simple: His clothing, His food; His stories, His parables; His language, His words. Yet His message is still studied today, for, although complicated by man, the order He gave was clear, concise, positive, and easy to understand, for He simply said, *"Follow me."*

I'd like you to remember three main points from this small section:

1. Don't take more time than your subject is worth.
2. Always quit before you're through. (Then you know they'll come back for more.)
3. Attention is lost when understanding is gone.

Why You Should Avoid Negative Words

In the previous chapter, I gave you various lists of words both to avoid and use in your writing and speaking. I want to give you some more useful information about words here. First, the negative ones to be avoided; then, certain positive ones most people like; third, specific trigger words that move a person's emotions.

A survey of 1,000 persons, in all walks of life, conducted by the University of Iowa's School of Journalism revealed that most people do not like the following words:

Abuse	Crooked	Imitation	Opinionated	Timid
Afraid	Deadline	Implication	Poverty	Unfair
Alibi	Discredit	Impossible	Prejudiced	Unsuccessful
Bankrupt	Failure	Improvident	Pretentious	Untimely
Blame	Fault	In vain	Quota	Verbiage
Calamity	Fear	Liable	Ruin	Waste
Cheap	Flimsy	Meager	Shirk	Weak
Complaint	Fraud	Misfortune	Slack	Worry
Crisis	Hardship	Negligence	Superficial	Wrong

As you'll note, most of these words have a negative flavor or a pessimistic note. People don't like negative ideas. The questionnaires also showed they did not like words beginning with -un, such as unsuccessful, uncertain, unconcerned, and the like. They much preferred the word not for presenting a negative idea, for instance, not successful, not certain, not concerned.

Not carries more emphasis than -un. If I say, "I'm not concerned about your welfare," it sounds more forceful and carries more weight than if I were to say, "I'm *un*concerned about your welfare."

"I'm *not* interested in your product is more emphatic than "I'm *un*interested in your product." Perhaps *not* and *-un* are identical in meaning, but they don't *feel* the same.

This is not to say this list is all inclusive or that all people do not like these words. But it's a good idea to stay away from negative sounding ones when you're speaking or composing a letter.

How to Use Positive Words People Like to Hear

That same University of Iowa survey found that most people like words that have a positive flavor like these:

Ability	Cooperate	Grateful	Loyalty	Sincerity
Abundant	Courage	Guarantee	Merit	Stability
Achieve	Courteous	Handsome	Notable	Substantial
Active	Definite	Harmonious	Opportunity	Success
Admire	Dependable	Helpful	Perseverance	Superior
Advance	Deserving	Honesty	Please	Thorough
Advantage	Desirable	Honor	Positive	Thoughtful
Ambition	Determined	Humor	Practical	Thrift
Appreciate	Distinction	Imagination	Proficient	Truth
Approve	Efficient	Improvement	Progress	Useful
Brave	Energy	Ingenuity	Promote	Valuable
Benefit	Enthusiasm	Initiative	Reasonable	Vigor
Capable	Excellence	Integrity	Recognize	Vital
Cheer	Exceptional	Intelligence	Recommend	Vivid
Comfort	Faith	Judgment	Reliable	Wisdom
Commendable	Fidelity	Justice	Reputable	Worthwhile
Confidence	Genuine	Kind	Responsible	You
Conscientious	Good	Lasting	Simplicity	Yours

How You Can Use "Trigger" Words that Rouse the Emotions

A few years ago a large western university, famous for its

research in applied psychology, conducted a scientific experiment for a well-known national advertising agency. Five hundred people were tested. The youngest subject tested was 14, the oldest 69. The majority fell in the 20-to 50-year age bracket.

The procedure was simple, yet the results extremely reliable. A lie detector was used. A list of words was then read to each subject and his reactions recorded by the polygraph.

The researchers found that all words with a *sexual connotation* caused the highest response in the subject, whether male or female, old or young. It is not surprising then to find sex used constantly to sell everything from cars to toilet paper.

Words such as *dandruff, halitosis, headache, heartburn, body odor, blowout, skid, accident, hospital, insurance* also elicited a high response from the lie detector. From this it's easy to see that a lot of advertising is aimed at certain basic fears almost all of us have at one time or another in life.

Fear is always on the opposite side of the coin of desire. Smart manufacturers and advertisers know this. They use our basic fears to their own advantage.

Other specific trigger words that caused a strong reaction on the polygraph were these:

Amazing	Guarantee	Listen	Money	Power	Results	See
Discovery	Health	Look	New	Proud	Safety	Watch
Easy	Important	Love	Now	Proven	Save	You

TECHNIQUES THAT WILL HELP YOU IMPROVE
YOUR SPEAKING ABILITIES

I'm not trying to make you into a public platform speaker, but I know that as a manager or an executive, you'll have to, on occasion, present your viewpoint to the board of directors . . . give a briefing for some visiting VIP's . . . speak at the annual stockholders' meeting . . . give an inspiring talk to a large group of employees to speed up production or increase sales . . . perhaps talk at a Kiwanis' luncheon or a Chamber of Commerce meeting.

The techniques in this section—five ways of controlling your nervousness when speaking to large groups of people . . . seven methods of getting into your subject without hesitation or fumbling around . . . six don'ts to remember and certain distracting mannerisms to avoid—come from the real professionals in the art of speaking or performing before large audiences: professional platform speakers; television and radio announcers, news broadcasters and commentators; college professors, nationally known religious leaders, and top-notch sales managers.

When you use their tips and put them into practice for yourself, you'll benefit by gaining more self-confidence. You'll be able to improve your delivery, sharpen your speaking style, and increase your overall ability to put yourself across with people.

How to Control Your Nervousness

Almost everyone experiences a few butterflies in the stomach when getting up in front of a group to talk, no matter how good he is or how long he's been at it. Here are five simple techniques you can use to help control your nervousness.

1. Be thoroughly prepared. Master your subject thoroughly. Be the authority.
2. Have a positive mental attitude. Be confident in yourself and have faith in your own abilities. *Act as if it were impossible to fail.*
3. Have your initial remarks well in mind. The first few moments are always the most critical.
4. Tell a story on yourself, Jack Benny style. This releases tension quickly and endears you to your audience.
5. Be deliberate . . . slow down. Force yourself to speak more slowly. Your normal poise and bearing will come back to you.

Seven Ways of Getting into Your Subject

To establish contact, gain attention, arouse interest, and get into your subject quickly and easily—you can use one or more of the following techniques:

1. *Use an Effective Opening Statement* That will show your audience immediately how they will benefit by listening to you. Make your opening statement a *grabber*.

2. *Make Reference to Some Previous Information.* This method is most often used when your contact with your listener is of a recurring nature. It refreshes his memory and re-establishes contact with him on common ground. It's best to renew that contact with your listener by talking about a benefit.

3. *Use a Startling Statement.* To get into your subject with a bang, find some eye-opening statement that can be used to punch home a benefit immediately. Be sure you can back up your startling statement with proof and facts when you use one.

4. *Ask a Question.* A question is one of the best ways to open a conversation or a group discussion. Your listener has to respond in some way to you. The moment he does, you've established contact with him.

5. *Use an Anecdote, a Story, an Illustration, an Example.* People are always more intersted in people than things. To prove your point, show your listener how it worked for Jim Brown, Sam Green, or Susie Smith. Tell your story or give an illustration for a definite and specific purpose. Don't tell a story for the sake of telling a story.

6. *Quote an Authority.* "A testimonial from a satisfied user is still the best way to convince a prospect," says Carl Williams, president of a Los Angeles advertising agency. "If that satisfied user is also an authority in some field, or if he's a celebrity and well known to the public, so much the better."

7. *Use a Demonstration.* When you use a demonstration to put your point across, you'll increase your chances of gaining attention and holding the interest of your audience. The lecture method is the poorest way of presenting a subject. Demonstrations and group participation get better results.

Six Don'ts to Remember

1. *Don't Bluff.* Never bluff to cover up a lack of knowledge. If you don't know the answer, say so. Find out what it is, and let the person know as soon as you can.
2. *Don't Use Profanity or Obscenity.* Not even a tiny "Damn!" or "Hell!" is permissible. The moment you use profanity, you run the risk of losing the respect and attention of some of your listeners.
3. *Don't Use Sarcasm or Ridicule.* This is especially true if you have a captive audience. Your listeners will resent it if they can't respond in the same sarcastic manner. If a person resents you, you'll never get him to do what you want him to do.
4. *Don't Talk Down to Your Listener.* You might be smarter than your listener, but only in one subject, and you selected that one. Never treat your listeners as ignorant if you want to keep them listening.
5. *Don't Lose Patience.* If your listener asks you to cover a point again, don't get upset. His inability to understand might be your failure to explain it clearly. Repeat the information or use other techniques to explain your point.
6. *Don't Make Excuses.* Don't start out saying, "Ill-prepared as I am . . . I didn't have a chance to go over this material . . . I'm not qualified to talk on this . . . I wouldn't be here, but . . ." This turns your listeners off immediately. Don't apologize or make excuses. Only amateurs do that; professionals never do. Be a pro.

Irritating Mannerisms to Avoid

I know you've listened to people who had some irritating mannerisms that distracted you and caused you to view them unfavorably. I went to a doctor once, who, when explaining my physical condition to me, had the habit of constantly asking, "Do you follow me?" with every third or fourth sentence. After a few minutes, this really got on my nerves. I found myself betting mentally when he would say it again, rather than listening to what he was telling me.

Others will use such phrases as *you know* over and over again. Tape yourself on a recorder and see if you pick up any repetitive phrases when you play it back. Have someone else—your wife, children, a friend, listen to your tape, too. They'll hear words or phrases you use over and over. You won't hear them because you're too used to them.

Physical mannerisms can include cracking your knuckles, drumming your fingers on a desk, excessive gum chewing, rubbing your nose, stroking your mustache, pulling your ear, adjusting your glasses, By themselves they're nothing, but when your listener sees them constantly he's distracted by them. He loses interest in what you're saying. Talk to the mirror to see if you have any physical mannerisms, nervous twitches, blinking of the eyes, whatever, you should eliminate.

For many years I chain-smoked cigarettes. When I quit, I went on the candy kick for a while, then gum, and finally ended up chewing toothpicks all the time. I became a connoisseur of toothpicks. I knew which brands tasted good, which ones had a bad flavor, the kinds of wood they were made from, how they held up under heavy chewing in a crisis, and so on.

I had a toothpick in my mouth all the time when I was awake except when I was eating, even in church or in the shower. People started referring to me as "that fellow with the toothpick," or they'd say, "He must eat all the time; he always has a toothpick in his mouth." So I finally broke the toothpick habit. You know, it was almost harder to quit them than it was to kick the cigarette habit.

THE "SILENT SKILL" AND HOW IT GETS RESULTS

Do you want to find out what's going on in your own organization? *Then listen to your people with an open mind.* Do you want your employees to like you? All you need do is *let them talk to you* about their personal problems, worries, and fears. Want a person to level with you, to tell you the truth? *Then give him the courtesy of listening* to what he says. To listen carefully and attentively is one of the highest compliments you can pay a person.

Here are some more benefits that can be yours when you properly use the *silent skill.*

1. Your employees will not only accept you, but they'll also like you when you pay them the compliment of listening.
2. When you listen to people's problems, you'll know and understand them better.
3. Listening lets your subordinates know you're really interested in them.
4. Listen to what your employees say; you'll learn a lot about your organization by listening *between the lines* to what they didn't say.
5. You'll become successful, for one of the hallmarks of a successful manager is that "he listens."

Talking cannot be all one-sided. If you're to learn anything from your employees, you'll need to listen to them. University of Chicago studies of top-level management in 100 firms showed that managers spend 40 percent of their time listening to their employees. Yet those managers retained only 25 percent of what they heard. I'm sure you'd like to do better than that. You can when you use these—

TEN TECHNIQUES TO HELP YOU IMPROVE
YOUR LISTENING ABILITIES

1. **Give Your Whole-Hearted Attention to the Other Person.** Listening with everything you have means putting aside your own interests, preoccupations, and problems, at least temporarily. For those few moments concentrate 100 percent on what the other person is saying. Focus all your attention on him. Listen with all the intensity and awareness you can command.

2. **Really Work at Listening.** Although you may not realize it, listening is hard work. When you listen intensely, your heart beat quickens, your pulse rate increases, and your blood circulates faster.

Even your body temperature rises slightly. You yourself will know whether you're really working at listening or just faking it.

3. Show an Interest in What the Speaker Says. One way of showing interest is to look at your speaker. Establish eyeball contact and keep it. Show by your alert posture and intense facial expression that you are deeply concerned with what he's saying. Whatever you do, don't fiddle with objects on your desk or clip your nails.

4. Resist Distractions. If the conversation takes place in your office, tell your secretary you don't want to be disturbed. Shut the door, cut off the telephone, the radio. Give the speaker the best opportunity to tell you what you need to know. If you don't, he might react the way I did once in a doctor's office in Omaha.

My wife and I were receiving a final report from a high-priced neurosurgeon about her physical condition. He was interrupted three times by phone calls from his secretary. The fourth time the phone rang, I picked it up and said, "The doctor is out. He won't be back for 30 minutes, period. Don't call again before 2.30."

5. Practice Patience. Patience is a matter of waiting, watching, listening, sitting silently until the person who's speaking is completely through. If he's your employee and you're the manager, chances are the tempo of his thinking is a lot slower than yours. If it weren't, your positions might be reversed. So understand why he's slower than you; have patience.

6. Keep an Open Mind. Remember you're listening to get new information. If his ideas don't coincide with yours, that doesn't mean you're right and he's wrong. Most innovations in business and industry often come from the rank-and-file worker as managers at AT&T, GM, 3M, Dow Chemical, Ford, GE, and hundreds of other large successful corporations will be quick to tell you.

7. Listen for Ideas. A good listener watches for ideas, concepts, and principles. A poor listener tends to get lost in factual details. If an employee has an idea to speed up production and eliminate waste, keep your eye on that objective. Don't fret if you can't remember by heart all the technical details. That can come later.

8. **Learn to Listen Between the Lines.** Lots of times you can learn more by what the other person didn't say than by what he did say. Just because he didn't say he doesn't want to do it your way is no sign that he does.

The speaker doesn't always put everything he's thinking into words. Watch for the changing tone and volume of his voice. Sometimes you'll find a meaning that's in direct contrast to his spoken words. Watch the facial expression, mannerisms, gestures, body movements. To be a good listener means you must use your eyes as well as your ears.

9. **Judge the Content . . . Not the Delivery.** I once worked for a man who'd been a college English professor. That bothered me for quite a while, until one day he said, "Look, Jim, I'm not grading you on your grammar, sentence structure, or choice of words. I'm interested only in *what* you're telling me—not how you're saying it."

Don't worry about a person's personality or his style of delivery. You should be interested in finding out what he knows. Judge the content . . . not the delivery.

10. **Hold Your Fire.** Many times a listener spends most of his time figuring how to rebut the speaker, rather than actually listening to what he's saying. Forget your own pet theories. You might learn something brand-new and extremely profitable if you *teach your ego to hold its breath.*

A Technique that Stimulates a Person to Talk

To simulate a person to open up and talk, all you need do is ask him a few leading questions about himself, his family, his job, or his ideas, his intereests, his problems. Then sit down and be ready to listen patiently for as long as you can spare. Let me give you a personal example to show you how easily that technique works:

I was recently invited to a small informal get-together at a friend's house. My hostess introduced me as a "real live author" to a good-looking young lady named Jenne' who was her house guest.

"A writer—how nice," this young woman said, and I could tell by the sound of her voice and the glazed look in her eyes that a "real live author" was the last person in this whole wide world she was interested in.

"You have an absolutely gorgeous tan," I said to her. "And in the middle of winter, too. How did you manage that? *Tell me*, where have you been? Miami Beach . . . Hawaii . . . Mexico?"

"Acapulco," she said. "Oh, it was so wonderful . . . so romantic."

"*Tell me all about it*," I said, and for the next two hours she did.

The next day my hostess called to say how much Jenne' had enjoyed talking with me the night before. "She told me what an interesting person you were to talk with," she said. But I hadn't said more than a dozen words all night long. See what I mean?

If you want to get a person to open up and talk, then ask him about himself, his interests, his bowling scores, his successes, his children, hobbies, and so on. Use a few questions to get him started; then listen with complete and full attention. People will love you for that.

When you pay attention to people and listen to them, good things are bound to come your way, sooner or later. Take Jenne', for example. She wanted an autographed copy of one of my books to show her friends. (And read, too, I hope.) Heaven only knows how many people will buy one of my books as a result of my listening attentively and patiently to her for a couple of hours. Do the same thing. You'll be able to reap the benefits of being a good listener, too.

How You Can Use This Powerful Tool to
Calm an Angry Employee

I know you've had the problem of the angry employee who comes to you steaming about some injustice that's been done to him. Imagined or real, it matters not. You want to solve the angry employee's problem so he can quickly become a cooperative productive member of your organization again. Here are five time-tested steps I've used to successfully calm down a person time after time.

1. Listen to the angry person's story from beginning to end without saying a single word.
2. Tell him you can't help but agree with him after looking at the problem from his viewpoint. (If you can't say you *agree*—at least say you *understand*.)
3. Ask him what he wants you to do.
4. Tell him you'll do your best to keep this problem from coming up again.
5. Say you'll always be ready to listen to him any time in the future if he ever needs your help again.

Remember every person has his own emotional breaking point. Some can take more than others, but sooner or later, all of us reach the point of no return where we simply cannot stand any more pain or criticism or punishment.

If you have an employee who's reached his emotional threshold, don't fight back. Let him get it all out of his system. Listen patiently with understanding until he exhausts himself. The important thing is to clear up the disagreement or solve his problem in such a way that good feelings and a warm, friendly, cooperative relationship can be re-established after the storm has passed.

There is no doubt in my mind that a person must master the art of oral communication before he can ever hope to aspire to a top-level corporate management position. *The person who can command words to serve his thoughts and feelings is well on the way to commanding people to serve his purposes.* I have in this chapter touched upon the high points you need to follow to perfect your speaking skills. It's up to you to expand and amplify the information I've given you here with more study and research of your own.

Now let's get on to the next chapter, *How Successful Managers Always Get the Job Done No Matter What*, where you'll learn how to use my *Sixth Master Key to Management Success*.

Chapter 6

How Successful Managers
Always Get the Job Done,
No Matter What

As a responsible and competent manager, you must be able to get the job done no matter what. Your superior will expect that from you. He's interested in results, not alibis . . . solutions, not problems.

Now it's easy enough to manage when everything is going your way—when you have more than enough manpower, materials, money, and time to get the job done. Almost anyone can do that.

It's when conditions aren't perfect that your ability to manage will become so important, for the best manager is often the best improviser. When you don't have enough trained people or all the equipment, time, and money you need, your management abilities will really be tested. The power to manage and get the job done in times of adversity is one of the most distinguishing characteristics of the successful manager.

That's why my *Sixth Master Key to Management Success* will be so valuable to you. It will show you the techniques you can use to get the job done, no matter what the obstacles. You'll also learn a reliable method to measure your abilities as a manager of people. This method will let you predict your organizational weather. You'll know ahead of time if it's going to be calm and fair, or whether you're in for a seige of stormy weather.

How You Can Be a "Can Do" Manager

"Here in our company, people are measured by what they get done rather than by what they say they're going to do," Fred

Walker, a top-level industrial manager told me. "About the finest reputation a person can make for himself is to have it said of him that *he always gets things done.* He'll become known throughout the organization as a *can-do manager.* That's the highest compliment he could receive. It says all we need to know about him."

Can-do managers are always highly sought after in business and industry for they're so few. That's why they're always highly appreciated. For instance, assistant managers who leave Procter and Gamble—and they're not many—are usually prized by other companies and recruited by them immediately.

The managerial ability to get things done is not an inherent quality. It can be developed. Over the years I've found these guidelines to be especially useful to me whenever I've encountered tough jobs to do. I recommend them highly to you.

1. Understand fully the specific job to be done. Know exactly what is required of you.

2. Break your job down into individual steps to identify its main components.

3. Organize your resources promptly. Determine the manpower, materials, money, and time you need. If certain elements are not available, you'll have to improvise with an acceptable substitute from what's at hand.

4. Figure out how many subordinate managers will be required to assume personal direction of the various phases of the operation. Pick your best personnel, for you'll need to give them full authority to do the job.

5. Issue your instructions to each one of your subordinate managers. Give them time to draw up their plans and issue their orders before you set the project into motion.

6. Give each manager the manpower, materials, money, and time he needs to do his job.

7. If you find your means inadequate to do the job, ask your superior for additional help. Don't be backward about requesting honestly needed assistance; just make sure it's really necessary before you ask.

8. Arrange for coordination and cooperation among your subordinate managers.

9. Set a time to start and a time to complete your project. Once you've made your decision, get on with it. Don't delay. Implement your order without waste of time or means.

10. Let your organization go ahead with a minimum of interference from you. Use your time for other management responsibilities: supervision, inspection, coordination, future planning.

Five major stumbling blocks here can keep the average manager from becoming an excellent can-do manager. Those who don't get the job done usually violate points 4, 5, 7, 9, and 10.

(4). They hesitate to release authority to their subordinate managers because they feel they can do a better job themselves. As a consequence, they find themselves swamped in a mass of details.

(5). They fail to give their subordinate managers enough time to make up their own plans. The end result is no coordination, confusion, and eventual failure.

(7). Average managers hesitate to ask for additional help when it's necessary, fearing it will show weakness on their part. When they finally do ask for assistance, it's often too late.

(9). They are reluctant to initiate action or commit themselves, fearing the possibility of error. Don't hesitate. As the professional gambler says, "Do your worrying before you place your bet, not afterward."

(10). Average managers fail to inspect and supervise to insure their orders are carried out.

The above-average can-do manager will not trip over these points. He will take them in stride. This simple ten-step procedure will work on big projects as well as small ones. Big responsibilities can be broken down into smaller tasks. These can be subdivided into even smaller specific jobs.

To be a successful can-do manager, you'll need the *vision* to see what needs to be done . . . the *wisdom* to plan and order the execution of your plans . . . the *courage* to act to gain your goals.

A Sure-fire Technique that Always Works
to Get the Job Done

In the introduction, I told you how Charles Schwab was able to increase lagging production in a steel mill by *throwing down a challenge*. I have used this same technique many times myself when every other method had failed.

One of the deep basic drives in every person is the desire to win. No one wants to lose. When you challenge a person, you touch his competitive quick, and the adrenalin starts flowing.

There's still enough boy in every man to accept a dare. Throw down a challenge and you excite a man's initiative and ingenuity. You arouse his enthusiasm and build his self-confidence.

Friendly competition between sections and departments is one good way of doing this. In the Sears Roebuck chain, stores in similar surroundings challenge each other on special sales days. The Topeka, Kansas and Springfield, Missouri stores have had a friendly feud going for years.

Another good way to throw down a challenge is to inspire a person to compete with himself. This can be done in production, sales, anywhere. Offer a prize or reward to the person who breaks his own previous record.

Many of a person's basic desires can be fulfilled with this one sure-fire technique. When you throw down a challenge and the challenged person wins, he'll gain these nine basic desires.

1. Recognition of efforts, reassurance of worth, praise.
2. Social or group approval; acceptance by one's peers.
3. Ego-gratification, a feeling of importance.
4. The desire to win, to be first, to excel.
5. The achievement of something worthwhile.
6. New experiences.
7. A sense of personal power.
8. A sense of self-respect, dignity, and self-esteem.
9. Emotional security.

What a huge return for such a small investment!

Many of the companies I've already mentioned use this technique successfully to build individual morale and organizational esprit. For instance, when IBM wants to be best in everything it does, it's offering each employee the fulfillment of his basic desire to excel. By wanting to be first in everything, IBM is able to inspire all its people to do their best.

Specific Guidelines for Issuing Clear, Concise, and Positive Orders

If you're having trouble getting the job done, could be you need specific guidelines to follow so you can issue clear, concise, and positive instructions to your people.

Ambiguity, vagueness, and incompleteness of orders are more to blame for failure than willful disobedience. Only by long and careful training and practice can a manager achieve perfection in giving orders. The following outline will help you more quickly attain that goal.

1. **Make sure the need for an order actually exists.** You don't need to issue an order to prove you're the boss. If you're in charge, people already know that.

2. **Give your orders in a manner that shows you expect immediate compliance.**

3. **Never issue orders you can't enforce.** This point is often violated by inexperienced managers, causing them great embarrassment when they can't back up their orders.

4. **Give clear and complete, correct and concise orders.** People must know exactly what you want done and when. They should not have to guess.

5. **Issue your orders as a gentleman would, not as a tyrant.** If possible, ask questions or use suggestions instead of giving

direct orders. The words in your order say *what* is to be done. The manner in which you issue it influences *how* it will be carried out.

6. **Oral orders must always be repeated to you.** I know of no exception to this important rule. Failure to do this can result in serious errors or grave misundersandings.

7. **A lack of orders does not relieve you of your management responsibility.** You should keep a complete picture of the situation in mind so you can take the necessary suitable action in any emergency or in the absence of orders from your superior.

8. **Supervise the execution of your orders.** An order without supervision is no order at all. This is such an important point—and the one most often neglected by the average manager—I will discuss it in complete detail in the next section.

SUPERVISION: A MANAGEMENT TOOL THAT CAN MAKE THE DIFFERENCE BETWEEN SUCCESS AND FAILURE

No order is complete without the supervisory phase. If all it took were orders to get the job done, you could sit in your easy chair and run your operation by telephone. But it doesn't work that way. An old phrase that's good to keep in mind is this:

Never Inspected . . . Always Neglected

Many times I've been called in to solve a company's labor problems, only to find the problem was management's failure to supervise.

I'm sure you've had subordinate managers say to you, "But it's not my fault . . . I told him what to do!" That age-old excuse is only an alibi for laziness, lack of supervision, failure to inspect to see that the work is actually done. If that's the story you're getting from your people, they need to use my fail-safe inspection procedure.

1. **Set aside a certain amount of time each day for your**

supervisory inspections. Always inspect some phase of your operation *every* day. Monday mornings and Friday afternoons are the most critical periods of the normal work week. People tend to slack off during these two times, so bear down on your inspections then.

2. **Vary your routine.** Don't inspect the same points every Wednesday, the same ones on Friday, and so on. Vary your time schedules, too. Employees shouldn't be able to set their watches by your inspection routine. Change things around; keep people on their toes.

3. **Review your inspection points before you inspect.** Study up and review your selected inspection points *before* you inspect. That way you won't get caught short; your employees won't be able to fool you. You'll always be the expert if you follow this procedure. Don't check more than eight different points during any one inspection. You can't trust your memory further than that.

4. **When you inspect, cover only the points you selected.** Carefully review your selected points before you inspect so you'll know everything there is to know about them. Barring an emergency, don't check anything else. Never try to be the expert on everything in one single day.

Your study before you inspect will refresh your memory. It will clear up any foggy points or minute details for you. Use this system and you'll always look like the absolute expert in your field. Time will make you one.

5. **To inspect is to emphasize.** Emphasize *your* selected points in your inspection, not the ones your subordinates are trying to select and emphasize for you. Remember who's doing what. You're doing the inspecting . . . they're being inspected. Not only that, when your subordinate seems ever so anxious to lead you away from the specific area you're interested in, you can be sure something's wrong with it.

6. **When you inspect, bypass the chain of authority.** This is an absolute must. No other kind of inspection is ever satisfactory. Your subordinate managers can and should go with you on your

inspections, but *don't question them. Always question their subordinates.*

7. **When you inspect, listen.** Don't talk except to ask questions. To keep from getting mousetrapped during an inspection, never ask a question to which you don't already know the answer. This technique does not apply if you're asking only for information, but you should do this at a time other than inspections. The point of an inspection is to make sure your people are doing what they're supposed to do. You're not inspecting to give out information about your operation; you're inspecting to get information.

8. **Re-check the mistakes you find.** An inspection is of no value unless you take the necessary action to correct the mistakes you find. So follow up; re-inspect. Supervise to make sure your corrective orders are carried out. Remember, always, that an order without supervision is the same as no order at all.

OTHER BENEFITS THAT CAN BE GAINED
FROM INSPECTIONS

1. **Inspections give you a personal contact with your people.** It's important to be seen by your employees. Even the best worker will get the feeling the boss doesn't give a continental hoot if he never sees you. So get out from behind your desk and out of your office. You establish the theme for your entire organization by your actions. Don't isolate yourself. Be friendly and approachable.

2. **Use inspections to keep people fully informed and up-to-date.** If you handle your inspections properly, you can make them appear to be primarily for the employees' benefit. Let them know you want to keep them fully informed about what's going on, especially in areas that could affect their paychecks, their fringe benefits, their personal welfare. You can make inspections seem to be secondary, off-hand, by saying, "Oh, by the way, George, I notice you're doing it this way. Is that the correct procedure?" If his answer is "Yes,"

follow up with "Why?" If it's "No," your next question should be "Why not?"

3. **Use inspections to improve human relations.** Don't inspect machines; inspect people. Managers work with people; technicians work with things. You're a manager, not a technician, so use showmanship during your inspections. Make each inspection a personal visit with your employees. Remember first names. Know everything you can about your people, their hobbies, outside interests, golf scores, and so on. Ask about the health of the wife and children. Sincere interest in your people and their welfare will improve morale, a point I'll discuss in detail before we finish this chapter.

4. **An employee's performance can be improved by inspections.** You can use your inspection as an opportunity to praise and encourage a person in his work. Performance is always improved by praise, not criticism. Ask for ideas on how to improve work procedures. This feeds a person's ego. It makes him feel more important. Never inspect for the purpose of harassment. Only amateurs do that. You're a professional.

HOW TO MEASURE YOUR ABILITIES
AS A MANAGER OF PEOPLE

Although the final success of management in a profit-making organization is always measured in dollars and cents on a balance sheet or in the annual report to the stockholders, not every manager in that organization is in a position to assess the direct results of his management that way. Not only that, in non-profit organizations or the military services, the methods I will describe here are the only reliable way an individual can actually evaluate his abilities or his success as a manager of people.

Take Earl Hopkins, for instance. Earl is the production superintendent of the Electronic Systems Division of the Pace Corporation. Earl has no way to measure his management success in actual dollars and cents as such. Of course, he can see his managerial results reflected in his production reports, but that in itself is not enough. Not only that, when Earl's production was down, he had no way of knowing specifically where his problem was before I was called in to help him.

"Before you showed me how to use the four indicators of good management to assess my results, I was really lost, Jim," Earl told me. "The controller always sent me regular financial reports to show how my division was doing, but these were of no tangible help to me in actually running my division. They were always after-action reports and of little use in my daily activities.

"'Your system helps me pin-point a potentially dangerous problem and resolve it while it's still small and manageable. For example, if production starts to slip, if quality falls off or waste increases, I can determine almost at once which of the four indicators of good management is at fault and go to work immediately to solve my problem.

"In fact, by watching these four indicators closely as you told me to do, I can actually forestall trouble by taking corrective action before it happens. I'm beginning to feel like a weather forecaster predicting thunderstorms, except I'm more accurate in my predictions of storm warnings than most of them are."

Even managers who depend primarily on financial reports, statistics, and profit and loss statements to evaluate their management abilities and success are still dependent on these four indicators of good management. The successful accomplishment of any mission always depends on the performance of people. Statistics and financial reports can point you in the right direction, but they alone will not answer the ultimate question of what's wrong. Only people can do that.

The Four Indicators of Good Management

Whenever I'm asked to help some company solve a people-management problem, I always use these four key indicators to measure the health of the organization and to identify and isolate their specific problems:

1. Individual morale,

2. Organizational esprit,

3. Work discipline,

4. Individual and organizational proficiency.

I can usually tell in short order whether a company is turning a profit or not just by evaluating these four basic indicators of good management. I can also determine what the problem is, which department is involved, and which one or more of the four indicators is at fault.

You, too, can use these four indicators of good management to evaluate and improve your own organizational performance. When used properly, they act as a weather barometer. You'll know if your organizational weather is going to be calm and fair or whether you're in for a siege of thunderstorms, perhaps even a tornado or hurricane.

Why The Four Indicators of Good Management
Are So Important to You

The levels of individual morale, organizational esprit, work discipline, individual and organizational proficiency are directly dependent on how good a job you're doing in helping your employees gain their basic desires.

If you, as a manager, neglect and disregard your employees' basic desires, they will have a low morale. This will cause a lowering of organizational esprit, work discipline, and overall proficiency. The end result could be an inferior product, customer complaints, loss of business, a lessened profit, even eventual bankruptcy.

However, if you direct your efforts toward helping your employees satisfy their basic desires, they'll have a favorable positive attitude toward you and the organization. Their morale will be high. Your people will be enthusiastic, confident, and anxious to do a good job. They'll cooperate and work together as a team, setting their own goals and working toward them with initiative and ingenuity.

This could be expressed in an ongoing mathematical formula

like this: Satisfaction of employees' basic desires = high morale = high organizational esprit = superior work discipline = top-notch individual and organizational proficiency.

When I'm called on to help some company, my first action is to determine how far the organization has deteriorated. If only morale has been affected, I know the problems can be resolved quickly if management will accept my recommendations.

However, if the organizational bad health has progressed to the point where all four indicators have been affected, I know it will take some time before the problems can be solved, for management has to win back their employees' confidence first.

As soon as I know the extent of organizational damage, I start digging to find out which basic desires are not being satisfied by management for their employees. I'll give you a solid example of my procedure at the end of this chapter. First, I want to cover each one of these four indicators of good management individually.

Evaluating Individual Morale

Morale is defined as a person's state of mind. It is the fertile ground in which you can sow the seeds of organizational esprit, work discipline, individual and organizational proficiency.

A person's morale depends on his attitude toward everything that affects him: his fellow workers, his superiors, his job, his home and family, life in general, and all other things that are important to him. As I stated previously, morale is dependent on a person's fulfillment of his basic needs and desires.

The state of morale never remains the same; it is constantly changing. The morale of your organization's members is an important index of your own management abilities. You can measure morale by watching your people closely in their work, by inspections, formal interviews and informal visits, evaluation and progress reports. Specific items to watch for are these:

1. Personal appearance.
2. Conduct, bearing, attitude, and courtesy.

3. Excessive quarreling or bickering.

4. Harmful or irresponsible rumors.

5. Response to orders and directives.

6. Personal motivation for achievement.

7. Tardiness, absenteeism.

8. Accident rate, safety record.

9. Complaints and gripes.

10. Pride in individual accomplishment.

11. Family problems, indebtedness, alcoholism.

I want to touch briefly on points 1 and 11. Take point 1, *personal appearance*. I know from past experience if a person is neat and clean in his dress and appearance, the quality of his work will usually be the same. If a person is sloppy and careless about the way he dresses or the way he looks, chances are he'll be sloppy and careless about his work, too.

When it comes to point 11, *family problems, indebtedness, alcoholism,* I'm not suggesting you should be a snoopy, nosy busybody or a nursemaid. But no person can do his best work if his mind is occupied with personal problems. So you should be concerned with a man's personal affairs *only as they affect his morale on the job.* If you can help him solve his personal problems, you'll have a more efficient employee.

Key Methods You Can Use to Improve Morale

You can take certain specific actions to keep morale at a high level. I have found the following measures to be extremely effective:

1. Always recognize a person's desire to retain his individuality. Treat him as an important person, not as a piece of machinery. Know his first name and use it. Find out each person's primary desires. Do your best to help him attain them. The carrot-and-stick method is out-of-date. All you need do is find out what each person wants and help him get it. Then he'll automatically do whatever you ask.

2. High morale comes from doing an important job well and receiving recognition for it. If any job in your organization is not important, then eliminate it. No person can feel wanted and needed if his job isn't really necessary to the organization's success. He must feel essential to your efforts to do his best for you.

Public praise always improves both morale and performance, so when a person does a good job, tell him so, and do that in front of others. A signed letter of commendation or certificate of achievement, as well as a photograph and an article in your organizational paper, make your praise more tangible and permanent. Giving a person recognition for doing an important job well satisfies no less than five of his basic desires:

1. Recognition of efforts, reassurance of worth.
2. Ego gratification, a feeling of importance.
3. The accomplishment or achievement of something worth while.
4. A sense of self-respect, dignity, and self-esteem.
5. Emotional security.

3. Good management makes for good morale. Employees must have confidence in their leaders. They have a right to expect their superiors to know their jobs. No one will have confidence in a manager who is unsure of himself. People enjoy working in an organization where things run smoothly, where work is planned properly, where they do not have to "hurry up and wait," or change work methods at the whim and fancy of the boss.

4. Keep people informed of organizational plans, policies, and procedures. They want especially to be told ahead of time of events that can possibly affect their paychecks, working conditions, or individual welfare. Adequate and timely information prevents gossip and stops rumors. There's no substitute for the plain, unvarnished truth to maintain high morale.

5. **Chances for advancement and opportunity for individual progress are essential for high morale.** No one wants to be in a dead-end job. Knowing that advancement is possible and that excellent performance in the present job as well as preparation for greater responsibility can lead to promotion helps a person's morale.

As Martin Rebman, a top executive with a large photographic manufacturer, says, "Successful managers today pay as much attention to their people as to their products. We give our employees real work to do and real responsibilities, often as soon as they join the company. We're receptive to new ideas and people speak up. Promotions are made from within and the right people are promoted. Management wins loyalty by being fair and competent."

6. **Physical working conditions affect a person's morale.** Dark, dingy, and dirty work areas, washrooms, and rest facilities leave a person feeling miserable and depressed. Morale can be raised effectively with well-lighted and well-ventilated work areas, clean and sanitary washrooms, comfortable and attractive lunch and rest facilities.

Evaluating Organizational Esprit

Morale is the total attitude of the individual; esprit is the total attitude of the entire organization. Esprit is the loyalty to, the pride in, and enthusiasm for a company shown by its employees. Esprit de corps is not applicable to the military alone. It is the common spirit reflected by all employees of any organization, either civilian or military.

Organizational esprit is best demonstrated by Japanese workers. In fact, theirs is the envy of the average American corporation manager. Japanese are basically team workers; Americans are primarily individualists. Management officials in Japan work hard to maintain a team spirit and organizational esprit among their employees. In many firms, the work day starts by singing the company song. Japanese workers cheer each other when changing shifts, like baseball players applauding a teammate who's just hit a home run.

Sometimes, whole plants are shut down so everyone can go off together on a company paid holiday. Most companies have management-labor councils that hold continuous year-round discussions with employees—not just on wages and fringe benefits, but also on production rates, new machinery, and how to improve working conditions.

As a result of such high organizational esprit, strikes are infrequent. When they do occur, they are symbolic. They usually end in a day. Workers don't want to let other companies get ahead of their own. As Niroshi Naruse, a 33-year-old checker in Kinokuniya, a Tokyo supermarket, said, "We all have pride working here, for we know it is the most reputable supermarket in Japan." That's organizational esprit.

But Japanese are not the only people with high organizational esprit. A salesman with 12 years at 3M told me, "What I really like about 3M is its constant commitment to excellence. In everything we do, we want to be the best.

Here are some of the factors managers in top-notch corporations look for in judging organizational esprit:

1. Expressions from employees showing enthusiasm for the company.

2. A strong competitive spirit. (Sears Roebuck has always been noted for this.)

3. Willing participation or support by employees in all outside company activities, bowling leagues, softball teams, etc.

4. Pride in organizational achievements.

5. An employee interest in company honesty, fairness, and quality.

6. Readiness on the part of employees to cooperate and help each other get the organizational job done.

7. Belief that their company is the best in its field.

8. Low employee turnover.

Key Methods You Can Use to Improve and Raise Organizational Esprit

1. Start new employees off on the right foot with an orientation program that includes an explanation of the company's history, achievements, and current objectives.

2. Establish goals to build organizational esprit. Sears Roebuck's goal in the early 1960's was to become the world's largest retailer. They achieved that goal in 1966. Their current goal is to retain that position.

3. Promote and develop the feeling that the organization must excel and produce a product of which employees can be proud.

4. Recognize organizational achievements; make sure they are properly publicized.

5. Make use of ceremonies, symbols, and slogans.

6. Use competition between sections and departments to develop teamwork.

Evaluating Work Discipline

Discipline is a term usually associated with military or police organizations, but without the proper discipline in a company or corporation, there'd be complete chaos. People may not say "Yes sir" and "No sir" or salute in civilian life as they do in the military, but discipline is still required and what the boss says goes.

Discipline is the individual or group attitude that insures prompt obedience to orders and the initiation of appropriate action in the absence of orders. Discipline within an organization insures stablity under stress; it is a prerequisite of predictable performance. The well-disciplined worker functions with a minimum of supervision. The person who works only when the boss is around isn't worth having.

Proper work discipline will assure to the individual the greatest freedom of thought and action, and at the same time promote his feeling of responsibility to the group.

Factors you should consider when you evaluate work discipline are these:

1. Care of individual tools and equipment. Regard for company machinery, property, and supplies.

2. Individual job proficiency.

3. Attention to quality and details.

4. Meeting deadlines.

5. Cooperation and harmonious relations among departments, sections, and individuals.

6. Proper and prompt response to orders and directives.

7. Respect (not servility) for superiors.

8. Cleanliness of individual work areas.

9. Ability and willingness to work effectively with little or no supervision.

Measures You Can Use to Improve Work Discipline

1. One of the best ways to demonstrate discipline to your people is by your own conduct and example. Don't expect people to give their all for the company unless you do, too.

2. Establish a fair and impartial system for dispensing justice and an equitable distribution of privileges and rewards. Don't play favorites or allow cliques to develop.

3. Strive for mutual confidence and respect with proper job training. Delegate responsibility wherever possible.

4. Encourage and foster the development of self-discipline in your people. *Rule by work—don't work by rules.*

5. Watch for conditions that lead to breaches of discipline. Eliminate them wherever possible. For instance, the op-

portunity to steal and get by with it will tempt even the most honest employee.

Evaluating Individual and Organizational Proficiency

Proficiency is the technical and physical ability of both the individual and the organization to do the job. Organizational proficiency is the sum of all the skills and abilities of the people in the company welded together by the manager into a smooth-functioning team.

Your company will attain proficiency when you require high standards of individual and group performance. Proficiency results largely from training, doing the job over and over again until it becomes perfect. As a manager, supervision of the actual work will take much of your time. Supervision or inspection is one of the most reliable ways to judge the proficiency of both the individual and the group. Use the system I gave you earlier to inspect. You can't miss when you do.

How to Improve Individual and Organizational Proficiency

1. Each person must be throughly trained in the individual duties of his job. If he needs more training to do the job properly, see that he gets it.
2. Emphasize and stress teamwork throughout.
3. Provide opportunities for cross-training.
4. Give people the opportunity to do the next highest job whenever feasible.
5. Insure by inspections that the work is being done and that constant forward progress is being maintained.
6. Set high standards of performance and insist that they be met.

An Example of Mis-Management and How It Was Corrected

Some years ago I was called on to help a midwestern corporation resolve its management problems with labor. The corporation headquarters was in Chicago; the problem plant in Missouri. The plant had deteriorated so badly in its personnel management procedures and management-labor relations, it was no longer operating at a profit. Waste was horrendous. Quality was so bad employees wouldn't buy their own product even at a favorable discount. There had been more than 20 cases of malicious sabotage. One act alone crippled the plant so badly machinery had to be airlifted at great expense from a sister plant to keep the place operational.

I could fill a whole book with this example alone, but I must be brief. I will say that all four management indicators were at the lowest level I've ever seen. I'll give you several incidents to demonstrate where management was at fault, and why they were failing to satisfy their employees' basic needs and desires.

1. **The Plant Manager.** "I hope you can find out what's wrong with these damned Ozark hillbillies," he said on our first meeting. "If you don't, I'm going to get the axe as manager here . . ."

2. **The Manager in Charge of Industrial Relations.** "I don't know what the hell these bastards want," he said. "Before we came here, these hill people didn't have anything. Most of them never had a suit in their life. All they ever wore were overalls, flannel shirts, and straw hats. Confounded yokels . . ."

3. **The Production Superintendent.** "You'll find they're all a bunch of rednecks, just as stubborn as their damned Missouri mules," he said. "The SOB's think they can tell us what to do. Why you could drop this whole town in Chicago and never find it again."

4. **A Department Foreman.** This department seemed to have more than its share of troubles, so I spent time with it on all three shifts. One particular morning I stood with the young foreman, Barton F., watching the change of shifts. It was just short of 7.00—the official plant time for punching out on the clock.

The day shift had already reported; they stood at their machines waiting to be told about the day's production. They needed only their supervisor's word to start rolling. The graveyard shift was tired; it was the end of their working day. They'd been hard at it since 11 the night before. Now that they were finished, they were squatting down on their haunches to rest, leaning against the iron railings around the heavy machinery, or sitting on stacks of rubber skids just waiting for the 7 o'clock whistle to blow.

The young foreman called his outgoing shift supervisor over. "Get those men on their feet!" he snapped. "You know I don't allow anyone to sit down while he's working in my department. I'm not running a damned rest home!"

"But Bart, my men are all through work," the night supervisor protested. "You know we have a 10-minute changeover period. They're tired and just waiting for the whistle to blow so they can punch out and leave. They're not working now."

"Don't talk back to me!" the foreman yelled. "I'm still the boss in this department. They're still on the clock, so get 'em up on their feet. And that's an order, damn it!"

5. **Production Employees.** (Extracted from the statements of more than 50 employees) "They make you feel like dirt . . . no one ever says thanks or has a good word for you . . . they're never satisfied no matter how good a job you do . . . management doesn't give a damn about our health. Did you see our washrooms? They're filthy. The lunch rooms and rest areas are just as bad . . . they have no respect for a human being . . . I treat my dog better than my foreman treats me . . ."

What basic desires was management not satisfying? Almost all of them, but specifically, these were not being fulfilled:

1. Recognition of efforts, reassurance of worth, praise.

2. Social or group approval; acceptance by one's peers.

3. Ego-gratification, a feeling of importance.

4. The desire to excel.

5. A sense of belonging.

6. The accomplishment or achievement of something worth while.

7. Good health; physical comfort.

8. A sense of self-respect, dignity, and self-esteem.

9. Emotional security.

6. **The Plant Manager.** When I gave my report to the local plant manager and told him what should be done to satisfy his employees' basic desires, he said, "Screw the damned employees. I'm not interested in what they want. I just want to get production back up where it belongs."

7. **The Vice-President in Charge of Operations.** My final report was made in Chicago to the vice-president in charge of operations. He put all my recommendations into effect immediately, including transferring all "foreign" managers and staffing the plant with locally recruited management personnel to restore confidence in the company.

Although it took nearly a year to restore that plant to normal, I'm happy to say it is now operating at maximum efficiency. Morale is high. So is organizational esprit. Work discipline and individual and organizational proficiency are both superior.

When profits are off, production is down, or sales are in a slump, the smart can-do manager, who always gets things done no matter what, will check the four indicators of management success to find out exactly where his problem is so he can quickly solve it.

And if he's really a top-notch can-do manager, he'll turn to his people for help in finding the answer to his problem. He'll encourage their initiative and ingenuity. That's my *7th Master Key to Management Success*, which we'll take up in the next chapter.

Chapter 7

Foolproof Methods

Ingenious Managers Use to

Encourage Initiative and Ingenuity

Initiative means to take the lead or the first step in any undertaking. Simply said, *it is the power of commencing.* Initiative, or seeing what has to be done—even in the absence of orders—is necessary at all levels of your company if progress is to be maintained. In fact, initiative in any organization should be pushed down to the lowest decision-making level possible by instilling a desire to excel in every employee.

You can encourage initiative by assigning tasks commensurate to each person's abilities and then allowing him to work out the details and finish the job. This does not mean you simply allocate the work and then go off fishing. You must know each individual job well enough to supervise the work properly.

Closely allied with initiative is ingenuity or resourcefulness, the ability to solve a problem in the absence of normal means or methods. Ingenuity means to be possessed of the faculty of invention, or as Hannibal, the Carthaginian general who was one of the greatest military geniuses of all time, said, "I will find a way or I will make one."

Your organization is no doubt well prepared to handle all its "normal" daily tasks. Unfortunately, the "normal" situation is usually described only in textbooks. It's the abnormal, or unusual, that always demands the manager's attention. Inactivity or passive acceptance of an unsatisfactory condition because of a lack of "normal means" to cope with it should be completely unacceptable to the ingenious manager. He will *find a way or make one* and then initiate the proper action to solve the problem at once.

From this you can see how well ingenuity and initiative go together. They may not be identical twins, but they surely belong in the same family.

When you inspire and motivate people to use their initiative and ingenuity to get the job done by telling them only what to do—but not how to do it—when you ask for their advice, their help, and their ideas in cutting costs, reducing waste, increasing production and sales, you will not only get the results you want, but you will also satisfy some of their basic natural desires, specifically:

1. Financial success; money and the things money will buy. (That is, if you offer cash awards or an increase in pay for money-saving ideas and cost-cutting suggestions.)
2. Recognition of efforts, reassurance of worth, praise.
3. Social or group approval; acceptance by one's peers.
4. Ego-gratification, a feeling of importance.
5. The desire to win, to be first, to excel. (This desire is especially useful to you in stimulating a person's initiative and ingenuity.)
6. The opportunity for creative expression.
7. The accomplishment or achievement of something worth while.
8. New experiences.
9. A sense of personal power.
10. Liberty and freedom. (You can fulfill this natural desire for your employees by giving them extra time off for cost-cutting suggestions or money-saving ideas.)
11. A sense of self-respect, dignity, and self-esteem.
12. Emotional security.

Managers Aren't Paid to Be Satisfied

I was once asked to help revitalize a company that had become stagnant, completely unproductive, and nearly bankrupt. A new general manager had been designated in the hope of getting the company back on its feet and operating profitably again.

"Do you have any special instructions for me before I start to work?" I asked the new manager.

"I most certainly do," he said firmly. "Let me know at once if any department managers in this company are satisfied with themselves, their subordinates, or their work output so I can get rid of them immediately. As far as I'm concerned, managers aren't paid to be satisfied."

I've long remembered those words: *Managers aren't paid to be satisfied*, for over the years I've found that the organization that's content with its status quo is dying.

The Ford Motor Company nearly went that route because of self-satisfaction before Henry Ford II brought it back to life. The Motorola Company is an outstanding example of corporation initiative and ingenuity in setting the pace in the electronics field. So is the Harris Corporation, another leader in a different sector of the electronics and communications field. Documation, Inc., a comparatively small Florida manufacturer of computer products, seems headed for the top because their management is aggressive and never satisfied with things as they are. All these firms depend greatly upon their employees' initiative and ingenuity to get the job done properly.

From my years of experience in management I've been able to pinpoint 12 specific signs of unjustified or premature managerial satisfaction that can lead to organizational decay and death. If you can identify any of these symptoms in your own organization, no doubt about it, you need my *Seventh Master Key to Management Success*. It will show you how to use your employeees' initiative and ingenuity to solve your problems and get you out of the doldrums.

SIGNS OF MANAGERIAL SATISFACTION THAT
CAN LEAD TO ORGANIZATIONAL DEATH

1. **Management takes no interest in what the economy or their competitors are doing.** Company officers are so self-satisfied they fail to keep up with consumer trends and have no interest in new ideas. This problem nearly caused the Ford Motor Company's de-

mise. Dozens of electronics firms went out of business after WWII simply because they couldn't turn to TV and other electrical products when radio was no longer king. Motorola is one marked exception.

2. Management is unwilling to accept new methods. "We've always done it this way!" is the death rattle of the dying organization. A person with initiative and ingenuity doesn't stay long in this kind of company.

3. Management is too dependent on only one product or only one customer. Experts like Peter F. Drucker say this is one of the three main causes of business failure. Diversification is the answer to this problem. Just for example, Colgate-Palmolive is best known by most people for its hand soap, but they also make all sorts of detergents, cleansers, bleaches, starches, personal care products, medical and hospital supplies, pharmaceuticals, fabrics, dyes, etc. Because of such wide diversification, they've been paying dividends since 1895.

4. Management demands conformity . . . not creativity. One of the biggest food chains in the world nearly went down the drain because of self-satisfaction. Management's attitude toward their employees was "Don't question our procedures . . . just do as we tell you to do." Recovery has come about only because of a change of attitude. It has been a long, slow, painful process that's still going on today.

5. Management is completely self-centered. When managers are interested only in protecting themselves and their prerogatives, even at the expense of their employees' welfare, the organization is automatically destined to fail. It cannot last long.

6. The emphasis is on rules rather than skill. When a person is judged more by what he did wrong, rather than what he did right . . . when promotion is based on seniority instead of intelligence, the organization is on the verge of being laid to rest permanently.

7. People are not interested in self-development. This is one sure sign of organizational decay and death when management is so self-satisfied it can see no need to improve performance, raise standards, or develop new and more efficient methods.

8. Management is not interested in educational development. Forward-looking companies and corporations will pay at least part of the costs when employees want to improve their education during their off-duty free hours. The dying organization has no interest in assisting its people in either their professional or personal development.

9. Management has no long-range plans or goals to achieve. The absence of a common purpose or unified goal is the chief cause of discontent and unhappiness in any collection of individuals. Most new religious movements fizzle out and die after a few years because of this. "Where there is no vision, the people perish." (Proverbs 29:18)

10. Employees are passive, dependent, "civil service" types. I am certainly not indicting all government employees when I use this terminology. But I've worked with enough of them to know that the majority's attitude is—if the regulation doesn't say exactly that you can, then you can't. I've always assumed the opposite position. *If the regulation doesn't say specifically that I can't, then I can.*

11. Management cannot face the facts directly. The organization that expects an employee to tell the boss what the boss wants to hear instead of what he has to hear is no place for an energetic person with a creative mind.

12. The dying company is a boring place to work. The dying organization becomes an industrial Korea or Vietnam. It may be "put in my 25 or 30 years and retire" instead of "do my 13 months and go home," but the principle is still the same. To work only for retirement, hating every minute of the job you do, is no way to live. As a wise friend of mine, Nick, once told me, "Life should be an experience to be enjoyed, not an ordeal to be endured."

International Telephone and Telegraph has had a lot of bricks thrown at it, but it cannot be considered as a boring place to work. In fact, as one company official told me, "ITT is the best place in the world for the individual with initiative and ingenuity. We can always use a person with the entrepreneurial spirit."

Developing Initiative and Ingenuity

Today we have transistors in our radios, our television sets, stereo systems, and tape recorders to replace the old-fashioned vacuum tube. Why? Because some ingenious person used his initiative and came up with a better idea.

Transistors, solid state systems, and computers are but a few examples of the tremendous technical progress that's been made simply because someone had a better idea or a better way of doing things. All the good things we enjoy today came into being because of people's initiative and ingenuity.

Never underestimate the brainpower of your people just because they are your subordinates. Good ideas come from a person with an active imagination, no matter who he is or what he does. Things we take for granted had to first start in someone's mind: simple things like the paper clip, safety pin, zipper, the velcro fastener.

Education and experience may be influential in the development of initiative, but they are not always the most important factors. Thomas Edison patented more than 1,000 inventions, but he had only three months of formal education. His teacher thought he was too dreamy, had an addled mind, and never would amount to anything, so his mother took him out of school and taught him herself.

Sometimes the best ideas come from people with no experience whatever in the area. The Wright brothers ran a bicycle repair shop in Dayton, Ohio, yet from their experiments came the aviation industry.

Most discoveries in the health field have not come from practicing physicians. Alexander Fleming, the discoverer of penicillin, was a Scottish bacteriologist. Pierre Curie and his wife, Marie, discovered radium; they were physicists and chemists. A German scientist named Roentgen discovered X-rays. Jonas Salk, after whom polio vaccine is named, was a virologist.

Two tips I'd like to give you here about developing initiative and ingenuity. The first one is this:

Act as if it were impossible to fail. Never give up on an idea that you really believe in. Thomas Edison spent more than 40 thousand dollars in fruitless experiments before he got the first electric light bulb to work. That was on the 21st of October, 1879, when 40 thousand dollars would buy a lot more than it will today. You probably don't remember, but at one time cosmetics had to be kept in the icebox or the refrigerator to keep them from spoiling. A chemist, who later became the president of an internationally known cosmetics firm, conducted 679 separate tests on how to keep cosmetics from spoiling on the store shelves before he discovered the answer. So if you really believe in something, never consider the possibility of failure. In fact, *always act as if it were impossible to fail and you can't help but succeed.*

One of the most thrilling examples of acting as if it were impossible to fail is the story of how the Polaroid-Land camera was invented. Some years ago a man named Henry Land took a picture of his little girl. She wanted to see the finished photograph right away. He told her the film must be taken out of the camera and developed in a darkroom by using certain chemicals.

He explained to her how negatives were obtained and how they were then used to make positive prints. His daughter listened to all this, but the explanation did not satisfy her at all. She wanted to see the finished picture right now.

"If they can do all that in a dark room, why can't they do it inside the camera?" she said. "It's dark in there, too, isn't it? Why do I have to wait so long to see my picture?"

As Mr. Land listened to his daughter, his mind began to take hold of this revolutionary idea. Why not build a camera that would produce finished pictures right on the spot? Just because no one had ever done it before didn't mean it couldn't be done.

Of course, anyone who knew anything at all about photography could have given Mr. Land a thousand reasons why this could not be done, but luckily, he didn't know all those reasons. You already know the rest of this story. Today you can buy several different kinds of Polaroid cameras that will do exactly what young Miss Land asked her father to do that day.

The next tip is a "don't" for you to follow:

Never criticize or laugh at a person's idea. If you want your people to use their initiative and ingenuity, never criticize or laugh at a person's idea, no matter how ridiculous it might sound to you. Destructive criticism on your part will completely destroy a person's initiative, wound his pride, and destroy his ego. Criticism will make your subordinates adopt a play-it-safe, security-first attitude. So always give a courteous hearing to a person's idea, no matter how farfetched it might seem. Don't make an enemy out of him by making fun of his idea.

If you think you've heard some fantastic ideas in your time, let me tell you how the Grand Coulee Dam was finally built. You see, the engineers building the dam had run up against a seemingly impossible problem to solve. Their normal construction methods would not work because of deep deposits of constantly shifting sand and mud. Tons of it would pour into newly excavated areas, ripping out pilings and scaffoldings. All kinds of engineering devices were tried with no results. For a while it looked hopeless. There seemed to be no answer to their dilemma. Some of the best engineering minds in the country were almost ready to give up the vast project.

Then one of the young engineers had an idea. "We can drive pipes down through all that sand and mud," he said. "Then we can circulate a refrigerant through them and freeze the whole muddy mess solid as a rock. Once it's frozen, we won't have to worry about it coming down on top of us while we work."

Although most of the engineers doubted if this idea would work, they decided to give it a try for it was almost a last resort. In a short time, the unmanageable and shifting wet sands and mud had been frozen into one huge solid block of earth. They could have built a skyscraper on it had they wanted to do so. So the Grand Coulee Dam was built and millions of people benefited because one man had a "crazy" idea that got the job done.

Let me close this section with a set of guidelines you can use to develop your own initiative and set the example for your people to follow so they can develop their initiative, too.

TEN GUIDELINES YOU CAN USE TO DEVELOP INITIATIVE AND INGENUITY

1. **Stay mentally and physically alert.** You simply can't

grasp the initiative or see what has to be done if you're physically or mentally asleep at the switch or walking around with your eyes closed. A tired mind and a tired body are not conducive to developing new ideas.

2. **Train yourself to recognize what needs to be done.** Once you see what has to be done, don't hesitate to do it. Don't wait to be told. Never use the excuse that you didn't know what to do because your superior hadn't told you.

3. **Think up new approaches to problems.** Let your imagination soar. Do some brainstorming with others to get some new ideas.

4. **Learn to anticipate by thinking ahead.** Plan ahead for the unexpected. Always think in terms of "what will happen if . . ." By doing this, you'll reduce the risk of being caught off-guard to the bare minimum.

5. **Make the most of promising new ideas or plans.** Give each new idea a *fair* trial before making a final decision about accepting or rejecting it.

6. **Look for and readily accept responsibility.** This forces you to use your abilities to the utmost. Many people try to look the other way when responsibility comes along. Don't be afraid. Look for responsibility and then readily accept it when opportunity comes your way.

This is an extremely important point. The president and chief executive officer of a nation-wide hardware chain told me, "The biggest mistakes I made as a young manager were when I should have done something but didn't. All my major blunders have been opportunities I missed because I didn't want to accept any real responsibility."

7. **Put into operation worthwhile suggestions made by others.** Don't hold up because you didn't think of it first. Just be glad the fellow who thought of the idea works for you. That way you can at least get some reflected glory out of it.

8. **Constantly encourage people to try new methods and new ideas.** You can't improve the status quo without trying new procedures.

9. **Use all your available resources** in the most effective and efficient way possible.

10. **Be adaptable.** Always be flexible enough to adjust to new and changing situations. Develop your ingenuity. Don't be afraid to venture into the unknown. Always be ready to take that calculated risk. Look for answers and solutions to problems, no matter what the obstacles.

Developing Initiative and Ingenuity
by Challenging People

One of the best ways I've found to develop initiative and ingenuity is to challenge people, to test their mettle. Doctor Jill Morrison, a biochemist with a pharmaceutical firm in New Jersey, agrees with me whole-heartedly. She, too, challenges people to find a better way of doing things. In doing so, she's helping people fulfill those 12 basic natutural desires I listed for your just a little while ago. But I'd like to ask Doctor Morrison herself to tell you how she does it.

"Initiative can be developed by challenging a person's capabilities to go a difficult task," says Doctor Morrison. "This forces him to use his initiative and ingenuity to solve the problem you've given him. As his abilities to handle tough assignments increase, you can make his next job even more difficult. You'll compel him to continually use his initiative to get the job done.

"One caution is to be observed, though. That is not to give a person a task too far beyond his capabilities to perform. That will do nothing but cause frustration and lead to a disgruntled employee. I constantly check and supervise my assignments to keep that from happening in my department."

Many companies today offer incentive and cash awards to

employees who use their initiative and ingenuity to come up with new methods, for money and the things money will buy is one of the most important of a person's basic natural desires. For instance, James Bellis, an employee of Eastman Kodak, was awarded a cash bonus of nearly $7,000 recently for finding a way to reduce the breakage of gears in the pocket-sized Instamatic camera.

As a result of stimulating their employees' initiative and ingenuity, the Minnesota Mining and Manufacturing (known primarily as the Scotch tape company to most people) is constantly branching out into new products that did not even exist a few years ago. General Electric also motivates its people to use their imagination to come up with new methods and new ideas. GE's only requirement is that the right people be kept informed about what's going on.

Even the stiff, sedate, formal procedures of the banking profession have changed. Banks no longer resemble funeral parlors where people speak only in whispers. Citicorp, parent of New York's Citibank, is full of innovation and opportunity for the ingenious manager who wants to use his initiative.

How Solving Problems Helps Stimulate
Initiative and Ingenuity

If everything is running smoothly and there are no problems, then no one needs to use his initiative and ingenuity. It's only when things aren't going right that a demand is made upon a person's imagination and creativity to come up with a better way of doing things.

Solving problems always reminds me of the story of the man who prayed for more strength to solve his. One day Sam complained to his minister that it seemed the more he prayed to God for strength to solve his problems, the more of them he had to solve.

"But there's no other method God can use, Sam," the preacher said. "The only way he can help you develop greater strength to solve your problems is to give you even more and tougher ones to solve."

Now I don't know if God gave Sam a specific set procedure to follow in solving his problems, but I can give you an exact technique that will help you tremendously. Use it and you'll be able to solve your toughest problems easily. People will think you're blessed with extra initiative and ingenuity. Your own employees can use this procedure profitably for your benefit, too.

No one has to be a genius to solve a tough problem. The ordinary average person can use his initiative and ingenuity when he learns how to properly focus his imagination on the problem and then channel his thinking along certain well-defined lines to solve it. I simply call this initiative and ingenuity-stimulating procedure. . . .

THE MANAGEMENT PROBLEM-SOLVING PROCESS

The management problem-solving process is a sound and analytical technique that will help you arrive at sound decisions for the solution of your toughest problems. This procedure has three main steps.

1. Recognize the problem.
2. Make an estimate of the situation.
3. Take appropriate action to solve the problem.

Recognize the Problem

You have a problem in your organization when an incident occurs or a situation exists that adversely affects one or more of the four indicators of good management that I discussed in the previous chapter: individual morale, organizational esprit, work discipline, individual and organizational proficiency.

However, to think of your problem only as one of morale, esprit, work discipline, or proficiency will not fully identify the problem for you. Too many different factors and conditions that will influence each one of these indicators are present in an organization.

So you must evaluate your problem, not only in the light of

these four important management indicators, but also in view of how well you're fulfilling (or not fulfilling, which is more likely since you have a problem) those natural basic desires all your employees have. Remember that the four indicators of good management are entirely dependent on how well you're satisfying your people's basic desires. When the barometer falls for one of these indicators, you should identify which basic desire is not being fulfilled or where you're at fault.

You must clearly define the problem you've uncovered. What are its boundaries . . . its limitations . . . its exact nature? Determine all the pertinent details and gather up all the facts bearing on the case. Once you've decided what your exact problem is, you're ready for the second step.

Make an Estimate of the Situation

To make a proper estimate of the situation; divide step number 2 into 4 separate sub-steps, namely:

1. Find out the exact cause of your problem.
2. Determine all the possible solutions.
3. Explore and evaluate all the possible solutions.
4. Select the best solution.

Find Out the Exact Cause of Your Problem

To determine the exact cause of your problem, get answers to these six specific questions:

1. *Who* is involved in this problem?
2. *What* are the precise circumstances, the exact conditions?
3. *When* did this problem first appear?
4. *Where* exactly did it take place?

5. *How* did it happen?

6. *WHY* did it happen?

After you've recognized your problem, isolated and defined it in Step One, you must find out *who* is involved in this situation. You'll also want to know exactly *what* circumstances and conditions really do exist. You'll be concerned about finding out *when, where,* and *how* it actually happened. And most important of all, you'll want to find out *WHY* this problem came up in the first place. Unless you can resolve the *WHY* of any problem, it will keep coming back at you again and again.

Now when it comes to the *why,* I've found that people cause 95 percent, if not more, of all management problems that you'll encounter. Only about 5 percent or less are caused by machinery breakdown or equipment failure. Even then, a lot of machinery breakdown is caused by improper maintenance and that comes right back to people again.

I've found that *the failure of management to satisfy their employees' basic desires is the primary cause of most problems encountered in business or industry.* So always review carefully the basic natural desires your employees have when you're determining the *why* of your problem.

In determining the cause of your problem, you'll want to know all other facts that bear on it or have a direct relationship to it. If certain parts of it cannot be substantiated by facts, then you'll have to make some logical assumptions. Here your past managerial experience, good judgment, and common sense will be most valuable to you.

Determine All the Possible Solutions

The second step in making your estimate of the situation is to consider all the possible solutions to your problem. Don't rule out a possible solution on your first trial examination of it. Even if it doesn't prove to be worthwhile for solving today's problem, it could well be the answer for tomorrow's.

Always stockpile your ideas. They can be of value to you later on. The more possible solutions you consider, the better your chances are that the one you finally select will be the right one.

Explore and Evaluate All the Possible Solutions

Your third step in making an estimate of the situation is to weigh the various courses of action, one against the other, by comparing their advantages and disadvantages.

First of all, *weigh the advantages of a single solution against its own disadvantages*. If the disadvantages are greater than the advantages, then that solution is no doubt unusable. After you've checked out each solution by itself, then compare the merits of one solution against the others to determine which one is best.

Don't let prejudice or personal preference influence your considerations. Above all, remember that a rash manager who jumps to conclusions without looking at all the facts will often create a more serious problem than the one he's trying to solve.

Select the Best Solution

Your last step in making an estimate of the situation is to select the best solution of those you've considered. An important point to keep in mind here is that your final solution could be a combination of two or more of the solutions you've had in mind. Don't limit yourself arbitrarily to a single solution.

Take the Appropriate Action to Solve the Problem

The last step in the management problem-solving process is to take the appropriate action to solve your problem. Once you've decided which solution you're going to use, then put it into effect immediately by issuing the proper order.

Don't content yourself with merely initiating the necessary

action to solve your problem. Your success will generally depend on your ability and willingness to supervise and check the results of your corrective action. One of the most significant characteristics that distinguishes the successful manager from the ordinary average one is the ability to select and vigorously carry out an effective course of action.

Let me summarize the management problem solving process for you:

1. Recognize the problem.
2. Make an estimate of the situation.
   a. Find out the exact cause of your problem.
   b. Determine all the possible solutions.
   c. Explore and evaluate all the possible solutions.
   d. Select the best solution.
3. Take the appropriate action to solve your problem.

The management problem-solving technique can be used at all decision-making levels. It is a format that helps to harness, control, and direct your people's initiative and ingenuity in the right channels. Initiative and ingenuity without direction or supervision waste energy without getting tangible results.

How a Mission-Type Order Challenges a
Person's Initiative and Ingenuity

Your subordinates will develop their initiative when you give them work to do without telling them exactly how to do it. They will be forced to use their imagination and ingenuity to develop specific methods or techniques to accomplish the tasks you've given them. This is essentially what a mission-type order is, telling a person *what* to do, but not *how* to do it.

A mission-type order says what your desired results are, but it doesn't tell a person what methods he must use to get those results for you. It emphasizes skill—not rules. When you use mission-type orders, you leave the door wide open for your employee to use his initiative, his imagination, and his resourcefulness to solve the problem you've handed him.

Structure and Function of a Mission-Type Order

Let me describe a mission-type order in detail for you so you can see exactly how it can work to get the results you want. A mission-type order has three basic fundamental parts or elements: *The mission, the limiting points, the resources available.*

1. **The mission.** A mission-type order should say clearly and concisely what is wanted. It must state the exact objective to be reached, the specific results to be obtained. In other words, *say precisely what it is that you want done.*

2. **The limiting points.** The limiting points or control factors, if any, must be spelled out in your order. How far can your subordinate go in his methods to carry out your order? Are there any methods he cannot use? What about a time element, a deadline that must be met? Can he coordinate with others to get the job done? *What exact limitations have you placed upon him?* Or is it a free-for-all, no holds barred, catch-as-catch-can affair? If so, will you back him all the way if he gets in trouble for you?

A good rule of thumb to follow here is *balance the welfare of your people against the accomplishment of the mission.* One cannot be sacrificed for the other. Do this and you won't have many problems or questions as to what limitations to place on your subordinates.

Some chemical companies have violated this principle in the past. They have placed accomplishment of the mission above the welfare of their workers. The end result was more problems than ever before.

3. **The resources available.** Your order should say clearly what resources you're making available to your subordinate to accomplish his assigned mission. Be specific. Spell out in exact and definite terms the amount of money, manpower, time, materials, and

facilities you're giving him to do the job for you. You also need to give him a clearcut indication as to whether he can expect any outside help or support should the need arise for assistance.

Using Mission-Type Orders for Maximum Results

Mission-type orders are a must if you want to get the maximum results from your organization. This is especially true in large corporations where the organization and operation are so complex and widespread geographically. Corporations with branch retail stores or industrial plants scattered throughout the country have no choice but to use mission-type orders. By the same token, the reason for much of their success is their willingness to use mission-type orders, for they always bring out the best in people.

The higher the level in the chain issuing the order, the broader must be the scope and the overall mission that is given. There's a world of difference in the orders given to a plant manager hundreds of miles from the corporate headquarters and a production foreman in a factory where his boss is only a few feet away.

However, mission-type orders tend to make managers at all levels of supervision use initiative, resourcefulness, and imagination to get the job done. Each one is comparatively free in his choice of options to accomplish the mission as long as he stays within the limits of previously defined boundaries and policies.

If you've never used mission-type orders in the past, you're in for a pleasant surprise. When you use them, they'll give your organization a flexibility it's never known before. Mission-type orders are designed to bring out the best in your employees. They'll either have to use their initiative and ingenuity or make way for those who can.

Not all people can handle mission-type orders, so using them is one of the most effective ways of weeding out quickly the inefficient and incompetent subordinate managers in your organization before they become a permanent burden to you. If you do have junior executives or middle managers in your company who can't handle this kind of order, get rid of them. Replace them with those who can.

Decentralizing Execution of the Work

When you use mission-type orders, it follows quite naturally that you must decentralize execution of the work. This comes hard for some managers who are unduly prone to do too much by themselves and leave too little responsibility and initiative for their subordinates. This is the road to small achievement.

A top-level manager must decentralize the work or he will fail. He has his own heavy responsibilities. He must make decisions, plan ahead, give orders, and supervise their execution. Success in a corporate undertaking is attained by each individual having an important job to do and a responsibility that taxes him to the utmost.

The three key words to success in decentralization of the work-load are these:

ORGANIZE . . . DEPUTIZE . . . SUPERVISE

These three words hold the secret to getting more work done than you ever thought humanly possible before. Use them. You'll be amazed at the results you get.

Where and How to Start Using Mission-Type Orders

Some managers have a tough time letting go and getting started with this concept if they've been used to doing most of the work themselves. A good way to initiate this program is to get your people to watch for places where you can save and economize. In view of today's continuing inflation, the smart manager will continue to look for ways to reduce overhead and cut costs without sacrificing quality.

Just raising prices to keep pace with inflation or to retain the same margin of profit is not the answer. The Donnelly Company of Holland, Michigan, found that out, remember? They turned to their employees for help in finding the answers.

A good place to start looking for profit leaks is in the maintenance department. In many companies, this is the worst profit leak of all. Studies have shown that plant maintenance workers spend only about 2 and 1/2 hours out of every 8-hour work day working productively. The rest of the time they sit around drinking coffee, playing cards, reading the paper, or gossiping. Points you can watch for in your own maintenance department are these:

1. Foremen who are too slow in assigning jobs in the morning to their maintenance workers.
2. Lack of a good preventive maintenance program.
3. Failure to supervise properly routine daily maintenance.
4. Vague and conflicting work orders.
5. Failure to establish proper priorities for work orders and maintenance.
6. Lack of coordination when more than one shop union is involved, for instance, when the work requires carpenters, plumbers, electricians.
7. Failure to order and stock the right parts and materials.

HELPFUL HINTS FOR USING
MISSION-TYPE ORDERS

1. Give each person a job to do and then let him do it.
2. Urge each employee to use his skill, initiative, and ingenuity to beat your established standards.
3. Offer him security in return for his knowledge when he translates his know-how into skills on the job for you.
4. Motivate him to set up his own goals and establish his own standards of performance.
5. Let him work in his own style as much as possible.
6. Set up a system to test an employee for his maximum potential.
7. Let him tell you how and where he needs to improve.
8. Let him work at the next higher level whenever possible.

9. Make corrections that encourage progress and development.
10. Fit the job to the person, not the person to the job.
11. Always recognize successful achievement in a tangible way.
12. Back people to the hilt when they make honest mistakes.

Chapter **8**

The Fine Art of Getting People

to Cooperate and Work Together:

a Time-Tested Management Formula

If you were to ask me which one of my 12 master keys to management success is the most important, I would be hard put to answer, for they are all valuable to you. However, I would be inclined to place my *Eighth Master Key to Management Success* up close to the top, if I were forced to make a choice, for this reason: You'll never be able to manage people properly and get the maximum results you want unless you know how to inspire and motivate them to cooperate and work together as a smooth-functioning team. Here's the precise formula you can use to get people to cooperate and work with you.

GIVE THEM YOUR COOPERATION AND TEAMWORK FIRST

If you want to get cooperation and teamwork from your people, you must make the first move. *You must give them your cooperation and teamwork first*. Top-notch managers know this secret. They've mastered the art of getting their employees to cooperate and work with management by giving them their cooperation first. The inexperienced or average manager doesn't understand this principle at all, says Craig Lambert, vice-president and general manager of the Haines Corporation.

"Most managers and executives say they don't *get* enough cooperation from their employees," Mr. Lambert says. "But why don't they? What's their problem? Who's actually at fault . . . the managers or their employees?

"I can tell you straight off the managers are at fault. Not only that, I can also tell you exactly where they're making their basic mistake. I know because I did the same thing myself for many years before I realized what I was doing wrong.

"Their mistake is in not giving cooperation to their employees first. That's why they're not getting any cooperation from their people in return. The essence of real cooperation is this: *You must always give before you can expect to get. When you do, you will always get back more than you give away.* When managers use this time-tested formula of human relationships, good things will start happening for them right away."

When you, too, use this time-tested formula and give your cooperation to your employees first,

YOU'LL GAIN THESE WORTHWHILE BENEFITS

1. Your employees will work together with you gladly.
2. Even your problem employees will want to cooperate, too.
3. Your people will respect you and have confidence in you.
4. You'll gain their willing obedience, unswerving loyalty, and whole-hearted support.
5. They'll work with initiative and ingenuity, eagerness and enthusiasm.
6. Your employees will work together as a team with high morale and esprit, with a definite purpose and direction toward a common goal.
7. You'll make them feel they belong where they are.
8. They'll work just as hard as you do to get the job done.

You can easily tell if you're *giving* cooperation to your employees. If they're prompt and cheerful, filled with enthusiasm, enjoy their work and are ready to put in an extra hour or so when it's necessary or when you ask them to do so—you can be sure you're doing a good job as a manager, for your people will be glad to cooperate and work together with you.

But if you're *not giving* your employees your cooperation, you can tell that quite easily, too. They'll be just as uninterested in cooperating or working with you as you are with them. They'll drag into work late, do a mediocre job all day, and run for the door even before the whistle blows. If that's the way your people act, don't make the mistake of asking them for anything extra. You'll not get it.

The rest of this chapter will be used to show you the various techniques you can use to put this time-tested management formula (giving your cooperation first) to work for yourself in all your daily relationships with other people: your employees, associates, superiors, customers, friends, yes, even your family. As you read, please keep this one fundamental concept in mind:

You must always give if you want to get, and you get back exactly what you give away, but the return will always be multiplied many times over.

That's the only sure way of gaining cooperation from all your employees so they'll work together with you as a team.

The 100 Percent Guaranteed Method of Gaining Cooperation from People

I have now in every chapter said over and over again that the only sure way to get people to do what you want them to do is to make sure you satisfy their basic needs and desires when they do as you ask. And I will say it again right here and now, for giving your people the opportunity to fulfill their fundamental needs and desires is the 100 percent guaranteed way of gaining their cooperation and getting them to work together with you. In short, *helping people attain their needs and desires is the best way you can give them your cooperation.*

I cannot emphasize this point too many times, for fulfillment of an employee's fundamental needs and desires is the first of the 12 keys to management success. Unless you unlock that first door, you won't be able to open the next 11. If you've forgotten what those basic needs and desires are, I'd suggest you look again at page 30 in Chapter 1 to refresh your memory.

Unfortunately, a great many managers have paid no attention whatever to their employee's basic needs and desires. That's why there's often such a wide gulf between those two great divisions in business and industry: management and labor.

In the majority of instances, each has existed only for itself without any respect or regard for the other. In fact, most of the time, except in some enlightened instances, management's attitude has been "to hell with labor!" and labor's attitude has been "to hell with management!"

Yet when these two major factions change their attitudes and work together for their mutual benefit, much can be gained. Later in this chapter, I'll give you three outstanding examples of what can be done when management and labor cooperate with each other to get the job done—the Lincoln Electric Company, Minneapolis Medtronics, and Bullock Garages and Home Builders.

Getting Cooperation Between Labor and Management

Japanese managers are masters of the art of giving everything possible to their workers so they can get the best possible cooperation from them. Management offers a tremendous number of benefits that help fulfill people's basic needs and desires. For instance, completely furnished, neat, clean, and extremely livable dormitories . . . separate cottages for married employees . . . cafeteria and recreation facilities including movies, tennis courts, golf courses, and bowling alleys . . . company discount store and credit union. Managers do everything they can to make an employee feel like a member of their family, not just another time-clock-number on the payroll.

In Japan, cooperation always begins at the top with management—not at the bottom with labor. Japanese firms take care of their employees almost from the cradle to the grave. If a man marries a girl employed by the same firm, there is great rejoicing on management's part. They feel the bond of loyalty to the company has been strengthened by having a husband and wife team working for them.

Don't make the mistake of comparing the Japanese system with the company store that used to exist and still does in some places—I've seen it myself close up in Florida—for the miner and the migrant farm worker in the United States. In America, the company store was for the benefit of the company, not the employees. The company tried to bind the workers to the organization by keeping them in debt to the company and making an exorbitant profit at the same time. This is not cooperation between management and labor; it is forced or involuntary servitude.

This is definitely not the way Japanese management cooperates with labor. If it were, it wouldn't work, any more than it does in this country. Japanese business and industry could not possibly gain the loyal cooperation of their employees the way they do.

If you have any lingering doubts about how successful Japanese methods of cooeration are, look around you at the many fine quality products they make, for instance, Sony tape recorders, Sansui and Panasonic stereo systems, Canon and Nikon cameras, Toyota and Datsun automobiles, Honda and Suzuki motorcycles. Or look at Japan's position as one of the world's leading exporters of fine lines of merchandise. It's right up there close to the top with a lot of quality products.

Some far-sighted American firms have seen the advantage of cooperating with their employees and going all out to fulfill their basic needs and desires just as the Japanese do. Just for instance, that's why IBM has never laid off anyone in the last 35 years for economic reasons. They always find new jobs for displaced employees, retraining them if necessary. Xerox pays all medical expenses for their employees and their families. They also have an excellent profit-sharing plan. J. C. Penney's employees enjoy stock bonuses, stock options, and profit-sharing plans. Bell Telephone, Kaiser Steel, General Motors, Chrysler, Hewlett-Packard, and dozens of others are moving rapidly to cooperate with their employees by giving them more freedom, authority, and responsibility to get the job done.

It Takes More than Money to Get Cooperation

Sometimes after a speaking engagement some young manager or business man or woman will come up to me and say, "But I'm not in a position to offer profit-sharing plans, medical and dental plans, or retirement benefits to my employees. What can I do?"

Of course, money is important. We all need a certain amount of it. But it is not the total answer. The University of Michigan's Survey Research Center asked over 1,500 employeed persons which of 25 different job factors was most important to them. *Interesting work ranked first. Good pay was way down in 5th place.* The Research Center found that only if employees could find in their jobs a sense of achievement, recognition, dignity, responsibility, a sense of belonging, advancement, and personal growth could they be inspired to work at their full capacity. Sounds familiar, doesn't it.

At the time I was working on this chapter, I watched a CBS news special called "Andy Rooney Goes to Work." Mr. Rooney found the same things to be true that I have been emphasizing throughout this book. That is that people want not only money and the things money will buy, but they also want and need recognition for their work and praise for their efforts. They want to be engaged in worthwhile work and feel that their efforts are important to the company.

Mr. Rooney discovered that when companies satisfied these basic needs and desires of their employees, they prospered. When they did not, they foundered. His conclusions were that the smart manager could get more done with a pat on the back and a word of praise, along with a decent wage, than the one who depended only on the dollar bill to get results.

Earl E. Bakken's Success Formula

I especially want to tell you about one striking example of attaining success through cooperation. This is the story of Earl E. Bakken, who, less than 30 years ago, lived in an attic. His main goal at that time was to have a good job as an electrical engineer.

Today, his company, Minneapolis Medtronics, Inc., is the

world's largest manufacturer of pace-makers for heart patients. The company also makes dorsal column stimulators to alleviate the symptoms of multiple sclerosis as well as other electronic devices to help people suffering with intractable pain. Mr. Bakken's Medtronic stock—12.8 percent of the total common stock issued—is valued at more than 40 million dollars.

When asked for the secret of his spectacular rise to success, Mr. Bakken simply said in effect, "My approach to management has always been to get other people to work *with* me rather than *for* me. I believe fully in the team concept, that we are a group of people cooperating and working together to reach a common and worthwhile goal.

"For instance, we have a comprehensive planning cycle in which everyone participates. The company managers set the major goals for each year. Then each of our divisions sets its own individual goals. This goes on down through all levels of the entire company, so that every single employee gets involved in the planning process.

"Then all this information comes back up and is compiled and consolidated until we finally produce a corporate master plan to which every employee has contributed something. This plan is published just before the beginning of the new year and copies are distributed to each one of our 2,000 employees so they will know exactly what our goals and plans are. This insures our cooperating and working together as one big team."

Getting People to Go All Out for You

The main reason for cooperating and working together is to get people to go all out for you. Remember that your job as a manager is to give your cooperation to your employees first by offering them the opportunity to fulfill their basic needs and desires. Your employee's obligation to you is to cooperate by giving you the best quality production (or sales) with the least waste in the shortest possible time. The Lincoln Electric Company exemplifies this concept.

I first heard of the Lincoln Electric Company, a manufacturer of arc welding equipment and electric welding machinery, back in 1969 when I was gathering material for my book, *Power with People.** I had addressed a group of industrial managers and executives, business men and women in Cleveland, Ohio, about how to use their employees' initiative, imagination, and ingenuity in getting the job done.

After my talk, a young lady, Barbara Howard, came up to me and said, "While you're here in Cleveland, be sure to visit the Lincoln Electric Company. They are the practical living example of everything you talked about tonight."

I did so the next day; Barbara was so right. The Lincoln Electric Company most certainly was the living down-to-earth example of how management and employees can cooperate and work together for everyone's benefit without the necessity for a labor union.

Mr. James F. Lincoln inaugurated his innovative profit-sharing program back in the mid-thirties. Together with his employees he worked out a plan that would let his workers share in the profits of the business. The basic concept of his plan was simple: the more the employees made for the company, the more they made for themselves. The end result was that all the employees worked harder, produced more, and figured out better and more efficient ways of doing things.

Instead of concentrating on how to "get" something out of the company or how to "con" the boss, the employees used their talent, brains, initiative, and ingenuity thinking up new ways to make more money for the company, and thus, more money for themselves. In a very real way, they were now part of the management team. Some amazing things happened in an extremely short time.

1. Ordinary average working men and women came up with ideas that would do credit to an inventive wizard like Thomas A. Edison.

2. There were no work slowdowns. All the employees realized they would be paid according to the company's ability to pay and that the company's ability to pay depended entirely upon their ability and willingness to produce.

---

*James K. Van Fleet, *Power with People.* (West Nyack, New York, Parker Publishing Company, Inc., 1970).

202

3. The company's volume of business jumped from 5 million a year to 33 million a year, an increase of nearly 700 percent in less than 10 years.

4. The cost of the manufactured product—arc welding equipment and electric welding machinery—was cut in half in spite of a continued inflationary rise in the cost of raw materials.

5. Dividends to stockholders increased four times or 400 percent.

6. The annual wage for Lincoln's 1,000 employees rose 540 percent during that time.

"Lincoln Electric people earn every dollar they make," Barbara told me. "They earn it by making a much better product to be sold to their customers at a much lower price than their competitors can meet. They produce many times as much as is produced in other places because of the development of their abilities to cooperate and work together as a team."

That conversation with Barbara Howard took place back in 1969. To bring this case history up to date and make sure the company was still using the same concept, I called her to double-check. The information I got from her was even more fantastic than the original figures.

Since I first wrote about the Lincoln Electric Company back in 1969, their sales have risen from $33,000,000 a year up to $310,000,000, an increase of more than 900 percent. If I were to use $5,000,000—the annual sales figure before the profit-sharing plan was instituted—as the base, the increase in yearly sales would be 62 times as great.

They now employ 2,350 people, an increase of 1,350 employees over their previous employment figures. A subsidiary plant has been opened in Toronto, Canada. Tangible assets of over $1,000,000 give them a AAAA rating from Standard and Poor.

And now for the most amazing figure of all. Including bonuses, the average employee working there earns $20,000 a year. As I'm sure you already realize, there is still no union to voice employee demands for better working conditions. There is no need for one. A long line of people is waiting to be hired, but this happens only when someone retires or dies. Employees seldom leave the firm for any other reason.

The Importance of Equalizing the Benefits

Curt Bullock, president of Bullock Garages and Home Builders, recognizes the importance of equalizing the benefits for his employees just as does the management at Lincoln Electric. Here's how he puts the formula of *giving people your cooperation and teamwork first* to work in his own business.

Mr. Bullock recently took 200 employees from the Danville and Moline, Illinois, divisions and their spouses on a five-day trip to Hawaii at company expense. Next year, employees and their spouses from the Ohio and Arizona divisions will be going.

"Why shouldn't the switchboard operator and the janitor go along with the sales people? Why should they be left behind?" Mr. Bullock said in effect. "After all, they're valuable to our united effort to satisfy customers. It takes everybody from the janitor to the company president to do the job, so everyone gets to go to Hawaii. Besides, in this company we've created a team in which every person participates and cooperates in a joint effort."

The company-paid trip to Hawaii is part of Mr. Bullock's management philosophy. That is that highly motivated employees, cooperating and working together as a team, can accomplish much more than people who aren't.

Mr. Bullock's business philosphy has paid off well for him. The company has recorded continuous growth in sales since he founded it 25 years ago in the backyard of his home. His company now has 90 offices in 12 states. Sales are nearly 3 million dollars a month, and that's a lot of garages.

One big reason for his spectacular growth and success, Mr. Bullock feels, is that his entire company uses the team concept, best seen in the assembly of their prefabricated garages.

Crews, consisting of 16 people, have a daily quota to meet: one garage per worker, or 16 for each crew. When that quota is met, they can quit and go home. "I don't ask my people to stand around for eight hours when their quota is filled," Mr. Bullock said. "There's no point whatever in that."

His employees make up most of their own rules to govern themselves. Anyone who doesn't do his full share of the work really feels the pressure from his fellow team members. If one person makes a mistake, the entire team is penalized, for the entire 16-man crew is docked for the time needed to correct the error.

Although the main reason for the Hawaii trip is rest, relaxation, and fun, employees still use part of the time to get to know each other personally and to understand the problems of other departments so they can cooperate and work together even better when they get back home. Sales managers get a chance to tell production employees whom they've never met before what problems they have in the field.

"No one objects to a few hours of work on a vacation," one carpenter said. "How many companies do you know of that send all their employees and their wives to Hawaii for five days and pay all the expenses? Anyone who'd object to a couple of hours a day talking shop would be plain nuts!"

When you emphasize skill rather than rules as Mr. Bullock, the Lincoln Electric Company, and Minneapolis Medtronic all do— when you let your employees use their imagination, initiative, and ingenuity to give you better quality production—when you let them cooperate and work together for everyone's benefit—you'll gain these very worthwhile benefits for yourself:

1. You can concentrate on results . . . not methods.
2. Production and/or sales will go up.
3. Costs, expenses, and waste will go down.
4. You'll attract a better class of employees.
5. Your people will put their heads to work for you.
6. They'll give you their maximum efforts.
7. Employee morale and organizational esprit will be high.
8. You'll have fewer management-labor problems.
9. Your employees will cooperate and work together.
10. Your company, like Bullock Garages, Lincoln Electric, and Minneapolis Medtronics, can become Number One in its own field.

Now that you've seen some examples of how smart and successful managers get people to cooperate and work together, let me give you some additional techniques you can use to get this same kind of cooperation from your own people. The time-tested formula—*give them your cooperation and teamwork first*—still applies. It is the basic principle or premise on which each technique is built.

Establishing an Emotional Rallying Point

One of the best ways to get your employees to cooperate and work together is to give them a goal to attain or a cause to fight for. People will unite solidly behind you if you can establish an emotional rallying point for them. Let me give you three examples of some extremely difficult causes to rally people to.

1. I have never known of a popular war. But if there ever was one, then World War II would have been it. Why? Because the American people were given an emotional rallying point to unite behind, not by their own leaders, but by the enemy.

You see, up through the 6th of December, 1941, the American people were wishy-washy and noncommittal about the war in Europe and on the Asiatic mainland. Actually, they could have cared less. They had little interest in foreign affairs. But when the Japanese attacked Pearl Harbor on the 7th of December 1941, people's attitudes changed immediately. No longer was the United States a disinterested bystander.

After the war was over, the Japanese high command admitted that attacking Pearl Harbor was their greatest mistake. "Our victory at Pearl Harbor was in reality our first defeat," a high-ranking Japanese admiral said. "Although it was a highly successful maneuver from a military point of view, for our attack crippled the powerful United States Pacific Fleet, it was our first in a series of mistakes in underestimating the will of the American people to fight. Pearl Harbor was the emotional rallying point for the United States in World War II. It marked the beginning of the end for Imperial Japan."

2. During that same war, the famous Japanese-American

regiment, the 442nd, was formed. It become known as the *Go for Broke* outfit. The men in the 442nd gave it their all. One battalion was called the *Purple Heart Battalion* because of its high number of casualties. It was one of the most decorated units in World War II.

These men not only had an emotional rallying point, but they also had a cause to fight for. They had to prove to all America that they were not Japanese, but loyal American citizens born of Japanese parents. And of course they did.

I have given you these two non-business examples of establishing an emotional rallying point for the following reason: If for some reason you cannot find an emotional rallying point within your organization for your people as Mr. Bullock, Lincoln Electric, and Mr. Bakken of Minneapolis Medtronics all have done, *you must look outside your organization to find one.* Look at your competition, for example, to find a weak point that you can exploit to your own advantage. Use it to establish a cause and then rally your people to it.

3. Back in the thirties, a comparatively small religious movement (it had a total of 216,000 members in 1977) established an emotional rallying point for its members by erecting a large headquarters building in Independence, Missouri. They called it the *Auditorium.* It seats thousands of people and was built primarily by small donations from its members right in the middle of the worst depression the United Sates has ever known.

But after the Auditorium was completed, the church began to stagnate. Today, it does not even retain its own natural increase. Why? Because when the Auditorium was finished, so were the people. They no longer had a tangible goal they could aim for. The church leadership failed to establish a new tangible emotional rallying point to which its members could be gathered.

I've given you this non-business-religious example of establishing an emotional rallying point for two reasons. One, when the goal you establish by the first emotional rallying point has been reached, you must immediately establish another one. Two, the goal should be tangible as was the Auditorium. Intangible goals are impossible for the average man to visualize for they are too vague and abstract. They do not inspire or stir a person to action. If you disregard either of these points, you are only inviting failure.

Now I did not say that establishing an emotional rallying point was an easy technique to use. It is not. But that's what makes this management game worth while. If it were easy to establish an emotional rallying point, then everyone could do it and there would be no challenge. So this is where you'll need to use your imagination, initiative, ingenuity, and all your management skills to get the job done.

Getting the Group's Key People to Cooperate First

As a manager, you're able to control many people through just a few. You don't need to personally supervise every last individual in your organization to get him to cooperate and work with you. You can direct the actions of dozens of people—yes, even hundreds—through just a few key persons. But not all these key personnel are always in management. Some will be found in the labor ranks, too.

In every group you'll always find at least one person to whom the other employees look for advice, help, and leadership. For example, I've seen this actually happen: A supervisor issues an order, turns his back, and walks away. Immediately, the workers in that group gather around one key individual. He speaks; they listen. Then they go back to work and carry out the supervisor's order. *But not until they get the unofficial go-ahead from the informal leader of their group.*

The speed of production and quality of workmanship will depend, not upon the order from the supervisor in management, but on the order from the informal leader in labor.

So if you want to get the best out of your people, if you want to get the entire group to cooperate and work with you, your first job is to find out who those informal leaders are. You'll want to know which people in your organization can help you the most. Do that, and you'll be able to save much time and energy by concentrating your efforts through your management people only on those individuals in labor who can help you achieve your goals.

Once you know who the key people are, you can use them as your unofficial communication system. You can have your managers feel out their groups by taking those key people aside and getting their opinions and ideas first. This doesn't make them the boss or take away any authority from your managers. It simply gets them on your side first. The basic-rule to use is this: *Find out who the key people are and get 'em on your side first; the rest will automatically follow.*

Above all, don't let your managers lock horns with these key individuals. There's nothing wrong with their having influence in their groups as long as they don't misuse their power and try to usurp yours. You'll get much further if you work with these people and use the power they have with their groups to your own advantage.

Kinds of Key People to Watch For

1. **The Unofficial Leader.** This person is part of the unofficial power chart found in every organization. He wields an influence that has no relationship at all to his actual position. Though he's not part of the official power line of authority, a word from him can often make or break a project.

His power may sometimes be negative rather than positive. For example, I've seen instances where long-time employees have quietly cornered power by getting the authority to initial plans or memos. Even though their initials actually mean nothing—neither approval nor disapproval—these employees can delay, sometimes even kill, a project by keeping it in their in-box too long. Even though that's negative power, not positive, it's still power. You need to know who and where that key person is.

2. **A Key Person Will Be Independent.** You can usually spot a key person in a group by his need for independent action. A great many times, this key individual will be a man or woman who has refused a position of management or supervision—even though he apparently has all the necessary leadership qualifications—simply because he doesn't want to be pinned down by official responsibility. He wants to be free to operate without being hampered by administrative rules and regulations or organizational red tape.

This kind of person you'll see in church groups, too. He will usually classify himself as a rebel or a non-conformist. He'll have ideas and opinions on most subjects. Much of the time his ideas are sound and sensible, but he still wants no part of any lay leadership position in the church. As one fellow like this told me, "I don't want to be a deacon or an elder. If I were, I could no longer speak my piece. I'd simply have to parrot the party line."

3. **A Key Person Is a Problem Solver.** A key person will often have a solution for your problem. A great many times the hardest part of solving any problem is simply getting started on it. A key person can help you get that action when you need it most. Often what you need is a supply of suggestions to help you solve your problem, no matter where those ideas come from or who supplies them. A key man will usually have several suggestions to make for solving your problems. His ideas may not always be the best, but they will help you get things moving again in a bogged-down situation. And as the old saying goes, "A poor plan carried out enthusiastically is better than a good plan not carried out at all."

4. **The Key Person Is a Creative Thinker.** A key person will be a creative thinker—a true non-conformist. A really creative person will be a wellspring of ideas. He will resist strongly any efforts to restrict and channel his thinking. If his creative urge is strong enough, it will show up in his efforts to get transferred to challenging jobs, or, at the least, to acquire additional knowledge of other departments and other people's work. This may well be your first clue to the presence of a key person who can help you solve your problems or achieve your goals.

5. **The "After Five O'Clock" Key Personality.** You may not care for this kind of key person—not many managers do—but he does exist, so you ought to know who he is. It will be to your advantage. This person will often have social contacts with top executives. These social connections may have been gained by a long-standing friendship of their spouses, membership in the same religious, political, or fraternal organization. Sometimes it's an office romance. However this relationship has been achieved is not important. But the fact that it exists is. This person may not be able to reach the boss at work, but he can sure do it after 5 o'clock. He can often hurt you as well as help

you, so you must know who this key person is so you can guard yourself at all times.

Ways People Can Participate in Management

Sometimes a manager has a hard time getting started with this new concept of giving employees his cooperation and teamwork first so he can get their cooperation and teamwork in return. To keep you from having that same problem, let me give you several methods you can use to do that.

1. GIVE Your Employees the Opportunity to Participate in Management. As Jimmy Durante always used to say, "Everybody wants to get into the act." Your employees are no different. They want to have a say in how things are run. You can make them feel it's their organization, too, when you *give* them the chance to take part in the planning, decision making, formulation of rules and regulations, policies and procedures.

You can use any number of methods to let them participate in management so you can gain their cooperation. Put your imagination, initiative, and ingenuity to work and come up with some ideas of just how to do it in your organization.

2. GIVE Them the Chance to Help Make the Rules. One of the problems in most organizations is the way rules are formulated and administered for employees. Traditionally, managers at the top dictate what is right and wrong for workers at the bottom.

Top management arbitrarily sets the rules for employees to follow. So do department managers and section supervisors. But people don't like to be told what to do or not to do. Rules and regulations restrict their individual liberties. So they tend to resist or violate them.

One of the best ways you can *give* cooperation to your employees is to let them work out their own rules and regulations to follow. You can still retain control by having them submit those rules to you for final approval. However, you'll find the average employee will be much stricter on himself than you are. And since those rules are *his* rules, the ones *he* made up, he'll be much more likely to obey them than if they were your rules alone.

An excellent way to put this technique to work is to allow your employees to establish their own working hours—within certain limits of course. This concept is called "flexitime" and has gained popularity with many companies and corporations. In Inglewood, California, city employees have been using "flexitime" since 1973. The city manager says they have all but eliminated the use of sick leave for medical and dental appointments. Premium pay for overtime has also been dramatically reduced. "People can now come in to city offices anywhere from 7.30 a.m. to 6 p.m.," he said. "The public likes it, the employees like it, and it's saving money for the city."

3. GIVE Your Employees a Chance to Take Part in Decisions. When you *give* your employees a chance to take part in the decision-making process, especially those decisions that affect them personally, they're much more likely to cooperate with you. If they agree with the decision, they'll regard it as their own. They'll back it to the hilt. If they don't agree, they'll still back it more strongly than they would otherwise, simply because you *gave* them the courtesy of listening to them and considering their points of view fully and fairly.

4. GIVE Your People a Chance to Contribute Their Own Ideas. People like to know the corporate goals. They also like to contribute their own ideas to help reach those goals. One huge world-wide organization with hundreds of retail stores has a policy of calling its employees together every Thursday morning for 15 minutes to discuss the next week's goals. At that meeting, management asks its employees to submit their own ideas in writing for meeting those goals. Employees whose suggestions are accepted are rewarded with extra time off, bonuses in their paychecks, promotion, and so on.

This kind of meeting is also a good time to encourage reports on problems or work difficulties so that better cooperation can be attained between sections and departments. It would also be an appropriate time to pass out bouquets. You can encourage your people to voice their complaints and let them work the steam out of their systems as long as you don't let it get out of hand.

To Wrap It All Up

In conclusion, let me say that the quickest way to gain cooperation from your people is to let them work *with* you, not *for* you, just as Earl Bakken does. When you *give* a person your cooperation and teamwork first, you make him feel important and necessary to your success. You build his ego and his status. When you show him how and where he's both needed and wanted, you increase his personal dignity and self-esteem. In fact, all you need do is tell him how you can't get along without him. Then step back and watch him go to town for you.

Now then. Let's get on into another of the most important chapters in my book, my *Ninth Master Key to Management Success,* "How Successful Managers Make Those Tough Decisions: Why Some Executives Are Worth $50,000 Plus."

Chapter **9**

How Successful Managers
Make Those Tough Decisions:
Why Some Executives Are
Worth $50,000 Plus

Every day a manager is required to make dozens of decisions. Some are minor and routine. But others demand the greatest skills a manager can muster, for certain decisions will have long-lasting and far-reaching effects.

The hesitant and indecisive manager who procrastinates, calls a meeting to get a "joint decision" from his subordinates so he can blame them if things go wrong, farms out the problem to a committee for "more study," or waits for "further developments" in the situation, is not destined to go far. That kind of manager will go out of his way to avoid making any sort of decision that might possibly be traced back to him.

This sort of indecisiveness is contagious. It infects the entire organization, causing hesitancy, loss of confidence, and confusion on the part of everyone. Such a manager will never become a $50,000 plus executive. He'll soon find himself shunted off on a siding in a dead-end position, or looking for another job with a different company. The executive suites of hundreds of company and corporations are overloaded with so-called managers and executives who are deathly afraid to make decisions about anything more consequential than the time of the morning and afternoon coffee breaks or when to let the secretary go to lunch.

If you want to avoid joining that crowd, you will develop your ability to make sound and timely decisions. I learned a long time ago that when you are in a position of authority, you must be willing to assume the responsibility for making the decisions required by that job. And after you have all the advice and detailed information you can get from your subordinates, you must make those decisions by yourself. I will always be thankful for this one lesson, if nothing else, I learned in the army away back when, and that is simply that *you cannot command by committee*. The same principle applies here in management.

My Ninth Master Key to Management Success will help you not only to improve your decision-making abilities by giving you certain specific techniques to use, but it will also fortify your courage to make those decisions as your skills improve. Constant study, training, planning and practice will give you the professional competence you need to make sound and timely decisions.

Here are some

SPECIFIC BENEFITS YOU'LL GAIN

when you make those tough decisions without fear or hesitation.

1. People Will Have Confidence in Your Skill and Abilities. Your employees will have confidence in you when you can make a rapid and accurate estimate of the situation to arrive at a sound, sensible, and timely decision. To be able to do this, you must gather together all the facts, analyze them, make up your mind, and issue your order with complete confidence that you've made the right decision. Always act as if it were impossible to fail.

2. Your Employees Will Do Their Best for You when you demonstrate good judgment and common sense in your decisions. If you're able to reason logically under the most trying of conditions and decide quickly what course of action is necessary to take advantage of opportunities as they arise, your employees will respect your good judgment and decision-making abilities. They'll want to do the best job they can for you.

3. Your People Will Become More Positive and Decisive in Their Own Actions. You, as the leader, establish the *climate of management* for your whole organization. When you are positive and decisive in your actions, your people will be positive and decisive in their actions, too. They automatically become a mirror reflection of what you are, what you do, and how you do it.

4. People Will Turn to You for Advice and Help. When you can make sound and timely decisions, people will be motivated to come to you for advice and help. You'll become known as an expert troubleshooter in solving the toughest problems. Such a reputation will enhance your stature throughout your entire organization.

Friends often call me to get advice or neighbors drop by to ask for help in solving some problem so they can make a sound decision. A nuisance? Yes, sometimes, but wow, does it ever build the ego!

5. You'll Rid Yourself of Frustration. The inability to make up one's mind is a leading source of frustration, not only in business and management, but also in solving the personal problems in one's life. In fact, the American philospher, Walter Kaufmann, once said that most people suffer from *decidophobia*—the fear of making decisions.

When you use the scientific methods of problem solving I gave you in the last chapter, along with the decision-making ones that you'll learn here, you'll rid yourself of that frustration. You'll have confidence in yourself and your own abilities to deal with pressure. And that's more than half the battle.

TECHNIQUES YOU CAN USE TO
GAIN THESE BENEFITS

Developing Your Powers of Decision

If you want to become a $50,000 a year and more executive, you'll need both courage and know-how. You must become adept at probing a problem's depths to find its basic cause. You'll be required to make a rapid and accurate estimate of the situation so you can arrive at a sound, sensible, and timely decision.

You must be able to use sound logic and reason, common sense and good judgment under the most trying conditions and decide quickly what action is necessary so you can take advantage of opportunities as they occur. To top off all these requirements, you'll also need foresight so you can predict the actions and reactions that might take place after your decision has been put into effect. When the situation demands a modification in your original plans, prompt decisive action on your part to make the necessary change will build your people's confidence in you as a manager and a leader.

Now exactly how to do all this? How can you put all this into practice for yourself? Well, Charles Summers, vice-president and general manager of Brevard Turbines, Inc., says here's one way you can develop your powers of decision very quickly.

"Before any of our division or department managers issue an order to activate a decision, they always ask themselves one simple question," Mr. Summers says. "That question is, 'What will happen if?'

"As long as each manager in our company does this, just as long as he keeps that phrase uppermost in his mind when he makes his decision or issues his order, the chances of his making a mistake are kept to a minimum.

"Before we established this simple management policy, we were constantly finding that today's solutions were often creating tomorrow's problems. Keeping in mind *what will happen if.* . . . helps our managers solve a lot of their problems even before they happen.

"I never cease to be amazed at the effectiveness of these four small words. We consider them so important we've posted placards and signs all over the place that say in big red letters WHAT WILL HAPPEN IF. . . . so that phrase will be drummed deep into everyone's subconscious mind."

Learning to Concentrate on the Essentials
to Establish Priorities

Let me give you now a concrete example of how to put your powers of decision to work. Most managers simply do not have enough time to do all the things they want to do. I assume you're no exception. So the first thing you need to decide is what is essential that you and you alone must do and what can be done by someone else.

As soon as you know what tasks can be done by someone else, make those assignments and get them off your mind and out of the way. Now you'll be left with only those problems that you alone can handle. The next thing you must decide is which one to work on first. Let me show you how you can solve that problem:

I once knew an industrial manager who created nothing but chaos in his plant simply because he didn't know how to make decisions and establish priorities in the work to be done. Every project to him was a crash. He sent out dozens of red-bordered memos marked "URGENT" to his administrative staff, his division managers, and his department foremen every week. But nothing ever got done for *when everything is always marked URGENT, then URGENT becomes ROUTINE.*

He finally gave up and called on me for help. This is the advice I gave him more than ten years ago. He still uses the same system today that I gave him back then.

"Roy, your problems can be solved only by properly establishing priorities," I told him. "Make up a list of the most urgent tasks facing you right now. Then give each job a different priority. *No two jobs can have the same number.*

"After you've established your job priorities, then dig right in on *Priority Number 1* and stick with it until it's done. Then go to *Priority Number 2* and do it the same way. Don't worry if you finish only one or two jobs each day. The point is that this way you'll be making progress where before you were completely stalemated. You'll get things done by taking care of your most urgent problems first.

"In short, Roy, use the approach of *first things first . . . one thing at a time.* If you can't solve your problems this way, chances are you couldn't handle them any other way either. Once you get this system rolling, stick with it. You'll clear away the debris on a daily basis one day at a time."

And I'll say the same thing to you. Use it. You'll be amazed at how much work you can get done by using this simple system. You need use your powers of decision to determine only three things:

1. The work that can be done by others.

2. The work that only you can do.

3. The job priorities on the work you keep for yourself.

Developing the Ability to Plan and Order

Once your decision about what to do has been made, your next step will be to develop a detailed plan to issue an order. A usable plan must be worked out to execute your decision if you are to get the results you want.

Definite tasks must be assigned to specific individuals. Allocation of supplies, equipment, and facilities must be made. The activity of individuals and groups will need to be coordinated to insure maximum cooperation. Definite deadlines must be fixed for completion of intermediate steps. In short, the plan that implements your decision must answer these questions:

1. *What* is to be done?

2. *Who* is going to do it?

3. *When* and *where* will it be done?

4. *How* will the job be done?

When your plan has been fully developed, you must issue it as either an oral or written order to your subordinates. Your instructions should be so clear there will be no chance of any misunderstanding. The ability to plan and then issue instructions that get the job done is an essential part of your responsibilities as a manager and leader.

How to Make Up an Operation Plan to
Implement Your Decisions

Some managers have no trouble whatever in reaching a decision. But then they have one devil of a time drawing up a proper operation plan to implement that decision and issue an order. They know exactly what they want to do, but they have problems in telling others how and what they want done. Most of the time they will forget to include some important details and their order becomes a piecemeal affair as subordinate managers and foremen are forced to come back again and again for more information and clarification of certain points that weren't properly covered.

The manager who has that problem has never developed a basic format to follow when issuing an order to put his plan into effect. Making a decision and drawing up the plan to implement it becomes a waste of time unless a manager knows how to issue the appropriate order to set his decision into motion.

But this need not be an obstacle to you if you will follow the outline for an operation plan or order that I've used for years now. If you have been having a problem with this particular aspect of decision making, I know you'll find this format extremely useful. You can use it as a guide to draw up your plans. Then when you issue your instructions to your subordinates, you can use the same format for your order.

FORMAT FOR AN OPERATION PLAN OR ORDER

1. General Information

a. *Competition.* Sometimes this subparagraph is not applicable to your particular circumstances. If it is, it should be used to give information about the general situation, the capabilities, and the indications of your closest competitors. In other words, what can your competitor do and what does he plan on doing? If you know, chances are you can beat him to the punch. Use the *who, what, when, where, why,* and *how* question words to get your answers. (Big corporations use an elaborate active intelligence system to keep up-to-date data for this subparagraph. For instance, the only way top corporations can stay at the top of the pyramid in their own field is to know what their closest competitors are planning on doing so they can do it first.)

b. *Your Own Organization.* Who will do the job for you? What resources are available to you to do the job? Can you expect outside assistance if it becomes necessary? In this subparagraph you cover your resources of *manpower, money, materials, time,* and *facilities.*

2. The Mission

In this paragraph you state the exact mission that you want to accomplish by issuing this operation order. Be specific. Say precisely what it is that you want done.

3. Execution of the Order

a. In this first subparagraph, you give your overall concept of how you are going to accomplish the assigned mission.

b. In each succeeding subparagraph, assign individual tasks to each division, department, or section within your organization. Always use one subparagraph for each individual element of your company. For instance, don't put instructions to sales and production in the same paragraph. Each one is entitled to its own.

c. In the last subparagraph, give your coordinating instructions that apply to two or more elements of your organization.

4. Administration and Support

In this paragraph you cover thoroughly the actions, duties, and assignments of your administrative or staff personnel, as well as any element of your organization that will not actually participate in the accomplishment of your primary mission, but which will support your active operational elements. Use as many subparagraphs as needed.

5. Special Instructions

a. *Miscellaneous.* Here you should cover all those miscellaneous items that are important to all elements of your company—including your own administrative and support people—but which are not necessarily a part of the execution as outlined in paragraph 3.

b. *Policies.* This subparagraph is used to outline the organizational policies and procedures of the manager or the executive who is issuing the order. If he cannot be reached at his usual location during this operation, this is the paragraph to indicate exactly where he will be.

This operation plan or order can be used for any activity or endeavor of any organization, either civilian or military, that you can imagine. In fact, it is the same format General Eisenhower used for the operation order that launched the Normandy invasion back in World War II. It can also be used by the employer with only three or four employees. The only difference is in the amount of detail and the number of annexes used. The basic principles remain the same. Will it work? Guaranteed. Let me show you why I say that.

Andrew Barlow is the production superintendent for a large rubber factory. For many years, they closed down for a week to ten days to take an annual inventory. And each time there was utter chaos in the plant—until last year, when Andy used this format to draw up a proper operation plan and issue the appropriate order. But I'd prefer that he tell you about it himself.

"When I first looked at this skeleton outline for your operation plan, Jim, I didn't think it would work," Andy said. "But after the fiasco we'd had the year before with the auditors from Akron who tried to take our annual stock inventory, I thought I'd better try it. It worked out much better than I'd expected.

"By following your detailed outline, I was able to come up with a complete operation plan for my inventory that was all inclusive. Nothing was left to chance. I was able to assign tasks and missions in a precise 1-2-3 fashion to the various divisions and departments and to give them the extra help and support they needed to get the job done. Everyone in the plant had something to do. No one was left out; no one was forgotten. Every detail was covered for a change.

"When we took our annual inventory this time, it went off like clockwork. The auditors were done in less than 24 hours. We had to close down production for only 72 hours: one day to prepare the plant for inventory, one day to do it, and one day to get our production lines set up again.

"The actual planning took us about one week. We had no problems; there were no foul ups anywhere for a change. In fact, I even got a letter of appreciation from the big boss up in Akron for a job well done."

See. It works. Try it for yourself.

Having the Courage to Act

Let's say a manager already has the power and the capability he needs to make sound and timely decisions. And he has the ability to draw up superb plans and orders based on those decisions. He still is a long way from achieving his goals unless he possesses this one most important and decisive attribute: *The courage to act.*

The ability to see what needs to be done, the wisdom to draw up magnificent plans and orders to execute a decision will be of no use whatever unless the manager has the courage to act when action is required.

How does one go about developing this kind of courage? I know of only one way. That is to *do the thing you fear to do so you will have the power to do it.* I consider this concept to be one of the most valuable ideas you can gain, not only from this chapter, but from the entire book, so I want to give you several examples of exactly how others have made this principle work to gain courage themselves. Then you can put this idea into practice for yourself.

Do the Thing You Fear to Do and You'll

Have the Power to Do It

If you do the thing you fear to do, you'll gain the power to do it. If you do not do the thing you fear to do, you'll never gain the power to do it. For instance, if you want to be a painter, you must first paint. There simply is no other way to become an artist. You can dream all day long about how famous and successful you could be as a painter, but until you actually pick up the brush and start painting, you will never gain the power to do it.

If you want to be a writer, then you must write. If you want to be an expert swimmer—then you must swim. The same thing can be said about golf, baseball, skiing, salesmanship, science, medicine, music, management, and on and on. You must make the first move yourself. Until you do that, you will never gain the power to do anything.

So if there do happen to be certain things in your life that you actually dread or fear to do, then force yourself to do those undesirable tasks until you've reached the point you no longer fear to do them. Making a decision and putting it into effect could be only one of the things you fear to do. This concept could improve your life in a great many other areas besides management.

When you are no longer afraid to do what you formerly feared to do, then you will have complete control over your fear. That is the real definition of courage: the control of fear. Courage is not the absence of fear as so many people think. *Courage is the control of fear.* Every battlefield hero, including Congressional Medal of Honor winners, will tell you that.

For instance, speaking in public strikes fear to the hearts of nearly everyone at first. I know I nearly panicked the first time I stood up in front of an audience. My throat was dry; my voice was raspy. My palms were sweaty—my heart was pounding.

But I spoke the first sentence and I felt better. As I continued to speak, my fears began to fade away. Confidence came back to me, for as soon as I did the thing I feared to do, I gained the power to do it.

HOW MARGARET SIMMONS CONQUERED
HER FEARS

Margaret Simmons, a popular author and lecturer, says she used to suffer untold agonies before every one of her talks. But gradually her fear lessened as she kept on speaking, until she finally completely overpowered it, simply by doing the thing she feared to do. Last year she spoke nearly 300 times and she said her only regret was that the year was only 365 days long.

The effectiveness of this idea of doing the thing you fear to do so you will have the power to do it is well illustrated by all the letters I've received from people who've heard me speak on the subject and put the formula to work for themselves. Let me quote from just a few:

HOW A SALESMAN PUT THIS IDEA TO WORK

Stanley D., a New Orleans salesman, wrote to say, "After I heard your talk on how to get rid of your fear of people, I felt I could take on anyone. Yesterday I walked into the office of a really tough purchasing agent—a man I'd always feared and who'd never once given me an order—and before he could say 'No,' I had my samples spread out on his desk. First time I'd ever opened my sample case in his office. He gave me one of the biggest orders I've ever received. Why? Because my attitude was positive and confident. I wasn't afraid of him and he knew it."

A SALES CLERK USES THIS PRINCIPLE SUCCESSFULLY

Gail R., a bashful Jacksonville, Florida, sales clerk, wrote me this: "I was so afraid of customers I gave them the feeling I was apologizing to them for waiting on them. I was even afraid to come hear you. I thought someone might see me there and laugh at me. Then I was scared to death to try your idea of doing the thing I feared to do so I would have the power to do it, but I really had no other choice. The personnel manager had given me exactly three weeks to get my sales up to par with the other clerks or be fired.

"But the moment I did as you said, I found I was suddenly speaking to customers with more assurance. My poise and self-confidence increased. I began to answer objections with authority. My sales went up nearly 40 percent last month. There's never been another word said about my dismissal. In fact, the store manager told me to start thinking about taking over the management of one of the departments."

HOUSEWIVES CAN USE THIS CONCEPT, TOO

Nancy L., an Atlanta, Georgia, housewife, says, "I was even afraid to invite my friends in for coffee for fear I wouldn't be able to keep a conversation going. But after listening to your talk at our church last Sunday night, I took the plunge and held a coffee call for half a dozen of my neighbors today. It was a great success. I had no trouble at all keeping things moving along interesting lines of talk. Thanks so much for your help."

EVEN ANIMALS AND BIRDS USE THIS PROCEDURE, TOO

Doing the thing you fear to do so you'll have the power to do it is not really man's idea. It is a law of nature. For instance, I've watched birds fly and I always figured it was automatic for them to do so. But that's not true. Last year a robin built a nest in the tree just outside my study window. I watched the growth of this little family, from the eggs in the nest until the day that four small heads popped up demanding to be fed. Then, one by one, the mother nudged her babies off into the air when the right time came.

But one little fellow was so afraid he couldn't fly. It took him nearly a week longer than the others. He would peer over the side of the nest and then cringe down in it in abject fear. Finally, the mother had no choice but to force him out of the nest. When she did, he suddenly flapped his wings and flew awkwardly away.

Now no one had taught him how to fly. Nature had given him the instinct to do it. But he had to fly first before he had the power to do it, for that is Nature's way of doing things. He had to do the thing he feared to do before he had the power to do it.

The same thing applies to people. Life will improve for you, too, not only in management, but in all other areas of your life, if you will remember and practice this one simple idea: Do the thing you fear to do and you'll have the power to do it. It's just that simple.

Let's say now you have all the prerequisites you need as a manager to make those tough decisions. You've developed your powers of decision by using your common sense, logic, reason, and good judgment. You've learned to concentrate on the essentials and establish priorities. You've developed the ability to plan and look ahead. You know how to announce your decision and not leave anything out by using the proper format for your operation order. You even have the courage to act; you are not afraid to trust your own decisions and move on them. Is this all you need? Perhaps, but I know from experience that certain areas give managers trouble in their decision making. So I want to give you a few guidelines you can use to avoid those trouble spots.

GUIDELINES YOU CAN USE TO HELP YOU
MAKE THOSE TOUGH DECISIONS

1. **Making an Estimate of the Situation.** You must have the ability to make a rapid and accurate estimate of the situation before you can hope to arrive at a sound and timely decision. You'll need to use a logical and orderly thought process like the one I gave you in Chapter 7, page 183. The only way you can sharpen your skills is to constantly practice making estimates of the situation until it becomes second nature to you. *Do it and you'll have the power to do it* applies here, too.

2. **Plan Ahead for Any Possible Emergency.** Always plan ahead for every possible event you can think of that might logically take place to ruin your plans. Making sound and timely decisions depends mainly upon your having a constant estimate of the situation in mind at all times. Use the phrase I gave you before—*what will happen if*—so you will force yourself to consider everything possible that might go wrong. The manager who fails to use foresight is inviting failure.

3. **Ask Your Key Subordinates for Their Advice.** Before you make your final decision and issue an order, always ask your subordinate managers for their opinions, their suggestions, and their advice. Take advantage of their experience and their ideas.

After you've listened to their recommendations, make your decisions and issue your order. When that has been done, the time for discussion is over. From then on you have the right to expect the full support and wholehearted loyalty of your subordinates to carry out your decision and obey your order.

4. **Knowing When to Announce Your Decision.** The timing of your announcement is extremely important. Don't leave your

subordinate managers out on a limb by not giving them enough time to develop their own plans, reach their own decisions, and issue the necessary orders to do the job for you. Above all, don't surprise your subordinate managers by announcing your plans and decisions to their subordinates. That's their job, not yours, so let them do it.

5. Encourage Continual Estimates and Continual Planning. No situation is ever static. Mistakes are going to be made; accidents are going to happen. Encourage your subordinate managers to continually make their own estimates of the situation and constantly plan on exactly what they would do when that mistake is made or that accident does happen.

6. Keeping People Fully Informed and Up-to-Date. When you make your sound and timely decisions, don't let all your efforts and time be wasted by failing to let the right people know. Make sure that everyone knows exactly what your decision is and what's going on. If you don't do that, costly errors will crop up simply because you forgot to tell one key person about your decision and your plan for action. Lack of communication causes more mistakes than wilful disobedience.

7. Evaluate the Long-Range Effect of Your Decisions. It is not enough to consider only the immediate effects your decision will have. You must be able to predict what the long-range effects are going to be. Remember that a chain reaction of events will be set off when you announce your decision and your subordinate managers put your plan into action. Don't let today's solution create tomorrow's problem.

Five Common Obstacles to Overcome in
Making Your Decisions

1. The Need to Always Be Right. Some people can't make up their minds on anything, even such minor matters as buying a suit, a dress, or a pair of shoes because they're so afraid of making a mistake. But no one can be right all the time. Even if you make a mistake, continual planning ahead at all times will keep you from getting too far down the wrong road. The moment you see that you've made a wrong decision, back up and start over.

> "I was having a hard time getting the trainees fed and back to the training area on time at noon," a young army captain told me. "So to speed things up I told the sergeants they would have to give up their reserved tables and mix with the troops to help keep things moving along more rapidly.
>
> "That was a mistake for it took away some of my sergeants' privileges. Their morale slipped and things immediately got worse instead of better. So I had to swallow my pride, admit I'd made an error, retract my order, and figure out some other way to resolve the problem."

When you refuse to admit you've made a mistake, things will usually get even worse than they were before. To admit you're wrong is not an admission of stupidity. But to stubbornly refuse to change your mind even when you know you're wrong is.

2. **Confusing Objective Facts and Subjective Opinions.** Management decisions should be based on hard facts, not on the way you feel about something at the moment. When you don't keep objective facts and subjective opinions separated, you're in for all sorts of trouble.

> "Spur of the moment decisions based on emotions have little objective value," Irene Norman, a local department store manager, told me. "Intuition has no place in management as far as I'm concerned. For instance, our personnel manager turned down the employment application of a brilliant young man who had all sorts of management potential just because he smoked a pipe. The personnel manager thought the fellow would be too dreamy and not hardheaded and practical enough. That makes as much sense as saying a man with a mustache can't be trusted—a favorite idea of my father—or that all red-headed women are supersexed."

Irene's remarks remind me of the old saying so often associated with religionists: "My mind's made up . . . don't confuse me with facts."

3. Failing to Get Enough Information to Reach a Decision. Decisions made on insufficient information will often be the wrong ones. Admittedly, there'll be times when you can't get all the facts. Then you will need to use your managerial experience, good judgment, and common sense to reach a logical decision. But to shortcut and not get all the facts you need when they're available is inexcusable.

For instance, a man I know, I'll just call him Sam, had a chance to get in on the ground floor of a risky but potentially profitable business deal. He couldn't afford to lose any money, but he was afraid if he asked too many questions or delayed his decision too long, he'd be left out in the cold. So without the proper facts, he said, "I want in." He lost everything. Why? Because he jumped in without getting enough information on which to reach a sound and sensible decision.

4. Fear of What Other People Might Think or Say. A lot of people are afraid to speak up because of what other people might think or say. That's why some managers hesitate to announce the decisions they've made for fear of criticism. That fact also influenced Sam's decision. He was afraid to appear hesitant and doubtful in front of other businessmen who were his friends. He wanted others to think well of him.

To desire another person's respect is one of our basic natural desires, but there is a limit. *You are not responsible for what others think or say, but only for what you say or do.*

5. Fear of Commitment. To some managers a decision is not a choice but a solid brick wall. It makes them feel helpless, powerless to do anything. This fear is closely allied to the fear of failure, which many psychologists say is a businessman's greatest obstacle.

However, if you don't commit yourself and take action, nothing will ever get done. And if you do see you're on the wrong road, then as I said before, back up and start over. Hardly anything is irrevocable except death and taxes. The ability to admit a mistake and change a wrong decision is one of the hallmarks of a wise, successful, and competent manager

How to Develop a Sense of Judgment in
Your Subordinate Managers

Unless you're running a one-man show, you'll have to depend on your subordinate managers to make some tough decisions, too. Management decisions always entail risks, but you can reduce those risks, not only by having your managers use the techniques I've given you in this chapter, but also by having them follow these four simple guidelines so they can develop a sense of judgment for themselves.

1. Have them practice making estimates of the situation.
2. Have them anticipate situations that will require decisions so they can be prepared when the need arises.
3. Have them avoid making rash or snap decisions.
4. Get them to approach problems with logic and reason.

Before moving on to the *Tenth Master Key to Management Success,* "How Top Executives Select and Develop Their Key Personnel," I'd like to recap briefly the ideas I've presented in this chapter.

As a manager, you should have the ability to make your decisions promptly and to announce them in a clear, forceful, and positive manner.

Many situations have more than one solution. You would be wise to get all the facts, weigh one solution against the other, and then calmly and quickly arrive at a sound and timely decision. Decisiveness is largely a matter of practice and experience.

To develop decisiveness, keep these specific points in mind:

1. Be positive in all your actions. Don't delay; don't beat around the bush. It takes more energy to fail than to succeed.
2. Get the facts, make up your mind, and issue your order with the complete confidence that you are right.
3. Recheck the decisions you have made only to determine if they were sound and timely.

4. Analyze the decisions made by others. If you do not agree, determine if your reasons for disagreement are sound.

5. Broaden your managerial viewpoint by studying the actions of others and profit from their successes or mistakes.

6. Be willing to accept full responsibility for your decisions.

7. Do the thing you fear to do and you will have the power to do it.

Chapter **10**

How Many Top Executives

Select and Develop Key

Management Personnel and

Why They Are Seldom Wrong

In Chapter 8, I pointed out the advantages of getting certain key people in the "labor" ranks to cooperate and work with you. In this chapter, my *Tenth Master Key to Management Success*, I am again talking about key personnel vital to your efforts, but this time they are in the ranks of management. That being so, your approach will be quite different.

First of all, key people in the ranks of "labor" who can help you achieve your goals are often there before you are. Your main efforts in that situation should be directed toward finding out who they are so you can get them to help you.

But in the case of management, it will many times be up to you to fill those key positions with the right people. You'll want to hire the best ones you can get and then develop their management potential on the job to your full advantage.

To bring you the most up-to-date, useful, and worthwhile information in this area, I talked directly to, or corresponded with, the personnel managers of a number of highly successful companies and corporations, including Lincoln Electric, Bullock Garages and Home Builders, Minneapolis Medtronics, Eastman Kodak, General Electric, Du Pont, J. C. Penney, Skyline Corporation, Bank of America, General Foods, Mobil Oil, the 3M Company, and IBM. I was also able to obtain some thoughts and ideas from several corporation vice-presidents and other high ranking officials in charge of the selection and development of management personnel in those same companies and corporations.

HOW MANY TOP EXECUTIVES SELECT THEIR KEY MANAGEMENT PERSONNEL

"What I Look For When Selecting a Key Manager . . ."

"Technical knowledge and know-how are, of course, musts when a person is being considered for selection or promotion to a key management position," says John B. MacDonald, an executive vice-president with a large U.S. corporation. "I expect a manager to know his job. So do his subordinates. If he does not know his business, he invites only ridicule and contempt from those who work with and for him.

"But technical knowledge is not the total answer. It alone will not earn a person the job. The individual I select must have much more than that to offer. For instance, I would expect this person to have an aptitude for long-range planning. He must be inventive and creative and able to bring new ideas to the company.

"And I would expect him to have the ability to carry on external relations with the many people who are important to our company: customers, stockholders, the community in which he lives, the corporate and financial world, among others. This is especially important if he is to progress to higher management positions.

"A manager in a key position with our company should also have certain desirable character traits. Above all, he must possess integrity. He should have a personality that instills confidence and respect. And he must be people-oriented. By that I mean he should have a natural leadership ability and a talent for judging people and placing his subordinates in positions that will maximize their strengths.

"I also look for intelligence, an open mind, the flexibility to learn from experience, the self-confidence to take calculated business risks, the ability to handle stress, the courage to make difficult decisions and carry them out.

"Many companies go outside to recruit their key management people. We do not. We promote from within. It's a standard policy with us that everyone must start at the bottom. Every top executive has done so. If you were to ask any of our 'associates'—that's what our employees are called—how the chairman of the board would be replaced if he died, the answer would probably be, 'Oh, we'd just hire a new office clerk.'

"Every sales clerk who rises to a managerial position with us knows he has the opportunity to become president of the company or chairman of the board. Our present chairman got his start as a salesman in a New York store's shoe department.

"To make sure we have enough homegrown talent for our top managerial jobs we give our younger managers the chance to gain general management experience and profit-and-loss responsibility at an early age. Also, in keeping with modern business trends, we are grooming more women executives—heretofore a relatively untapped source of senior management talent—for top-level management responsibilities."

Character Traits Most Executives Consider

Important in a Manager

Mr. MacDonald mentioned several desirable character traits he feels key managers should possess. These are integrity, leadership ability, a talent for judging people, an open mind, the flexibility to learn from experience, the confidence to take calculated risks, the ability to handle stress, the courage to make difficult decisions and carry them out.

All these are important. Admittedly, it is difficult to determine from an interview whether the person has all these desirable character traits or not. If he is from outside your company, you must depend on the information you get from previous employers, character references, and the like. If he is already in your organization, it will be much easier to assess an individual's desirable character traits.

I personally consider integrity to be one of the most important qualities I look for when hiring a manager. If a person is a liar, if he cannot be depended on to tell the truth, he is of no value to me, even if he's a genius. William Porter, an industrial executive, agrees with me.

"Integrity is one of the first qualities I look for when hiring a person for a top management position," Mr. Porter says. "It is one of the most important character traits an individual can posses. It is absolutely essential if a person is ever to rise to the top ranks of management.

"A person with integrity is always able to determine right from wrong and he will have the moral courage to do what is right. He will be a person of honor, one who can be trusted, a man of his word. He will not lie, cheat, steal, or chisel. Integrity is a must for the manager who wants to succeed."

Other top executives with whom I've spoken confirm Mr. Porter's statements. They, too, feel that integrity is one of the most important character traits to determine when selecting a person for a key management position.

Short-Range Objectives to Consider When
Hiring Key Management Personnel

Of course, the major present objective in selecting a person for a key management position is to get an individual who can carry out the duties and responsibilities and fulfill the requirements of the specific job.

If you're working for a firm like J. C. Penney or Sears Roebuck—who also promote primarily from within and seldom hire key management personnel *off-the-street*—you'll have plenty of opportunity to observe the work of those considered qualified for the job. You'll also be able to review personnel records and job performance reports as well as talk with the person's superiors face-to-face.

However, if the person is being hired from the outside, the task becomes more difficult. Educational development, past managerial experience, letters of recommendation from former employers, pertinent personal data such as habits, hobbies, and outside interests, all these are factors to consider.

Hiring the right person for a key management slot isn't done by making a snap decision after a 20- or 30-minute interview. It's highly important that you take sufficient time to talk to applicants for key management positions in depth if you want to get the best results. Here's what Ellis Ramsey, personnel manager for a large New Jersey based corporation, says about this:

> "I take plenty of time in my hiring interviews," Mr. Ramsey says. "My prospect might not have 20 years of experience as his resume indicates. He could have only one year of experience repeated 20 times. It's up to me to determine which he has.
>
> "I've found that several hours spent in interviewing each person can pay off in the long run. It's much easier and cheaper to pick the right person for a top management slot than to train the wrong individual to do the job.
>
> "As a general rule, I spend at least 4 to 6 hours interviewing our sales personnel . . . 6 to 8 hours hiring a person for an engineering or other technical job . . . 8 to 12 hours with an applicant for the position of a department foreman or division manager. These figures are minimum. I don't stop interviewing until I'm sure I have all the information I can possibly get so I can make the best possible decision."

Whatever number of hours you yourself establish for interviewing personnel for key management positions is up to you, but you would be wise to err on the side of too many rather than too few. Get every worthwhile detail you can possibly get from an individual. It is a maxim that a company or corporation reveals the value it places on people by the thoroughness with which it hires them.

Long-Range Objectives to Consider When
Hiring Key Management Personnel

Even when you're considering the short-range objectives in hiring or selecting key management personnel, that is, whether the person can do the specific job you're selecting him for, you should still keep certain long-range objectives in the back of your mind. Is he qualified for higher management positions, or is this the end of the line for him?

Ideally, every manager you hire should be kept until his retirement from the company. But if that's to happen, the person will
have to establish some long-range goals and objectives of his own.
And you can help him do that, says David Grant, the official in charge
of the selection and development of management personnel for one of
the largest manufacturers of mobile and modular homes in the United
States.

"Not only do I determine whether a person is qualified for
further promotion, but I also check to find out if he has further goals
in mind," Mr. Grant says. "I simply ask a person to outline his life
goals for me and to indicate what his plans are for his own career
development.

"I also ask him to list his qualifications for such advancement
and to tell me what he plans on doing to improve his weak areas. I
have him do this in writing at home between his first and second
interviews so he has plenty of time to think about it. This will often
open an individual's eyes for the first time to his own future potential and promotion possibilities.

"If the person I'm interviewing is a young college graduate,
this requirement forces him to crystallize and focus his thinking. I
will not accept vague and abstract statements like 'I plan to be
division manager or president of the company or chairman of the
board some day.' A statement like this has to be backed up by a
definite plan for achieving the specified goal."

Raising a person's sights to a higher goal can bring out the
best in him and that's what you should want from your management
people, their best. When Earl E. Bakken started out, his goal was
just to have a steady job with an electrical engineering firm. When he
raised his sights, he became the president of Minneapolis Medtronics
and a multi-millionaire. The first goal of Donald V. Seibert, J. C.
Penney's chairman of the board, was to run the company's largest
shoe department. But he soon changed his goal when he found out it
took as much time and energy to run the shoe department as it did to
manage the whole men's clothing department or the entire store.
Right then he raised his sights.

Paul J. Meyer, founder and president of Success Motivation

Institute, the world's largest producer of personal motivation, supervision, leadership development, executive and management courses, says, "If you are not making the progress you would like and are capable of making, it is simply because your goals are not clearly defined. If a person has a long-range goal, if he is motivated by the end result, he will overcome obstacles, situations, circumstances—and nothing can deter him. Goal-setting is the most important thing in life."

If your company has the same promotion policy Sears Roebuck or J. C. Penney use for their managers, who knows, the next person you hire could become president or chairman of the board if you motivate him to establish some goals for himself.

If your company doesn't have such a management development policy, institute one. When people know that opportunity is unlimited and they can go all the way to the top, they'll do their best for you, and that's what you want from every manager you hire.

Drawing a Person Out in an Interview

Getting the information you need from people during an interview so you can select the best qualified person requires skill. It is not an art that can be learned overnight. However, constant practice and the use of the right guidelines to draw a person out can make you a skilled interviewer. I'll give you the guidelines I learned from Elaine Martin, one of the sharpest personnel managers I've ever met. The practice is all up to you.

"To draw a person out during an interview so he'll answer your questions completely, you must *make the session enjoyable for him,*' Mrs. Martin says. "Most people enjoy talking about themselves; it feeds their ego. And your goal is to get him to talk about himself, so ask him leading questions and give him plenty of time to answer.

"Too many rapid-fire questions one after the other make the person feel as if he's being interrogated by a lawyer or a policeman. You can't establish rapport that way. Slow down. Let him expand and amplify all he wants. Just pay attention; that's all you need do. You'll learn much more about him when you listen patiently.

"Always Start with Questions that Are Easy to Answer," Mrs. Martin goes on to say. "The person knows he's being interviewed for a specific purpose, so he expects questions from you. He could well be nervous and questions that are easy to answer help him relax. A person becomes more comfortable when he can answer your questions without effort. The nervous tension begins to fade away, he drops his guard, and he's soon at ease with you.

"For instance, I always start with questions like, 'Where do you live? Are you married? How many children do you have? Then I move into such questions as, 'Would you tell me something about your past managerial experience? Why did you leave your previous employer? Why do you want to work for our company? How do you think you might improve the situation as it now is? How did you feel about your last job? Then I move on to tighter, more specific questions like, 'Exactly what did you like about your last job? Precisely what was your opinion of your last supervisor? Why did you like him or dislike him? Did you like or dislike your job? Why? Why did you leave?'

"I use any one or all of four different methods to ask questions that draw a person out in an interview. For instance,

'I Ask Questions that Require an Explanatory Answer. Questions that can be answered yes or no in an interview don't get enough information. You'll end up doing all the talking. Ask questions that require the person to explain his answer, for example, *'What* do you think of the policy of flexitime? *How* do you feel about having a woman as your superior? *How* would you handle an employee's complaint of favoritism?' Much can be learned about how a person *thinks* and *feels* with questions like these.

"Key Words Like 'How About' or 'What About' Stimulate a Person to Talk. Your initial questions can be followed up by questions that require even more explanation by saying, 'But *what about* this point? *How about* this factor?' These two phrases, *how about* and *what about,* are quite useful in keeping a person talking so you can draw him out more and more.

"Repeating Key Words Is Another Technique that Stimulates Conversation. Suppose you ask a person how he feels about his last company, and he says, 'It was all right, but I had some problems with my subordinates.' Your immediate comeback should be, 'Trouble with your subordinates?' The implication is you want more in-

formation about the subject. Your applicant will at once say, 'Yes,' and then give you a further explanation. All you need do is watch for key words and use them to draw him out even further. For instance,

" 'I liked my job, but my superiors wouldn't back me up.' 'Your superiors wouldn't back you up?' 'I liked my work, but I didn't have enough freedom to make my own decisions.' 'Didn't have enough freedom to make your own decisions?' You can see from these two examples how the repetition of key words digs deep into how a person thinks and how he feels and the kind of personality he has.

"My Fourth Technique to Draw a Person Out Is to Summarize Back to Him. Here's how I use this method. I'll say, 'If I understand you correctly, you mean . . .' His answer might possibly be, 'Yes, that's right, that's what I mean.' In that case, I'll move on immediately to something new. But that answer is rare. Most of the time, the answer will be, 'No, that's not quite what I meant,' or 'Yes, that's partially correct, but . . .' Either way, further explanation is necessary on his part.

"Of course, there's much more to successful interviewing than this, but these four little guidelines will do much to help you become a skillful interviewer so you can make the right decisions in your personnel work."

Such techniques as these might seem awkward to you to use at first, but with practice, they'll become an easy part of your hiring interviews and in other conversations as well where getting information is important to you. You now have the guidelines of one of the most skillful personnel managers I've ever met. The practice that leads to perfection is, as I said before, entirely up to you.

Before I leave this subject of interviewing an applicant for a management position, I want to say that 'body language" cannot be depend upon as a reliable method to determine how a person thinks or feels about something.

Some personnel managers try to read too much into a person's mannerisms, for instance, his cracking of knuckles, drumming of fingers, tapping of toes, excessive perspiration, frowns, scowls, gestures, and the like. These individual peculiarities or idiosyncrasies are unreliable and cannot be depended upon to reveal accurate information about a person.

For instance, one manager I know perspires quite heavily most of the time, in winter as well as summer. Because he's nervous? No, because his metabolic rate is higher than the average person's. His body temperature is 99.6 rather than the normal 98.6. That's why he always perspires more freely than the rest of us.

Another highly successful executive who is an asset to his company was once turned down by a personnel manager because he wore a perpetual scowl. The personnel manager thought the man was too much of a sourpuss and didn't hire him. What he didn't know was that the 'scowl" was permanent and the result of facial surgery after an automobile accident.

Six Keys to Hiring a Winner

It is possible time after time to find managers who have talent and who are winners. Discovering them takes patience, time, and the proper methods. Here are six specific techniques recommended by Harrison Ryan, president of the Ryan Management Company, a Los Angeles executive and management search firm.

"First of All, Pinpoint Responsibility," Mr. Ryan says. "Make one person responsible for finding the manager you want, whether it's a company executive or an outside agency like ours. If it's a company executive, of course, the personnel manager can help. But the primary responsibility for getting the right person should be given to only one person, preferably the executive or manager for whom the hired individual will be working.

"Second, Draw an Exact Profile of the Kind of Person You Want. Not only should you write up a detailed job description that indicates the duties and responsibilities of the position, but you should also list the specific personal qualities the manager must have along with his educational requirements and the personal background desired.

"Third, Don't Limit Your Search. Find the greatest number

of potential candidates you can for the position. An advertisement in the newspaper is not enough. The person you want is probably already employed so he's not reading the help wanted ads. That's why a firm like ours is so useful to a company looking for the best. We specialize in finding top-notch executives and management personnel and can find and develop more leads than the average company's personnel manager can ever hope to.

"*Fourth, Make Your Interview Tough.* Ask demanding questions in your interview. You need a lot more than 20 or 30 minutes to get the information you need to hire the best. Your interview at a minimum needs to cover fully the applicant's goals and objectives, his previous job experience and background, his outstanding personal characteristics, and the reason he's interested in working for your firm more than anyone else's.

"*Fifth, Always Check His References.* Too many personnel managers don't take the time to check out an applicant's references. They assume he wouldn't list them unless they were the best he had. But even the best reference is not always all favorable, so be sure to talk with all his previous employers, associates, and character references he has listed on his resume. Don't ask for their statements in writing. Most people are hesitant to sign their names to derogatory information. You'll get more candid and straightforward opinions in person or over the phone.

"*Last, Go for a Positive Selection.* Don't let a person win by default. You should be able to get enough applicants to end up choosing between two or three outstanding candidates. If only one person is interviewed, keep searching. You just haven't looked far enough or long enough."

These techniques are good to use whether you promote from within or whether you go outside to get your management talent. Perhaps these methods seem too painstaking or time-consuming to you, but they're not. When you're hiring a person for the rest of his management life—and that should be your goal at all times—you want to make sure you get a real winner. Hiring a manager is a lot like getting married. You have to look at a lot of prospects if you want to make sure you get the best.

METHODS TOP EXECUTIVES USE TO MEASURE
PROGRESS AND DEVELOPMENT OF
KEY MANAGEMENT PERSONNEL

A recent survey of more than 500 executives in several large blue-chip corporations found the following eight managerial weaknesses to be the most noticeable.

1. Lack of organization and planning ability.
2. Lack of initiative.
3. Improper delegation of responsibility and authority.
4. Inability to make sound and timely decisions.
5. Poor communications.
6. Lack of imagination and laxness in developing subordinates.
7. Inability to promote effective human relationships.
8. Failure to set reasonable standards of achievement.

These eight factors are the most critical in the development of management personnel. To help you measure the progress and development of your own key management people, I've drawn up a list of revealing questions that cover these eight vital areas. I was aided in this task by information I obtained from department and division heads and personnel managers of ten extremely successful companies and corporations. These questions represent the latest thinking of some of the best management minds in America.

Planning and Organizing the Work for His Department

1. Does he understand his job responsibilities and the authority he has to carry them out?
2. Can he draw up sensible plans with realistic time schedules to get the job done?

3. Does he subdivide the work into easier and progressive phases, setting intermediate goals to be attained?

4. Does he use his resources (money, manpower, time, materials, facilities) properly to get the job done with as little waste of any of them as possible?

5. Does he use overtime only as a last resort or does he use it routinely to get the job done on time? When overtime is necessary, does he inform his people as soon as possible to prevent inconvenience and worker dissatisfaction?

6. Does he re-evaluate the workload of each person periodically to cut down on overtime and to insure that every individual is doing a full day's productive work?

7. Can he effectively establish priorities for the work to be done, both by himself and by his people?

8. Does he conduct effective meetings only when required, avoiding unnecessary or routine ones that waste manpower and productive time?

9. Are his meetings held to help people or harass them?

10. Does he make sure each person knows the duties and responsibilities of his primary job? Is each one doing his job in a satisfactory manner?

11. Does he make full use of all the skills and abilities of his people?

12. Does he have a program for cross-training?

13. Does he make sure his people have the equipment and materials they need when they need them?

14. Does he have a method of accounting for each person during duty hours?

Showing Initiative in His Job

1. Does he recognize problems and solve them or correct situations that need improvement even in the absence of his superior?

2. Can he come up with new solutions and fresh ideas for solving problems?

3. Does he make the most of a new plan or promising idea?

4. Does he use worthwhile suggestions made by his subordinates?
5. Does he encourage his people to submit new methods and new ideas?
6. Does he anticipate by thinking and looking ahead?
7. Does he look for additional responsibility?

Delegation of Authority

1. Does he effectively delegate authority to do the job?
2. Does he avoid interfering once he passes on the authority to do the job?
3. Does he realize he still must retain the final responsibility for the success or failure of the mission?
4. Can he use mission-type orders effectively?
5. Does he push the decision making down to the lowest level possible?
6. Does he keep from getting bogged down in details that belong to someone else?
7. Does he do the difficult jobs himself for fear they will not get done?
8. Does he supervise to make sure the job is being done properly?
9. Does he ask his people to participate in setting work objectives and work schedules?

Making Those Really Tough Decisions

1. Does he make those tough decisions or does he try to pass the buck upstairs?
2. Are his decisions consistent with established company policies and procedures?
3. Does he stay within the bounds of his own authority in making his decisions?
4. Does he use a realistic problem-solving-process in reaching his decisions?

5. Does he ask for the advice and help of others in reaching his decisions?

6. Does he give his employees a chance to actively participate in the decisions that affect them?

7. Does he accept full responsibility for his decisions?

8. Can he make up his mind without unnecessary delay?

9. Does he have the courage to act after his decision is made?

The Ability to Communicate with People

1. Does he know the actual status of his people's morale?

2. Does he encourage his employees to express their opinions?

3. Does he get the feeling of the group on important matters that affect them, before going ahead?

4. Does he listen with patience and understanding to new ideas?

5. Does he answer his subordinates' questions satisfactorily?

6. Does he have an "open door, open mind" policy for listening to complaints, recommendations, and so on?

7. Does he keep people informed on changes in company policies and procedures affecting their work?

8. Do his subordinates know what qualities he values most in them?

9. Does he recognize good work and express appreciation for their efforts?

10. Does he show his people how each individual job is important and essential to the total group effort?

11. Does he explain the "why's" of his decision?

12. Does he inform his superiors of the accomplishments and development of his subordinates?

Developing His People's Potential

1. Does he select properly qualified people for jobs in his department?

2. Does he help new employees adjust to the job and the group?

3. Does he motivate his people to do a better job?

4. Does he systematically evaluate the job performance of each one of his people and keep them informed on how they're doing?

5. Does he have a standard and consistent procedure in recommending his people for promotion?

6. Has he apprised any of his employees of weaknesses and strengths in job performance in the past 90 days?

7. Is he always willing to help his employees solve their work problems?

8. When someone fails to meet his established commitment, does he determine the cause and take corrective action?

9. Does he use constructive criticism, reflecting a helpful attitude?

10. Does he discuss career opportunities with his people?

11. Does his assistant or the senior individual know of upcoming projects in his department? Would his assistant be able to carry them out in his absence?

12. Is he training an assistant to take his place in case of temporary absence or promotion?

Getting Along with People

1. Is he able to give a brief background on each person he supervises?

2. Is he firm and fair in dealing with all his people?

3. Does he give recognition for a job well done and compensate for overtime to prevent low morale?

4. Does he enjoy working with his people?

5. Do people enjoy being a member of his group?

6. Does he make it easy for people to talk with him?

7. Does he visit his people and his associates in their offices and work places?

8. Does he participate suitably in social events of his employees?

9. Can he tactfully adjust to diverse personalities?

Setting Reasonably High Standards to Maintain

1. Is his credibility high with his subordinates?
2. Does he use systematic methods to measure performance and progress?
3. Does he give his people goals, a sense of direction, something to strive for, an objective to achieve?
4. Does he establish the proper climate of management for his people to work in?
5. Does he evaluate continually to raise the work standards of his group?

JUDGING THE END RESULT

Now that you've seen some of the techniques many top executives use to select and develop their key management personnel, you might want to know how well these methods work. Well, let's take a look at some of the results they get so you can see for yourself.

Take the Lincoln Electric Company, for example. Managers there don't leave the company. They stay until they retire. There's a long waiting list of currently employed people waiting to be hired, not only in management, but also in labor. The same can be said for Bullock Garages and Home Builders, Minneapolis Medtronics, and the Skyline Corporation.

A spokesman for IBM told me that they always find new jobs for their displaced managers, retraining them if need be. Eastman Kodak promotes from within, just as do Sears Roebuck and J. C. Penney. Few managers or executives ever leave these companies.

Managers and executives don't leave the 3M Company either. It's been decades since 3M has put an outsider into a top management job. A senior Du Pont executive says, "You don't find many jobhoppers here. Managers come to stay and expect to remain until they retire." General Foods also selects and develops the best managers it can get. Bright young people there can rise as high as product manager even before they're in their thirties. Mobil Oil gives young managers responsibility quickly and lets them go up as fast as their individual abilities will allow.

Xerox has always attracted exceptional people as has Procter and Gamble. As a result, both companies are often "raided" for management personnel by other corporations, but the majority stay for their entire business career.

All these companies are leaders in their respective fields. In most instances, their names are synonymous with their products. For instance, if you were to ask the average person to give you a company name for cameras, he'd say "Eastman Kodak." Soap means Procter and Gamble . . . office equipment and business machines, IBM . . . timber and lumber supplies, Weyerhaeuser . . . electrical appliances, General Electric . . . cereals, General Foods . . . chemicals, Du Pont . . . Scotch tape, the 3M Company, and so on down the line.

You can't build reputations like this with management personnel that's below par. The results they've obtained with their managers and executives speak for themselves; I need say nothing more. If you're not getting the same results these companies are, I'd suggest you review and check your hiring procedures. Could be they need up-dating and modernizing.

QUALIFICATIONS THE MANAGER
OF TOMORROW WILL NEED

To get the answer to this question, I contacted the presidents and chief executive officers of several large corporations. The consensus of their thoughts and ideas is summarized for you in this section:

1. Managers in the future will need a much greater understanding of human nature than in the past if they are to provide the kind of leadership needed to accomplish the goals and objectives of both the business enterprise and the people who constitute it.

2. People work most productively when the pattern of organized human relations satisfies reasonably well the basic needs and desires of employees. The manager of tomorrow, besides understanding the needs and desires of each individual, will also be required to understand organization as a process of relations between persons, as well as a means for attaining the corporate objectives. He will be expected to know how to maintain conditions in which people can work most efficiently to obtain their basic needs and desires and gain the corporate goals at the same time.

3. Since knowledge is becoming so vast and complex, multiplying year after year, no one person will be able to know everything he needs to know about any one particular field. This situation will demand more teamwork and cooperation from employees than ever before. To lead this kind of complex enterprise, a manager will need to understand fully all the facets of human behavior. He will be required to become an expert in the field of human relations and applied psychology.

4. The manager of tomorrow will be acutely aware of the importance of human relationships. He will tap both individual and group resources to get the maximum results. Management will mean developing and using the skills of people more than ever before. Despite our advances in computer technology, profits in the future will depend increasingly upon the human performance in business and industry. The manager who can lead and direct people will be in demand as never before.

Now that we've discussed how to find and develop the cream of the crop in management, let's go clear to the other end of the spectrum and take a look at the problem people you're bound to have in your organization so you'll know what to do about them. I've yet to meet the manager who could not gain some marked benefits from my *Eleventh Master Key to Management Success:* "Master Methods Wise Managers Use for Controlling Problem People."

Chapter 11

Master Methods Wise Managers
Use for Controlling
Problem People

Studies conducted by a number of research firms and several universities reveal that no less than 10 percent of the employees in the nation's work force are plagued with problems that result in a lack of productivity on the job.

Yet some organizations, for instance, the Donnelly Company, Lincoln Electric, Minneapolis Medtronics, Bullock Garages and Home Builders, the Skyline Corporation, among others I've discussed with you, literally have no real problem employees at all. Why not? Because the management of those companies has been wise and discerning enough to satisfy the basic needs and desires of all their employees. They've done that by using the same methods and procedures I've been telling you about for the past ten chapters.

If you, too, will use the techniques you've learned so far, If you will determine the basic needs and desires of all your employees and do your level best to satisfy them, you'll find that many of the problems you used to have in managing people will simply disappear into thin air. For those few problem people who remain, and they'll be far less than that national 10 percent, you can use my *Eleventh Key to Management Success* to handle them.

Why It's Important to Protect
Your Investment in People

Unskilled labor may be easy to come by. But today most companies don't need unskilled labor; they need well-trained, highly skilled, dependable, loyal, and productive employees. The competent technician, the well-trained assembly line worker, the able administrator, the capable manager, and the top-notch executive didn't get that way overnight. All those people are expensive to train and difficult to replace. It's to your advantage to keep as many of them as you can from turning into problem people. It's also to your benefit to help a problem person salvage his job, his career, his livelihood before it's too late for him to do so.

To save a problem person (who is not completely incorrigible) is not only the right and decent thing to do, but it is also the best way to protect a valuable investment. And most companies do have a sizable investment in their people. Just for example, when the Zenith Radio and Television Corporation opened a plant in Springfield, Missouri, they trained over 4,000 new employees for 16 weeks at company expense. Woolworth conducts a comprehensive retail training program for their junior executives. Some companies help their managers and executives get advanced degrees. For instance, Columbia University has an adult education course called *Master's Degree for Executives*. The company pays $7,500 for the course which consists of classes one day a week, three week-long sessions each calendar quarter, and 15 hours of homework a week. The studies last for two years and upon successful completion, a Master's Degree is awarded the graduate. Several hundred business and industrial managers and executives have already taken this course.

So with all this organizational time and money invested in people, what are you going to do with the ball of fire who ends up burned out at 40? Or the highly skilled employee who decides to retire on the job at 45 feeling the company still owes him a living even for low quality production? Or the brilliant executive who becomes an alcoholic? Or the chronic absentee, the hand-sitter, the loner, the bogged-down, the too-busy, even the genius who can cause you problems?

Are you going to get rid of them all? I doubt it. That's not the answer, except perhaps in the case of the completely incorrigible employee. The rest of these problem people, at least in the majority of instances, can be salvaged and turned into good, loyal, dependable employees again. The most valuable asset your company has is not its physical plant, its real estate, its equipment and machinery, but its people: specifically, the individual performance of each and every employee.

So few companies realize that. They spend thousands of dollars on elaborate security systems complete with fences, guards, and dogs to protect three of their management resources: money, materials, facilities. But they do nothing to protect their huge investment in their most important management resource: people. If you don't do that, you'll end up like the armed services replacing a good man or woman every couple of years. Few companies can afford to do that. I'll show you in this chapter how you can protect and save your investment in people.

Primary Causes of Job Dissatisfaction

What causes people to become problem cases and troublemakers instead of good and productive, happy and satisfied workers? In the majority of cases, it's *management's failure to understand and satisfy their employees' basic needs and desires*. That's it in a nutshell.

"Too often employees are a neglected corporate resource," says Harry O'Neill, executive vice president of Opinion Research, Inc., of Princeton, New Jersey. "Not only are your people important to the day-to-day functioning and future growth of your company, but they can also play a very useful role as company ambassadors in their community.

"But first you must understand your employees—their needs, expectations, knowledge, misconceptions. Only then will you be in a position to maximize their productivity, both on and off the job."

Mr. O'Neill says that in spite of shorter hours, better pay, and greater benefits, there is still too big a gap in understanding and rapport between management and labor, especially workers at the lower levels. He recommends that managers and executives conduct more in-depth employee-relations activities to help solve this problem.

Each of us has 15 normal basic needs that must be fulfilled to some extent before we can be completely satisfied and happy with our lives. Some of these desires can be satisfied only in our personal lives with our familes and in our homes. But a great many others are completely dependent upon our jobs and our work.

Numerous research organizations have found that when people become unhappy with their jobs or become problems to their superiors, management has often failed to satisfy their needs in one or more of the following five areas. So you would do well to concentrate your major efforts in these five specific areas to keep people from developing into problem cases.

1. A Person Needs the Chance to Use His Skills. A job that challenges a person's ingenuity and skills gives him a sense of accomplishment. Repetitive or routine work seems endless and boring, even to a dull individual. When you give a person a chance to use his skills on the job, you satisfy at least four, possibly even more, of his basic desires.

You build up his ego and give him a feeling of importance when you let him use his initiative and ingenuity to do the job. By giving him a chance to use his skills, you offer him the opportunity to excel. This also gives him the opportunity to be creative in his work and to enjoy new experiences on the job.

2. The Person Needs to Know that the Work He Does Is Useful. If a person knows the product or service he helps to produce is worthwhile and valued by others, he feels good about his job. If he can't see the point of his labors, his self-esteem suffers.

Let a person know the work he does is important to your efforts, and you'll fulfill at least five of his basic desires. You'll reassure him of his worth when you praise him for his work. This also feeds his ego and makes him feel important, not only to you, but also to himself. Knowing that his work is useful and worthwhile wins him social and group approval and enables him to be accepted as an equal by his peers and co-workers. When he knows that the job he does for you is useful, it also satisfies his basic desire to achieve or accomplish something worthwhile. Finally, knowing that the work he does is valued by you fulfills his desire for self-respect, dignity, and self-esteem.

3. **An Employee Wants the Opportunity to Participate in the Decisions that Affect Him.** Most employees consider themselves to be responsible individuals. Too much supervision or overly authoritarian direction often creates friction on the job. On assembly lines especially, workers are usually much happier if they can have a say in determining the pace of their work and if they can suggest improvements in their own working conditions.

When you give your people a chance to participate in the decisions that affect them, you'll gain some mighty big benefits, too. First off, you'll find your workers will be much better disciplined, for people will always obey the rules they make for themselves more readily than they will obey the ones you make for them to follow.

And you'll satisfy no less than four of your employees' basic desires when you let them help make the decisions affecting them. To be specific, you'll lend to their feeling of importance . . . you'll give them a sense of roots or belonging to the organization . . . you'll increase their feeling of personal power . . . and you'll give them a feeling of liberty and freedom. If they can suggest improvements in their own working conditions, you'll no doubt be able to contribute to their good health and well-being for they'll usually ask for improvements that help their physical comfort and general welfare.

4. **A Person Needs a Sense of Security.** Although a person's job may be just about perfect, he won't be happy in it for very long if he lives in constant fear of being fired or demoted. Of course, you have the right as a manager to expect decent work from a person, but you should never use threats or intimidation to get what you want. *Fear always leads to hate*, and that's all you'll get from your employees if you try to make them afraid of you.

5. **A Person Needs to Feel Important,** not only to you, but also to himself. That's why so many housewives and mothers go back to work after the children are raised and gone. They feel completely useless staying at home and get jobs to fulfill their basic need for feeling important and useful to others again.

When you fulfill a person's needs in these first four areas—giving him a chance to use his skills . . . letting him know that the work he does is useful . . . allowing him to take part in the decisions that affect him . . . giving him a feeling of security—you fulfill his fifth need automatically and make him feel important.

But don't stop there. Go out of your way to use other methods and techniques to make a person feel important, too. You'll prevent many problems from occuring when you do. Rememember that the desire to be important is one of the strongest drives in human nature. Treat your people based on this principle, and you'll never go wrong. In fact, the benefits you gain will often amaze you.

Of course, there are other job factors that matter to people in varying degrees, for example, pay and chances for promotion. But these five areas I've just discussed, when properly handled, will help satisfy 13 of the 15 normal basic desires every person has and that's an excellent score in anybody's ballpark.

Although some outside pressures may cause a person to become a problem to you—personal debts, an unhappy marriage, and the like—a job influences a person's social life and recreational activities far more than most managers realize. Mixing with co-workers and customers gives a person new acquaintances and friendships. Not only that, the job a person has often decides his status in the community. That also helps determine the kind of people he'll meet socially.

It's not surprising, then, that dissatisfaction at work can cause personal discontent and sometimes damage one's physical and mental health. The wise and discerning manager will do his best to keep his workers satisfied on the job, for he knows that will help his employees enjoy a fuller and happier life in general. And that pays dividends for the manager, too, for a happy and contented employee will produce a better quality product faster than a discontented and unhappy employee.

Helping a Person Analyze His Job

A great many times a wise manager can keep an unhappy

worker from becoming a true problem case simply by sitting down with him and helping him analyze his job in detail. Mismatches between a worker's needs and capabilities and the demands of his work may explain his dissatisfaction. The following four questions can serve as a guide to help you and your employee properly evaluate his job and his attitude toward it.

1. **Is the Employee Expecting Too Much from His Job?** Typically, a young, inexperienced worker expects a lot more intrinsic reward from his job than he gets. An older employee tends to be more satisfied with his work, sometimes because he's moved into a more fulfilling position or because he doesn't look for all of life's joys and pleasures to be found only in his work.

2. **Is the Job Too Demanding for the Employee?** Perhaps the job is beyond the capabilities of the worker. It presents more challenges than he can handle. As an end result, he will feel frustrated and insecure. If this is so, you must either help him develop his abilities to do the job, or move him to one that is less demanding.

3. **Does the Job Demand Too Little of the Person?** This is just as frustrating to a person as being overworked for it leads to boredom. It also invites problems from other employees who view the individual with envy, jealousy, and suspicion.

4. **Is the Job Taking Him Where He Wants to Go?** If a person's goal is to make a lot of money, he definitely won't be satisfied in a dead-end job that offers no opportunity for promotion or financial reward. You can best help this type of individual by letting him know how and where he needs to improve so he can be better qualified for promotion to the next higher job.

PINPOINTING THE PROBLEM PERSON

Although you may have done everything you can think of to eliminate the primary causes of job dissatisfaction and you've helped some potential trouble-makers analyze their jobs to keep them happy and contented, you're still going to have some problem people to handle and control.

Problem people require your special attention because they can actually wreck your organization in short order. They can hurt your production, your sales, and your profit. They can ruin your plans, break up friendships, lose customers, harm your company's reputation, and create friction wherever they are.

However, you cannot use your subjective opinions, your intuition, or how you "feel" about somone to determine who is or is not a problem person. Just because you don't like the person doesn't mean he's a problem. Beards and mustaches, red hair and short dresses have nothing at all to do with this. You must be completely objective in determining who and what a problem person is.

All you need do is get the correct answers to three simple questions to determine if a person really constitutes a problem for you. If you cannot honestly answer *yes* to at least one of these questions, then that person is not a problem, no matter how much you personally dislike him.

Is the Person Failing to Properly Carry Out the Duties of His Assigned Job?

In other words, is he *under*performing on his job? For instance, if he's working in production, is his work below the established standard in both quantity and quality? Does he produce fewer units than he should in a normal work day? Does he have excessive waste or a higher turn-back rate from quality control than his co-workers?

If he's in sales, does he waste company time? Is he making the number of sales he should each week? Is he making fresh contacts, finding new prospects, getting more customers for you?

Or if he's in management, is his division or department or section doing the job it's supposed to do? Is he getting the results he should for you?

No matter who the person is or what his position might be, you should be interested only in whether he's getting the job done for you or not. In other words, *does he in some tangible and visible way fail to measure up to the reasonable performance standards you've set for him?* If your answer is "Yes" to this question, you have a definite problem on your hands. But if it's "No," he's not a problem, at least not yet. You must go on to the next question to make sure.

Does He Interfere with the Work of Other Employees?

Do you constantly find the same person involved in employee disturbances? Does he just "happen to be" at the scene of the "crime" each time? Does his inferior quality of workmanship keep another department from functioning properly? Does his failure to produce the proper amount of units cause another worker or another section to shut down temporarily?

The days of the one-man show are long gone. Most business and industry today is a cooperative team effort. I've seen sales ruined by the shipping department sending out the wrong product and customers lost when inferior quality items are made by production employees on the assembly line. If any employee, then, *consistently* interferes with the work of any other individual, no matter where that other employee works, you definitely have a problem person to take care of.

Does He Cause Harm to His Group,
Either On or Off the Job?

Of course, as you've already seen in question 2, he can cause harm to his group by interfering with the work of others. However, a problem person can often cause trouble in other ways for members of his group. Not only can he cause his team members financial loss by his actions, but he can also create friction and discontent within the group by gossiping and starting rumors.

You can usually tell if a particular group has this kind of problem person in it when members of that work unit try hard to leave it. Or when other people refuse to be transferred into it. Or when you have no in-plant applications for an extremely good job that's open in that group. If any of these things happen, comb through the group until you find out who the problem person is. There's bound to be one, and that's for sure.

Remember, too, a person can harm his group by what he does off the job as well as on it. If a high-ranking senior vice-president or division manager is seen night after night drinking heavily in a bar, questions are bound to come up about the standards of the company he works for. If an employee's name shows up in the police statistics section of the newspaper, this, too, can harm the group.

Few things tarnish the reputation of a group as much as having one of its members get into trouble. That's why the United States Armies of Occupation in Europe and Japan after World War II had to work overtime to live down the actions of a small minority of irresponsible soldiers. The entire army was improperly judged by the actions of just a few. But that's human nature to do that; that's the way we are.

To sum up, then, ask yourself these three questions to determine if a particular individual is or is not a problem person?

1. Is the person failing to properly carry out the duties of his assigned job? Does he in some tangible and visible way fail to measure up to the reasonable performance standards you've set for him?
2. Does he interfere with the work of other employees?
3. Does he cause harm to his group, either on or off the job?

No matter who the person is, what he does, or what his position in your organization might be, if he's causing you trouble in one of these three basic problem areas, if you can honestly answer "Yes" to any one of these three questions, then that person is a problem to you. He will require your special attention so you can help him solve his problem.

Helping the Person Solve His Problem

Remember that most problem people get that way because

many times somewhere along the line *management failed to understand and satisfy their basic needs and desires.* Please also keep in mind that if you will make sure to give an individual the chance to use his skills, let him know that the work he does is useful to you, offer him the opportunity to participate in the decisions that affect him, and give him a sense of security, you'll be able to satisfy at least 13 of the 15 basic desires every normal person has.

Now that you realize that the primary cause of a person's problems can often be a manager's failure to satisfy one or more of that individual's basic needs and desires, your next step will be to do a bit of detective work so you can determine which specific one is not being fulfilled. You must decide this on an individual basis for no two people are ever exactly alike.

You don't need to be a psychiatrist or a psychologist or have a degree in abnormal psychology to deal with problem people. Just follow the number one rule in all human relationships and you can't go far wrong, for it's the master key that controls all human behavior, both normal and abnormal. That number one rule in case you've forgotten it is to. . . .

FIND OUT WHAT PEOPLE WANT
AND HELP THEM GET IT

When you do that, you'll be able to get what you want, too. Finding out what people want and helping them get it has always been the management policy of the Lincoln Electric Company of Cleveland, Ohio.

James F. Lincoln, when he was president, established the policy of biweekly conferences between management and labor representatives to discuss employee problems. That same policy is still in force.

If any employee has a complaint, a question, or a problem, he is urged and encouraged to attend these conferences and speak his piece. Managers listen so they can find out what the person's problem is and what can be done about it. The company does not want disgruntled employees building up steam inside or harboring a grudge.

The end result of this procedure? Complete harmony between management and labor. The company has no labor problems. They have never had a strike. There is no union representation for none is needed.

If you want to obtain the same good results that the Lincoln Electric Company had, then find out what your own employees want and help them get it. Let them talk to you about their problems and their complaints, their worries and their fears. Do that and you'll be able to keep your potential problem people from turning into real trouble makers.

Before I give you some more examples to show you how well this procedure of finding out what people want and helping them get it works in management to help a person solve his problems, I want to point out that an employee's fears can also create problems for you. You see, a primary motivator for many people is self-centered fear—the fear they will lose something they already possess, or the fear they will fail to gain something they are trying to attain. In short, *fear is always to be found on the opposite side of the coin of desire.*

For instance, if a person feels his job is in jeopardy, even though it might not be, his actions and reactions will be the same as if it were. The manager who uses an authoritarian manner in dealing with people is afraid he will appear weak and powerless in front of his subordinates so he comes on too strong with them. The one who tries to get results by being a good guy is fearful of losing social or group approval. He wants to be accepted by others so badly he will do almost anything to be friends with them.

When the fear he will not achieve his basic needs becomes greater than his normal desire to gain them, an individual crosses over the line to abnormal behavior. His drives are no longer normal, they are compulsive. They become an obsession with him. Sometimes his fear of not gaining his desires will lead to overaction on his part. At other times, his fear of losing his desires by making a mistake will lead to inaction. Either way, such a person can easily become a problem to you. Let me give you an example now so you will know—

How to Interpret and Understand a Person's Motives

"Every human motive has both a positive aspect and a negative aspect," says Dr. Clifford Lawrence, a Chicago psycholgist. "When an individual says or does something, he is striving to achieve a goal, a reward, or something he wants very much. At the same time, he is making an effort to separate himself as far as possible from that which he hates or fears.

"For instance, the average normal individual wants everyone to like him. His actions are therefore motivated by his desire for acceptance. Simultaneously, from the negative viewpoint, he is goaded by the fear of not being accepted by others. His actions will depend on which emotion is greater—desire or fear. If his fear of not having friends is greater than his normal desire to have them, his manner will be ingratiating, even servile. A child who gives away his toys trying to win friends is suffering with this same problem.

"The man who hoards money is driven by an abnormal fear of poverty. The one who insists on being center-stage at all times is obsessed by the fear of not being important. The man who indulges constantly in extramarital affairs is filled with a compulsion to prove his masculinity and his virility.

"The greater the desire to win approval and acceptance from others, to hoard money, to be important, or to make love to many women—the greater can be the internal fear that drives the individual to do as he does."

Examples of Master Methods Wise Managers Use
to Help Problem People

PROBLEM: "I once had a problem employee I'll just call Bill," Douglas Ellison, an Ohio industrial plant manager, told me. "Bill was a constant critic of management. Whenever he was told to do something, he always wanted to do it the opposite way. If there was an argument or disagreement of some sort, Bill was sure to be in on it. And he worked overtime to get in the last word. He demanded the attention of management, it seemed, and he always got it. He fulfilled all three requirements that constitute a problem person. He was underperforming in his job, constantly interfering with the work of others, and harming the members of his team by causing them loss of incentive pay because of lowered production."

ANALYSIS: "Well, I was at wit's end until I met you, Jim," Doug went on to say. "Then I sat down and analyzed Bill's problem and determined he was simply going out of his way to get attention. Bill had an ego problem and he needed to feel important. The next question was how to give him that feeling of importance he needed so much."

SOLUTION: "I decided to follow your advice, Jim. I gave Bill the responsibility of heading up the employee safety team for his section. It was his job to establish safety rules and regulations and to work out emergency rescue procedures with the plant safety officer in case of an industrial accident in his section. Wonder of wonders, it worked. Bill's desire for importance was fulfilled. People were actually listening to what he said when he talked. His ego was gratified and now everyone's happy."

PROBLEM: "I had hired an ex-army major as a section supervisor in the mill department," Joel Galloway, a rubber factory division manager, said. "But his manner was too much like that of an army drill sergeant. He issued orders right and left in a loud demanding voice and was extremely impatient and critical of everyone's work. Yet I knew he had a lot of potential management ability and I didn't want to let him go unless I absolutely had to."

ANALYSIS: "It was comparatively simple to analyze Tom's problem. He was simply too authoritarian as a result of his many years in the armed forces."

SOLUTION: "I didn't have much trouble in getting Tom to see my point. His brisk and curt military bearing was not caused by a compulsive desire for power, but simply resulted from his army training. When he spoke, he expected people to listen and not ask questions. He now realizes his subordinates can have some good ideas, too, so he listens to them and cooperates with them without being at all permissive. He's still strong and firm, no doubt about that, but in such a way that he's well accepted by all his people. They like and respect him a great deal."

PROBLEM: "Neal S. was promoted to section supervisor from the labor force and retained in the same department so we could use his technical skills and experience to the maximum," Elston Richards, a division manager in a North Carolina furniture manufacturing company said. "Neal wanted to succeed in his new job, but he was also anxious to keep his friendships intact with his former co-workers and associates so they wouldn't think he was putting on airs and lording it over them. Trouble was, he became too permissive and let his former buddies run over the top of him. He overlooked their mistakes. Absenteeism rose . . . quality went down . . . accidents increased . . . soon the section was a complete disaster area."

ANALYSIS: "I was at fault for waiting too long before I took action to correct the problem. When I did, I pointed out to Neal that his problem was his abnormal desire to win the social approval of his subordinates and that as a result, he was being far too permissive with them and letting them get away with murder."

SOLUTION: "It was almost too late, but Neal asserted his authority and natural leadership ability, and within 30 days things were back to normal again. I realize now I made a mistake in keeping Neal in the same department when he was promoted. It's now a standing rule in our company that when a man from the labor force is promoted to a position in management, he must be moved to a different department."

There will always be exceptions to the rule. By that I mean, although a person is a problem to you because he's underperforming in his job, interfering with the work of other employees, or causing harm to his group either on or off the job, you cannot always tie the cause of his problem down to a specific need or desire that's not being fulfilled. If that's the situation, then you'll need to do some more detective work to find out the cause of his problem. The best way to do that is to use the management problem solving process I gave you back in Chapter 7. Let me give you now several examples I've encountered in my own experience.

PROBLEM: Just for instance, take the alcoholic. No doubt about it, he's a problem. He'll come to work late, do a poor job, call in sick several days a week. And no one knows why he drinks the way he does. He doesn't know for he doesn't understand himself. Yet sometimes he can be salvaged. Not every alcoholic is a total loss or destined to become a flop-house bum.

SOLUTION: The only solution I've ever found to be successful is to get in touch with a member of Alcoholics Anonymous. Have him (or her) get in touch with your problem person and talk with him. Chances are you have a recovered alcoholic working for you right now and you don't even know it. Tell your employee what you're going to do and let him know it's either AA or his job. The point is you've offered him a way out, but you can go no further than that. He has to solve his own problem. You can't do it for him.

PROBLEM: Gladys K., a programmer in a data processing organization, changed almost overnight from a pleasant hard-working employee to a sullen, resentful, and insubordinate person.

ANALYSIS: A little digging and some personnel work showed that a new male employee who was also a programmer was hired at about the same time Gladys's personality changed. Further investigation showed that the new employee was being paid more than Gladys simply because he was a man. They were both doing the same work.

SOLUTION: Since it was impossible to lower the new man's salary without losing him, the only fair thing to do was to raise Gladys's salary up to equal his. When that was done, the problem was solved. Gladys became her own pleasant normal self again.

PROBLEM: Joe was not doing his job properly. Quality control turned back 75 percent of his production. Yet Joe was a hard worker. He was serious and sincere about his work and seemed to be trying hard to do a good job.

ANALYSIS: If an employee doesn't have the basic skills to do the job, then he should receive further training and instruction until he is properly qualified. If this doesn't work, then it could be the job is beyond his capabilities. If so, he should be given less demanding duties to perform.

SOLUTION: In this particular case, Joe was transferred to a different job that he was able to do properly.

PROBLEM: Jerry was a constant source of irritation to his supervisor. There seemed to be a definite personality clash between them. He was a good worker and his supervisor was also a good employee. The company didn't want to lose either one.

ANALYSIS: Sometimes people do clash without any logical or visible reason. If the friction between an employee and his supervisor can't be ironed out peacefully, then transfer the employee to a new department. I must admit that I, too, have met a few people in my time I wouldn't care to work with or for. Nor would I want them as next door neighbors either.

SOLUTION: In this specific instance, that was done. Jerry was transferred to a different department. He gets along well with his new supervisor and is doing a good job.

Don't Make His Problem Your Problem

The principle here is to help the person solve his problem, but not to make it your problem. Show the man how to carry his load, but don't carry it for him. It's easy to become too sympathetic and soft when a person cries on your shoulder about his sick mother, his bedfast wife, the broken-down car, and so on, but you must establish a line somewhere. We all have personal problems to resolve and we all have to take care of them and work at the same time. Your problem person will have to do the same thing.

ELEVEN GUIDELINES YOU CAN USE
TO KEEP MINOR COMPLAINTS FROM
TURNING INTO MAJOR PROBLEMS

If you have a good method of handling employee grievances, you can often keep minor complaints from turning into major problems. Here's a set of guidelines I've used successfully for a long time.

1. Make It Easy for Your Employees to Come to You. You don't have to be overly chummy, but you shouldn't be cold and distant with your employees either. The important thing is to free your subordinate from the fear that his complaint might antagonize you and create a bigger problem than he already has.

2. Get Rid of Red Tape. I have absolutely no use for government bureaucrats who use red tape to keep from making a decision or giving a person an answer. Don't clutter up your grievance procedure with cumbersome rules and regulations that defeat your purpose. Keep it plain and simple. You want to get to the problem and its solution in the least possible time. A good way to do this is to keep your door physically open at all times.

3. Explain Your Grievance Procedure to Everyone. It does no good to keep your door open for your employees unless they know why it's open. So pass the word along . . . let them all know . . . keep everyone informed. State clearly and precisely how an employee should present a grievance and say what will happen when he does. Explain your procedure, step by step, so that everybody will understand it.

4. Help a Person Voice His Grievance. Sometimes an employee may not be skilled in putting his grievance into words. If he feels that the successful correction of his problem will depend on his verbal ability, he may give up even before he starts and bottle up his discontent inside where it will fester and continue to grow.

5. Always Grant a Hearing to an Employee with a Grievance. No matter how trivial his complaint might sound to you, it's important to him, so always give your employee the chance to air his gripe and get it off his chest.

6. Practice Patience. I know you're busy and that you have many other things to do that demand your attention. But be patient; hear the person out. If you don't, chances are he'll go to the union with his grievance. Next time you see him could be in a formal arbitration hearing. Then you'll have to listen even when you don't want to, and it will be even more expensive and time consuming.

7. Ask Him What He Wants You to Do. Here's how you can turn a grievance into a profit for you. Just ask, "What would you like me to do?" This one phrase will do more to oil any rusty relationships between management and labor than any other that you can use.

8. Don't Make Biased or Hasty Decisions. Even though you're a manager, you must not make your decisions with the biased view of management, but with the wisdom of an impartial judge. Nor should you make any hasty or snap judgments. If you need more time to get more information, do so. A wise decision is much more important than a hasty one.

9. Get All the Facts First. Sometimes you'll need to hear someone else's side of the story before you make your decision. If this is necessary to get all the facts, do so, no matter how much time it takes. But don't use this as an excuse to put things off.

10. Let the Employee Know What Your Decision Is. Once you've made your decisions, let the person know what it is. Tell him yourself. Call him back to your office if necessary. Don't pass the word to him via your clerk or secretary. If you do, he'll know for sure you weren't really interested after all.

11. Double-Check Your Results. Later on, check back with your employee to make sure his grievance has been taken care of to his complete satisfaction. Follow up and he'll know for sure you really are interested in him and in his welfare.

I'm not implying for a moment that you can solve all the personal problems of your employees just by listening to their complaints. But I do know if you have a good grievance procedure in your organization, you can often keep minor complaints from turning into major problems. I also know that paying close attention to your employees and trying to help them will improve their attitudes toward you and your company, for listening to people is one of the best ways I know of to keep good, harmonious relations between labor and management. Doctor Paul Jansen, a Birmingham, Alabama, industrial psychologist, agrees with me.

> "You must pay attention to your employees and their problems if you want to help them," Dr. Jansen says. "I don't mean to give them your casual attention either. *To pay means to part with something of value.* In this instance, that something of value is your precious time and your preoccupation with your own interests and desires.
> "When you fail to pay attention to your employees and listen to their problems, their complaints, and their grievances, you reject them. Rejection hurts; attention heals. It's just that simple."

One final recommendation that is extremely important and well worth mentioning here is this: *Be concerned.* There's absolutely no use in your listening to a person and paying attention to him unless you really are willing to help him solve his problems. To be sincerely concerned about the other person is the basic foundation for all deep and lasting human relationships. It is the heart of all friendship and a real key to power with people.

You Can't Win Them All

No matter how hard you try, you're not going to be able to salvage every single problem employee. A small percentage of people seem to be constitutionally incapable of working with others, obeying orders, accepting discipline from a higher authority, or disciplining themselves.

Perhaps they are not at fault. I do not know. I am not a psychiatrist. Not only that, the study of abnormal psychology is beyond the scope of this book. From a management point of view, the important thing for you to do is identify the incorrigible employee as quickly as possible so you can get rid of him before he contaminates and ruins the rest of your people.

Many of these incorrigibles seem to have been born that way. They are by their very nature unable to grasp and develop a manner of living that demands simple honesty. Unfortunately, this small segment of humanity seems destined for the gutter or prison and nothing on earth you or I can do will stop them.

The answer, then, to this kind of problem person? There is none as far as you or I as managers are concerned. You are not a social worker and neither am I. You can't win them all, and this is one of those you can't win. Since you're not running a rehabilitation center or a rest home, you really have no choice in the matter. If the individual is a member of your management team—*fire him*. If he's a member of organized labor, you'll have to do the same thing. It might take just a little longer, that's all.

And now for the last, but one of the most important chapters, my *Twelfth Master Key to Management Success*, "Secrets Top-Notch Managers Use to Make the Most of Their Time." If you are one of the thousands of executives and managers who carry a briefcase full of office work home each night, it will be extremely valuable to you.

Chapter **12**

Secrets Top-Notch Managers

Use to Make the

Most of Their Time

Since this is a book primarily on managing people, you might wonder why this chapter on the use of time is included. However, *time is also one of the primary resources of management.* Not only that, I have yet to meet the business man or woman or the industrial manager who does not want more time to get the job done. Finally, people are more responsible for using up your time than any other reason, so managing your time properly to get the job done comes right back to managing people, including yourself.

Many managers work 60 and more hours each week, including at least ten hours outside the office. Some of them use not only their lunch hours to conduct business and solve problems, but also their dinner hours as well. At the end of an already overly long day, they carry home briefcases full of even more work to be done during their "leisure" time, when they should be free to be with their families or enjoying some relaxing pastime with their friends.

The end result of all this frenzied activity can be what is called *"hurry sickness"*: the fear that time is running out and more must be produced than already is. Hurry sickness, also known as the "stress syndrome," causes an excessive amount of adrenalin to be pumped into the body's vascular system. The heart beats faster . . . the lungs work harder. All the body's metabolic processes speed up and the person burns energy more quickly than normal.

This kind of stress can lead to duodenal ulcers, high blood pressure, heart attacks, headache, low back pain, diarrhea, even asthma and eczema, as well as a long list of other physical and psychological problems. Too much time spent on the job is also one of the leading causes of marital conflict, tension, and divorce.

One of the symptoms of the hurry sickness is the erroneous belief that by doing the work faster more time can be gained. First of all, a person can work only so fast before he starts making more and more mistakes. Of course, I'm not implying that a person shouldn't try to improve himself, but there is a limit to all things.

Take your own secretary, for instance. If she can type 50 words a minute with only one or two mistakes a page, leave well enough alone. Let her improve her performance gradually by herself. If you force her to increase her typing speed, her mistakes will automatically increase. Whatever time she saves by typing faster, she'll lose by correcting her errors or typing the letter over again. Not only that, the faster she tries to work, the greater the stress and strain, the quicker she tires, and the more her errors will increase. The same thing holds true for the production line employee, the department foreman, division manager, and right on up the line. There is much truth in the old adage: "The hurrier I go, the behinder I get."

If you think you don't overwork or even if you're not yet afflicted with any of these symptoms of the hurry sickness, let me ask you just one question: Do you ever rush through your work to get out to the golf course only to hurry through your golf game so you can run back to your office because you feel guilty about taking some no doubt well-deserved time off? No further questions. If you don't have the hurry sickness yet, you're sure on the verge of getting it, so my *Twelfth Master Key to Management Success* will be most valuable to you.

BENEFITS YOU'LL GAIN FROM THIS CHAPTER

I'll give you certain key methods and techniques that top-notch managers use to make the most of their time. You'll also benefit by seeing how they plan and organize their workday so they can get the most out of every available minute, yet have more time left over for their families and leisure activities. I'll show you what you can do about the 14 leading wasters of time. When you use the techniques that you'll learn in this chapter, you'll also be able to avoid the hurry sickness that causes so many severe physical and psychological problems for a great number of business managers and executives.

However, the most important benefit you can gain from this chapter is a radical change in your basic attitude or viewpoint toward the management of your time. You see, the real key to your management of time as you'll find out is not through the use of gimmicks, but by the management of yourself.

Why Gimmicks Will Not Solve the
Management of Time Problems

For many years I did as most managers and executives do. I tried every gimmick I ran across trying to save time. But the use of a gimmick to improve time usage falls in the same category as the doctor who treats only the symptoms of a disease without ever determining the actual cause. It may help the situation temporarily, but it does nothing to cure the major illness.

Let me give you an example of one such "time-saving" gimmick. A certain company has a policy of using a timer clock for conducting all its staff meetings. If the meeting is to last one hour, the clock is set at 60 minutes and ticks on down to zero as the meeting progresses. Then a bell rings to signal that time is up much like the buzzer on your kitchen range signals when the pie is done.

Does a gimmick like this help you save time? No, definitely not. The man who speaks first tends to dawdle along as usual. The one who speaks last is forced to leave out points he needed to include so he has to cover them later on individually with every person who was present at the meeting. This kind of gimmick does not save time. In fact, it can actually waste time as well as cause costly errors when people are forced to cover important material too rapidly or leave out certain factual data in an effort to save time.

Other gimmicks I've seen tried are conference rooms without tables and chairs to cut meetings short and offices without chairs to discourage visitors. But whatever business is not covered in a conference or meeting because of the lack of comfort will be taken up later on an individual basis either face to face or over the telephone, so again, time will not be saved by these measures. It will actually be lost.

Another gimmick I want to mention is the manager's office without a desk for paperwork to pile up on. This method will not solve the basic problem of wasting time either. It, too, treats only the symptoms of the disease without ever getting to the basic root cause of the ailment. For instance, without a desk for paperwork, the executive or manager will simply use a filing cabinet or place his essential paperwork on the floor beside his chair. A desk doesn't cause paperwork to pile up; the person sitting at the desk does that. He's the problem to be solved . . . not the desk.

One other misconception about the management of time is that by proper scheduling of one's work, all of a manager's problems of time usage can be solved. According to these "experts," all a manager needs do to get the most out of his time is this:

1. Make a list of all the jobs that have to be done.

2. Establish the order or priority for each job.

3. Determine the steps necessary to complete the job.

4. Establish the order of priority for each step.

5. Schedule all work by following these established priorities, not only for each job, but also for each step.

6. Stick to this schedule "as best you can" despite interruptions, mistakes, and frustrations.

This is a good system for controlling your work, but it does very little for managing your time. It does not help you reduce your workload and you'll never gain any additional time for yourself until you do that.

So enough of gimmicks. The only reason I've discussed them is to help you realize they are not the answer to your management of time. The only answer is to take complete control of the situation by managing yourself.

THE MASTER KEY TO YOUR USE OF TIME
IS MANAGING YOURSELF

The master key to the proper utilization of time is not by the use of gimmicks or scheduling your workload. Nor is it by watching the clock and managing your activities by it. *How you control, train, discipline, and manage yourself and your activities is the master key to the management of your time.* The clock has absolutely nothing at all to do with it. It is only a convenience, not a necessity.

Watching the clock will not break your bad habits of procrastinating and wasting time; only self-discipline will do that. Once you understand and accept the basic premise that you, not the clock, are the master of time, then everything else will naturally fall into its proper place. Then the management of time will become easy for you.

When you stop watching the clock and stop measuring your activities by it, you'll really learn to concentrate fully on the job at hand. Of all the principles of time management, none is more basic than concentration. People who have trouble getting things done on time are invariably trying to do too many things at once. The total amount of time spent on a job as measured by the clock is not the determining factor for getting it done. It's the amount of *uninterrupted time* spent on the job that really counts.

This discovery of not watching the clock but watching myself and my activities to manage time is not original or unique with me as I've found out since. Other managers and executives have learned how to use the same master key of controlling themselves to control their use of time, but each person has had to find out this secret for himself, usually through long and hard experience. Carl J. Shelton, an executive vice-president with a large automobile manufacturer, is one such manager.

"I never really learned to manage my time so I could make the most of it until I trained myself to discipline and control my feelings and emotions," Mr. Shelton says. "I believe my hardest job was forcing myself not to get involved in the details of the work that others should do. I had to drive myself to delegate every detail possible to my subordinates. I eliminated all the unnecessary jobs I was doing and learned to manage my time by organizing and planning my work schedule. Managing and disciplining myself was the only way I was ever able to manage and control my time."

Specific techniques I'll discuss that you can use to manage yourself in relation to the usage of time are these:

1. Deciding what you and you alone *must* do.
2. Delegating the work that others can do.
3. How to delegate authority and retain control.
4. How to organize and plan your own work.
5. Determining what you should and shouldn't see.
6. How to save time handling your correspondence.
7. How to determine if your workload is too great.
8. What you can do about the 14 leading wasters of time.
9. Using a daily checklist to measure your progress.
10. Using the time you save.

Deciding What You and You <u>Alone</u> Must Do

The first step in managing yourself and your activities so you can control your use of time is to *decide exactly what you and you alone must do*. The best way to do this is to go over your job description so you can *determine precisely what your specific duties and responsibilities are*. These are the only areas in which you, and only you, should be responsible for making the final decisions.

If you are doing any jobs other than these, get rid of them. They are not your responsibility, and therefore, do not belong to you. Some managers, after reviewing their work like this, find that certain jobs are not even essential and do not require doing at all. The best way to determine whether a job is actually essential or not is to assess the harm or damage that would result from not doing it. If nothing serious would happen, then that job isn't even worth doing. Should that be your situation, you won't have to delegate the work to someone else to do. You can eliminate the job completely.

Another good way to get rid of all the unnecessary work you are doing is to *eliminate completely any job that does not help you achieve your goals*. If you follow this principle, you'll stop wasting your time on matters that do not contribute to the important ends you want to achieve.

Reviewing your job description can simplify the situation for you quickly as Roger Minton, a division manager in the Dayton Corporation, found out.

"When I took over my position as the plastics division manager, I found myself doing all sorts of tasks that had no relationship whatever to my actual job," Mr. Minton says. "I was working three or four hours a day on problems completely unrelated to my own job. I found I had little time left to do my own work unless I took it home with me at night. So I began asking why certain work was being sent to me. The answer I got was, 'It's always been done that way.'

"Further investigation on my part revealed that the previous division manager, who'd been in that position for ten years before his retirement, had taken on many jobs that other people didn't want. He was a widower, had no children, no outside interests, and didn't mind spending his leisure time in the office, for he had nothing else to do. People took advantage of him and he became a dumping ground for all the vague, ill-defined tasks that no one wanted or that didn't seem to belong to anyone in particular.

"After going over my job description with a fine-toothed comb, I either eliminated completely, or gave away, those jobs that were not my specific responsibility to the proper person for doing. Only then was I able to get my own work done."

That should be your first step in saving time for yourself. Go over your job description carefully. Eliminate all unnecessary jobs. Give to others any unrelated work you're doing that rightfully belongs to them. *Decide what you and you alone must do. Then do that, only that, and nothing else.*

Delegating the Work that Others Can Do

After you've eliminated all the unnecessary or unproductive

work and given away all the unrelated jobs to the proper responsible people, you'll be left with only two kinds of tasks: those that you, and you alone, must do, and those that others who work for you can do.

Your next step is to *delegate to others all the work that rightfully can be delegated to them.* This is the only way you can free yourself from time-consuming details and make it possible to cut down on the number of your working hours without sacrificing productivity.

I will admit immediately that effective delegation is not easy to do. You need to manage and discipline yourself vigorously. Don't make the mistake of delegating to others only the work you don't like to do and keeping those jobs that you enjoy doing. That is not delegation, that's *assignment,* and that is not the proper way to delegate authority nor is it the correct method to use to utilize your own time profitably.

The major reason for a manager's hesitancy to delegate authority is his fear that his subordinates will fail to do the job properly and thus jeopardize his position. If you feel that way, let me show you how a top-notch manager solves that problem:

How to Delegate Authority and Still Retain Control

"The fear of failure causes a lot of managers to hang on to the details of work that belong to their subordinates," says Patricia Harrison, a product manager for an electronics corporation. "They're afraid that if they delegate authority to their people, something might happen that could seriously endanger their position. They imagine all sorts of problems and troubles that could come up if they surrender any part of their authority to their subordinates.

"To tell the truth, most managers feel they could do a better job than anyone else. They view the delegation of authority as a loss of control. But it doesn't have to work that way at all.

"The smart manager will delegate the authority to carry out all the details of the work *only after he has established the proper control measures that will let him take immediate corrective action if things do go wrong.* Here's what those control measures are:

"First, make sure the employee is thoroughly trained, qualified, and capable of doing the job you've given him to do.

"Second, give him his responsibilities, not all at once, but in increments, step by step.

"Third, correct his mistakes and praise his successes as he proceeds with his new assignments and responsibilities.

"Fourth, at each critical point, set up your controls in such a way that you can move in at once to stop or take over any action that might seriously jeopardize successful completion of the job.

"When you delegate the authority to do the details of the job, it will build a feeling of self-confidence in your subordinates. It's definite proof on your part that you have faith in them and in their abilities."

Patricia Harrison is not the only manager and executive who has learned how to delegate authority to save time. Ralph Cordiner, former chairman of General Electric, is perhaps the best example of this concept. He left all the operating decisions to his trusted subordinates and made as few as half a dozen decisions a year himself.

If you do as both Mrs. Harrison and Mr. Cordiner did, you'll give your employees the chance to learn, grow, and make a contribution they can definitely call their own. When you do that, you'll gain more time for yourself.

Organizing and Planning Your Own Work

After you've decided what you and you alone must do, after you've eliminated any job that does not actually need doing or does not help you achieve your goals, and after you've delegated all the work that others can do, then it's finally time to organize and plan your own work.

The best time to organize and plan your weekly schedule is at the end of the preceding week, either on a Friday or a Saturday. You may not be able to pin down exactly what you're going to be doing every single hour, but you should be able to program quite accurately what you expect to get done each day.

Perhaps you feel you cannot spare the time and energy it takes to think and plan ahead. However, I can assure you that the small amount of time you spend in organizing and planning your weekly activities will be more than made up by the large amount of time you'll save in the long run.

When you plan and organize your work, you'll find you're able to establish the proper priorities for getting the work done. You'll perform tasks in their appropriate order of importance, and that's a far better method than a catch-as-catch-can, random system of doing things as they come to your attention, which is really no system at all.

If you think you can't work on a daily or weekly schedule or regular routine, I'm sorry to say that I must disagree with you. Whether you realize it or not, you're already working and living on a schedule. If it's not your own, you can be sure it's someone else's. As long as you have to do things on some sort of a planned timetable, you'd be far better off to have one of your own, rather than be guided by one that someone else has made up.

Someone else's schedule will be planned to serve his interests, not yours. It'll be completely unproductive for you. Even the most efficient of secretaries will schedule your appointments to serve her convenience, not yours, if you allow her to do so. If you want to retain complete control of your own situation, then make up your own schedule. Plan your daily and weekly activities. Let your secretary assist you in the planning, but don't let her do it for you.

You can be sure that the executives, managers, and salesmen in all large and successful companies and corporations work on a planned and organized schedule and timetable. For example, an executive with IBM, a corporation noted for its enthusiastic people, says that a weekly work sheet is an absolute must in their organization.

"We give all our sales people certain tools which we know from experience are essential in their work," he said. "One of the most important tools is our weekly *Organization and Planning Work Sheet*. This must be completed by each sales person, giving the names and addresses of all the firms they plan on seeing during the coming week. A copy of this must be turned in before each week's work.

"Is this a standing operating procedure for all your sales personnel all over the country?" I asked.

"It most certainly is," he replied. "There are absolutely no exceptions of any sort."

"What would happen if a salesman wouldn't go along with your procedures and refused to make out his organization and planning work sheet for the next week?" I asked.

"That would never happen," he said. "But if it ever did, that salesman would no longer work for us."

This is not to say that IBM's success is all due to their sales personnel making out weekly organization and planning work sheets. But it does indicate that people at IBM know exactly what they're doing and where they're going. It also shows they know the value of time and how to use it properly. That's a big part of the reason for their spectacular business achievements over the years.

Determining What You Should and Shouldn't See

To conserve your time, you should delegate as much of the paper work as you can to your subordinates. Let them furnish you with a synopsis or summary of it along with whatever action they took. If you don't do that, the paper work has to come to you. There simply is no other choice.

Before you can institute this kind of procedure, your people have to know *what papers you must see and what correspondence you have to sign.* When they know that, they will also automatically know *what papers you don't have to see and what correspondence you don't have to sign.* The best way to set up guidelines for them to follow is to establish your own *Standing Operating Procedure.* If you don't know how or where to start, let me help you out with the following SOP which is called quite simply,

KEEPING THE BOSS INFORMED

I want the following matters brought to my personal attention at once.

1. Any important subject that will require some *immediate*

action on my part and which is not specifically covered in some previously published policy or directive.

2. Letters of disapproval of any sort from my superiors.

3. Any and all errors, irregularities, or deficiencies in my area of responsibility that have been pointed out by my superiors.

4. Any letters or reports that indicate neglect or dereliction of duty on the part of any of my subordinates, or that carry even the slightest hint of criticism, censure, or reprimand.

5. Written appeals made by any subordinate about decisions that I or my staff or anyone else in management has made.

6. Any subject that would injure the good name or reputation of the company.

7. Any serious accidents or incidents, either on or off duty, involving any of my personnel.

8. Any reports of financial irregularities or discrepancies or any shortages of property or materials.

The following matters will be sent to me for my personal action and/or my signature.

1. Any non-routine letter or report that contains a request or recommendation to be made to my superiors.

2. Letters or certificates of commendation, award, or appreciation that are to be given to any of my subordinates.

3. Any letter or report that will cast a shadow of doubt on the good name or reputation of any person or department within my area of responsibility.

4. Letters of disapproval or negative replies on requests or suggestions from my subordinates.

5. Any letter that contains even the slightest hint of criticism, censure, or reprimand of any of my subordinates.

6. Any non-routine letters or reports that are to be sent to any governmental agency.

7. Letters and reports that have to do with future planning.

8. Any letters and reports of *exceptional or outstanding information* that are not specifically covered in this memorandum.

I am indebted to Walter Park, manager of an automotive assembly plant in Missouri, for this SOP. Each one of his department managers has a copy of this memorandum on his desk. Each supervisor carries a copy in his pocket. His administrative staff uses it for guidance in routing paperwork.

"This is not the total answer for your management of time," Walter says, "but it sure helps. When people know exactly what matters I want to know about, and specifically which papers to route through my office, 95 percent of their questions are already answered. This memorandum speeds up their work and my desk is kept clear, too."

I'm not going to say that Walter's Standing Operating Procedure or one like it will solve all your management problems either, but it will sure give you a lot more time to work on the ones that you have left.

How to Save Time Handling Your Correspondence

Now that your SOP has helped you determine exactly what paperwork and correspondence you don't have to see, let me show you how to save time on the remainder that you do have to see.

Most of the paperwork that comes across the average manager's desk will be correspondence, either internal or external. When to read it and answer it will depend a lot on your own office routine, when the mail is delivered, and other office details.

For the most efficient use of your time, establish your own standing operating procedure. Then things will move along properly under your control. Doing things as they come to you is not the best solution. Let me give you an example of this. It may not fit your own individual timetable, but it will give you some ideas of how to organize and operate your own system.

"I read my correspondence only twice a day," says Jacob Steiner, an industrial plant manager. "The first time is early in the morning as soon as the mail is picked up from our postoffice box. The second time is immediately after lunch.

"I dictate my answers to the letters in the morning mail at once. This gives my secretary the rest of the day to type them for my signature and get them in the mail by the end of our business day. If any other box mail is picked up later in the day, my secretary holds it until the next morning unless it is urgent enough to require a telephone call to clear the matter up.

"Several years ago, I used to read the morning mail, then set it aside to do other things and come back to it as time permitted. Then I would have to reread it and answer it if a reply was necessary. That procedure wasted too much of my time. Besides, I found I never had enough time during business hours because something else always seemed more important. I was working until 9 or 10 o'clock almost every night just keeping up with my correspondence.

"Now I read my mail only once. As soon as I read a letter, *I decide right then and there before I ever read the second one* whether an answer is needed or not. If it is, I dictate the reply to my secretary *before reading the next letter.* If more information is needed to prepare a reply, I set that letter aside only until the necessary data has been obtained. Then I dictate the answer.

"My afternoon mail is primarily inter-office memoranda, buck slips, internal correspondence and reports, that sort of thing. This method lets me keep the two kinds of paperwork distinctly separate. It prevents confusion, overlapping, lost paperwork, and it keeps my desk clear."

The key to making this system work for yourself is to *complete whatever action is necessary on each piece of paper before you pick up the next one.* If you don't do that, you'll find yourself doing as Mr. Steiner was in the beginning. You'll be rereading every letter that comes across your desk. *You should never handle the same piece of paper twice.* Your fidelity to this one simple rule will help keep your desk clear and give you more time to use on other important matters.

How to Find Out if Your Workload Is Too Great

If you find you still have too much to do, even after you've put all these techniques I've just given you into effect, then your workload is just too heavy for you. How can you determine that and then prove your point to your boss when you do? The best way is to check out your job against the *Management Span of Control* to see if you have too many duties to perform or too many subordinates to supervise.

Take several average weeks to determine your normal workload. Don't use one exceptionally busy week or heavy time period to do so. Several times during the year, the pressure of business will compel any manager to work long hours until a specific job is done. That's part of the management game and it's to be expected. But you shouldn't have to work 12 to 14 hours a day, 5 days a week, 52 weeks out of the year.

One factor affecting the span of control is the *span of attention,* or the ability of a person to divide his attention between two or more tasks. Each individual has an upper limit beyond which he cannot pay attention to any additional work, no matter how important it is. Even below this limit, assignment of a new task tends to distract from the efficient completion of those already undertaken.

The interaction of human relationships also affects the span of control. For instance, if a manager has only 2 subordinates, he has 2 human relationships—one with each subordinate. But each of these relationships is also affected by a third human relationship, the one that exists between the 2 subordinates. The greater the span of control, for example, if a manager has 8 subordinates, the more complex will become the effects of those interacting relationships, and the more difficult will become those subordinates to manage and control.

Most management authorities agree that the economically minimum span of control is 3 *immediate* subordinates. The maximum span of control varies greatly with the capabilities of the individual. However, even the best of managers can seldom handle more than 8 *immediate* subordinates. If this maximum number is exceeded, the organization will become cumbersome, unwieldy, and difficult to manage.

Unfortunately, an organization trying to economize will often violate the span of control by giving each manager far too many people to supervise and far too many tasks to do. This only makes things worse. The end result will not be a saving in manpower, but an actual decrease in the efficiency and quality of workmanship. To violate the management span of control by trying to save money spent on management salaries is a false economy.

If these figures, 3 and 8, seem too small to you, remember the clue lies in the word *immediate* when considering the number of subordinates a manager can properly handle. The management span of control is based on a pyramidal concept. If you have 8 immediate subordinates who also have 8 immediate subordinates, you are actually controlling a total of 72 people altogether. If each of these 8 subordinates has 8 more subordinates, the figure suddenly jumps to 584.

When you properly use the management span of control (no less than 3 but no more than 8 *immediate* subordinates) you'll be able to control many people through just a few. You see, you don't need to control the whole human race to be successful. But you can control dozens of people—yes, even hundreds—through just a few key subordinates.

Genghis Khan controlled his vast far-flung empire through just a few key people—his loyal tribal chieftans. His was a military empire won by armed conquest. The same span of control he used also applies to the economic empire of General Motors. The president of GM is head of an organization that has more than three-quarters of a million employees. He also uses that same management span of control I've been telling you about. He could not possibly control and direct this vast, modern, sprawling economic giant in any other way.

Some of the factors that can influence the upper limits of your own span of control are these:

1. Your own experience, background, and training.
2. The experience, background, and training of your subordinates.
3. The degree of similarity in your subordinates' jobs.
4. The distance by which you and your subordinates are spearated.
5. The time available to translate your decisions into actions.
6. Your personality and the personality of your subordinates.

7. The mental and physical conditioning of your subordinates.

8. The complexity of your organization.

Although you must consider all these factors in determining what your final span of control should be, if it is less than 3 immediate subordinates or less than 3 separate and distinct areas of supervision, you will not have enough work to do. I cannot imagine that situation with any capable manager.

If you have more than 8 immediate subordinates or if you have more than 8 separate and distinct areas of supervision, you will no doubt have too much work to do. This is the situation I have found to exist time after time in nearly every company and corporation I've been called on to help solve some management problem.

If you do have more than 8 immediate subordinates or if you have more than 8 separate and distinct areas of supervision, you'll never be able to get all your work done, no matter how well you plan, organize, and use your time.

The management span of control, then, furnishes you a clue to the proper utilization of your time. You can use the same procedure to determine whether your own subordinates are underworked or whether they have too much to take care of in a normal work day. I know of no better guide to properly determine your subordinates' time usage than the management span of control.

What You Can Do About the Leading Wasters of Time

Based on the experiences of top-notch managers from all over the country from a hundred different companies and corporations, the 14 leading wasters of time are these:

1. Telephone interruptions.

2. Visitors dropping in without appointments.

3. Meetings, both routine and special.

4. Situations for which no plans were made.

5. A lack of management goals and objectives.

6. Cluttered desk, stacked up paperwork, and personal disorganization.

7. Inability to concentrate fully on the job at hand.

8. Trying to do too many things at once.

9. Involvement in details of work that should be delegated to others.

10. Failure to establish clear lines of authority and responsibility.

11. Personal indecision and procrastination.

12. Inaccurate or untimely information from others.

13. Failure to issue clear and concise orders and instructions.

14. Inability to say "No" and stick to it.

If you review this list carefully, I'm sure you'll notice that in not one single case is the actual management of time the basic problem. The real problem is the management of one's self. Training and self-discipline on your part will eliminate these 14 time wasters for you.

For instance, no gimmick can stop telephone interruptions or get rid of unwanted visitors. Only you, the disciplined manager, can do that. Unnecessary meetings won't cancel themselves, but you can. A lack of goals and objectives is not the fault of the clock; it is the fault of management.

A cluttered desk, stacked up paperwork, and personal disorganization don't come from insufficient time to get the job done. They prevent the job from getting done and result from a lack of self-discipline, will-power, and self-control. Again, only you can correct that problem by managing yourself. The clock has absolutely nothing at all to do with it. Not concentrating fully on the job at hand or trying to do too many things at once can be corrected only by positive action on your part.

Involvement in details that should be delegated to others, failure to set up clear lines of authority and responsibility, personal indecision and procrastination, lack of clear communication and issuance of proper orders, the ability to say "No," and stick to it—all these are not the consequence of the improper use of time. Instead, they are all the end result of improper management, and improper management is the real cause of wasted time.

As you can plainly see, we've come full circle back to my original statement in this chapter that *the master key to your use of time is managing yourself.* If you learn to control, train, manage, and discipline yourself, as well as your people, then these 14 leading time wasters will no longer be a problem to you.

A DAILY CHECKLIST TO MEASURE
YOUR PROGRESS IN THE
UTILIZATION OF TIME

You can make up your own list to check your daily activities so you can measure your progress in the proper utilization of your time. However, to help you get started, I want to give you one I have used successfully for many years. Of course, to make the most of your time, you should also have in writing a clearly defined set of life-time goals as well as annual goals, but for our purposes here, a daily checklist is sufficient to use for guidance.

1. Did I do anything today to move me closer to my established goals?
2. Did I plan and organize my activities for the day or was it just a hit-or-miss proposition?
3. Was my use of time today determined by me, or by circumstances and other people's wishes and desires?
4. Could I do tomorrow the same things I did today in less time? How? Where could I begin to save time?
5. Where did I lose time today? How much time did I actually throw away by plain old procrastination?
6. How much time did I waste today on things I like to do rather than the things I should do?

7. Did I delegate as much work as I possibly could to my subordinates?

8. Did I waste the time of my subordinates and associates as well as my own? Did I waste someone else's time by not being punctual for my appointments?

9. Did I issue clear and concise instructions to my subordinates so they won't have to waste time coming back tomorrow for further information?

10. How much time was wasted today in clarification of orders and instructions I issued yesterday or the day before?

11. Did I keep my subordinates from bringing to me the tasks they found difficult to do or the decisions they found hard to make?

12. Did I wait for others to do something that I could have done more quickly and easily myself? (This does not mean you should get involved in details of work that belong to others, but that you should not expect to get waited on hand and foot simply because of your status or position.)

13. Did I leave my secretary with enough to keep her busy while I was away from my office?

14. Were any routine meetings held that were not necessary?

15. Did I write a letter or a memo when a phone call would have done the job just as well?

16. How much time did I throw away in useless chatter and pointless conversation?

17. Did I try to do my most important tasks during my prime time?

18. Did I use the shortest and quickest, yet most accurate and dependable, methods available to me?

19. Did I establish work priorities based on their actual importance rather than doing the easier jobs first?

20. Did I concentrate on my objectives and judge myself by what I actually got done rather than by my activity?

21. Did I take some time out to recharge my batteries by relaxing once in a while throughout the day?

22. Did I use my idle waiting time to read, think, make notes, plan, or did I just daydream it all way?

23. Did I live in today, the *ever-present now*, rather than rehashing the victories and defeats of the past?

24. Do I know what specific jobs I want to get done tomorrow? What is the first project on which I should get started in the morning?

How to Use the Time You Save

When you use the specific techniques I've given you to manage yourself in relation to the use of time, you'll find that you'll gain a weekly time dividend for yourself. How well you invest this valuable dividend is, of course, up to you.

Unfortunately, some managers use the extra time they've gained to take on additional managerial tasks and duties or try to move some of their current projects along at an even faster pace. I hope you will not do that.

If you are wise, you'll see fit to use your time dividend for your own pleasure, be that your family, self-development, community service, sports, a hobby, or whatever suits you. For instance, J. C. Penney's Chairman of the Board, Mr. Donald V. Seibert, busy as he is, finds enough time to be an amateur musician and composer.

Mr. Seibert plays the saxophone, clarinet, and piano. His music is often squeezed into his busy work schedule. Several years ago, when his youngest child was in high school, Mr. Seibert was part of a church group that played contemporary music they wrote themselves.

"One time I started a musical composition in a bathtub in Paris and finished it on the plane coming back to the United States," Mr. Seibert said. "Our group performed it the next night. It didn't sound bad, but it probably would have sounded better if there'd been a piano in the tub."

If the chairman of the board of the third largest retailer in the United States, a nationwide chain with more than 1,600 stores, can find enough time to do some of the things he wants and likes to do, I'm sure you and I can, too.

It is my sincere desire that this chapter will help you get started in the right direction in your management of time. If you now realize that disciplining and managing yourself is the master key to the management of your time, I have accomplished my purpose.